Other Middle Ages

THE MIDDLE AGES SERIES

Ruth Mazo Karras, General Editor
Edward Peters, Founding Editor

A complete list of books in the series
is available from the publisher.

Other Middle Ages

Witnesses at the
Margins of Medieval Society

Edited by Michael Goodich

PENN

University of Pennsylvania Press

Philadelphia

10 9 8 7 6 5 4 3 2 1

Published by
University of Pennsylvania Press
Philadelphia, Pennsylvania 19104-4011

Library of Congress Cataloging-in-Publication Data

Other Middle Ages : witnesses at the margins of medieval society /
edited by Michael Goodich.
     p.   cm. — (The Middle Ages series)
   Includes bibliographical references (p.   ) and index.
ISBN 0-8122-3448-0 (hardcover : acid-free paper). — ISBN
0-8122-1654-7 (pbk. : acid-free paper)
   1. Social history — Medieval, 500–1500 — Sources.   2. Marginality,
Social — Europe — History — Sources.   3. Marginality, Social, in
literature.   I. Goodich, Michael, 1944–   .   II. Series.
HN11.087   1998
306'.09'02 — dc21   98-13308
                                                               CIP

To the Memory of
William Goodich (1911–1996),
a fighter for justice

Contents

Introduction

The aim of this volume is to provide a voice to those persons and groups in medieval society who have often been ignored in traditional sourcebooks of medieval history. In the past, economic, institutional, and ecclesiastical history had largely been presented through documents and literary sources produced by the official agents of church and state and reflected the ideology of the dominant classes, that is, the clergy and nobility. Charters, papal bulls, conciliar decisions, philosophical tracts, and royal law codes, for example, have remained the focus of most source collections, and those interested in the lives, aspirations, and problems of the unlettered classes and members of minority groups have often had to be satisfied with sources produced by others or turn to works devoted exclusively to such groups as the Jews, heretics, or women. All the texts included in this volume, however, deal with persons excluded, either permanently or temporarily, from full participation in civil society, and an effort has been made to include material that was probably written or attested to by such persons themselves.

This book has been divided into chapters dealing with: (1) the Jewish community; (2) apostates and converts; (3) sexual nonconformists; (4) victims of the Devil; (5) Christian heretics; and (6) the liminal and temporarily marginalized. Each chapter is introduced by a brief essay on the particular group involved. Although most of these texts were written for spiritual reasons, there is nevertheless much concerning the more mundane affairs of daily life.

A close reading of these texts will allow the reader to experience vicarious contact with medieval people. The lives of persons drawn from a variety of backgrounds come into relief. Among the speakers are the daughter of a sheriff (Joan of Marden), a Jewish merchant (Baruch of Languedoc), and a notary (Berardo Appillaterre). Such themes as child rearing, social life, economic difficulties, sexuality, family life, dreams, emotional instability, and gender relations appear in these sources. Testimony concerning Giacomuccio Fatteboni of Belforte, for example, describes the reactions of village folk to his attempted suicide. The recollections of a resident of a village near Hereford, Joan of Marden, recounting her resuscitation after drowning in a local pond deals with contemporary perceptions of space and distance, family structure, affectional ties, and popular medical knowledge. The testimony of Baruch the German of Languedoc (found in an Inquisitorial protocol), forcibly converted to Christianity under pressure from the Pastoureaux in 1320, sheds light on the complex ties binding Jew and Christian. Arnaud of Verniolle's trial record, drawn from the same source, represents a unique report of homosexual relations on the fringes of society in southern France. It presents a far more textured picture of sexuality in the Middle Ages than one finds in more conventional historical sources, such as chronicles, sermons and moral treatises.

Marginality in Medieval Society

These persons suffered certain liabilities that identified them as members of a "marginal" group living on the geographical or legal peripheries of society. Bronisław Geremek has noted that marginal persons or groups are primarily known to us on the basis of judicial records, in which they are condemned by the authorities and by public opinion for their manner of living or conduct.[1] In some cases, marginality could be a function of personality. Those identified as "out of their minds" or "possessed by the Devil," for example, probably suffered from some kind of mental illness that led to their confinement and physical separation from the community. Others, such as Jews, heretics, or prostitutes, whose beliefs or ways of life did not conform to societal norms were marginalized as a consequence of their social situation. Such persons tended to live in a permanent position of social exclusion, burdened with a series of legal liabilities.

A third group of persons experienced temporary marginalization during a period of liminal transition from one condition to another. Typically, after an early period of isolation and hostility, they sought official recognition from ecclesiastical authorities who might confirm their way of life in the framework of a new religious order under the controlling authority of the church. Peter of Murrone, for example, later elected Pope Celestine V, was a hermit who had dwelt in rural isolation in the Abruzzi before his order was granted recognition. Ramon Llull, after abandoning his wife and children and the life of the Majorcan court, spent some time as a hermit, composed philosophical tracts, and eventually sought papal approval for

1. Bronisław Geremek, "The Marginal Man," in *The Medieval World*, ed. Jacques Le Goff, trans. Lydia Cochrane (London: Collins and Brown, 1990), 347–73.

his reform schemes. Similarly, the chronicler Salimbene de Adam had been reared in a prominent family of Parma with close ties to the emperor. His decision in adolescence to abandon family, friends, and inheritance to join the recently founded Franciscan order thrust him into a liminal state, rejected and abhorred by his family, prior to his integration into a new religious order. Likewise, Clare of Assisi temporarily occupied an undefined position, having rejected marriage and family before founding a new order very different from its predecessors.

Significantly, many of these groups, although marginalized, established their own subcultures, each characterized by its own rules of honor, meeting places, garments, skills, jargon, and signs of group identity. The Cathar heretics, for example, created a semi-secret private world that included a religious hierarchy and special rites, beliefs, terminology (the Cathars called themselves "good Christians"), dietary restrictions, and so forth. The criminal class likewise possessed its own rules, argot or secret language, code of solidarity, and meeting places, which can sometimes be identified through the few surviving criminal court records, such as those of the Paris Châtelet. Some of these groups, like the urban-dwelling merchants and craftsmen of the eleventh century who first appeared in opposition to the economic structure of feudal society, successfully fought against exclusion and outlaw status, achieving formal legal recognition of their condition through a charter of liberties defining their rights and place of residence. Others, like the Jews, although also granted limited liberty, usually under the patronage of a local nobleman or bishop, remained in a permanent position of social and cultural inequality due to the overwhelming domination of Christian values during the medieval period. With the rise of the city in the twelfth century, some groups received official recognition, as neighborhoods were set aside where prostitutes and tanners could carry on their trade and Jews were allowed to dwell with relative freedom in "ghettoes."

Because of the paucity of first-hand evidence, not all those groups generally regarded as "marginal" have been included herein. A very broad definition of marginality would perhaps encompass too wide a cross-section of persons and groups not fully integrated into medieval society. The following groups, for example, shared many of the disadvantages identified with marginal status: (1) women, who by virtue of their status in both secular law and Christian theology lacked the rights and privileges accorded to men; (2) rural folk, who were largely excluded from the burgeoning monetary economy of the central and later Middle Ages; (3) persons dwelling in the remote regions of Europe, such as Lapps and Lithuanians, who lived far from the centers of political power and often retained the norms and values of a pre-Christian society; (4) convicted criminals, who were denied freedom of movement and other basic liberties; (5) the unemployed, who, lacking skills and regarded as outsiders (*advenae*) wherever they lived, often roamed about from place to place in search of employment; and, (6) practitioners of certain professions, such as executioners, usurers, actors, gravediggers, and minstrels, who were reviled as unworthy of being numbered among "respectable" folk. Although no chapter is devoted specifically to any one of these groups, women, criminals, and peasant folk are well-represented throughout. Furthermore, an individual may be marginalized or branded with a mark of infamy for more than one reason: the Jewish usurer and the heretical homosexual, for example, were doubly damned.

Women and rural folk, two groups whose testimonies are included, although not under a separate rubric, were often institutionally marginalized by the clerical elite, even though they were regarded as members of the body of Christ. Evidence of male ecclesiastical fear and animus toward women abounds, bolstered by a religious ideology that often justified women's subservience, beginning with the claim that womankind was created out of the loins of Adam and that Eve was the agent for the temptation of the first sin and the expulsion from Eden.[2] Scholastic theology defined women as incomplete men; the patriarchal family was regarded as a reflection of the heavenly hierarchy; and female orders like the Poor Clares and beguines (despite the independence displayed by Clare of Assisi and Christina of Stommeln) were placed under the watchful control of their male counterparts. This perhaps explains the disproportionate involvement of women in heretical sects, which often granted them the right to preach and even to perform clerical duties (see, for example, the testimonies of the Cathar Arnauda da Lamotha and Guglielmite Flordebellina of Milan). It should come as no surprise that many persons whose voices are heard in this volume are female saints. As Anna Benvenuti Papi has pointed out, "certain types of women keep cropping up in the hagiographical writings . . . widows, orphans, victims of familial breakdown, social disruption, and economic dislocation."[3] Suffering the "destabilization of the ordinary

2. Bonnie S. Anderson and Judith P. Zinsser, *A History of Their Own: Women in Europe from Prehistory to the Present*, 2 vols. (New York: Harper and Row, 1988), 1: 78–79; and Marina Warner, *Alone of All Her Sex: The Myth and the Cult of the Virgin Mary* (New York: Vintage Books, 1983), 59–60.

3. This and the following quotation come from Anna Benvenuti Papi, "Mendicant Friars

framework for female life: the family and its conceptual synonym, the convent," these women were marginalized as servants, shepherdesses, or members of peripheral tertiary and penitential orders or heretical sects.

Rural layfolk were the economic and demographic foundation of Europe. Nevertheless, the learned regarded them more often as the naive objects of ideological hegemonism than as the progenitors of an independent popular culture. Preachers and exemplarists such as Humbert of Romans and Stephan of Bourbon attempted to deepen rural belief and uproot the remnants of "superstition" and immorality. The effectiveness of mobilizing countryfolk for the faith is evident in the testimonies of Joan of Marden and Yves of Penguennan. Pope Celestine V likewise describes the vicissitudes of his rural upbringing in the Marches of Southern Italy and the hunger and poverty that faced a large, fatherless family. The personal experiences of rural folk found in this volume suggest that they adhered to the Catholic cult of the saints while at the same time partaking in the ancient, pre-Christian principles of "gift exchange," a kind of quid pro quo between divine patron and human client.

The classic members of a marginal and infamous profession were the wandering poets of the eleventh century and their successors, the minstrels, who lacked a fixed domicile and roamed from place to place seeking employment under a local bishop or nobleman. Their trade involved the utterance of blasphemies, scurrilous language, and trivialities (at least in the eyes of contemporary moralists), accompanied by obscene and grotesque gestures and the use of cosmetics. Their enemies excluded them from the communion of the faithful, and along with actors they were regarded as demoniacal enemies of God. As the twelfth-century theologian and natural philosopher Honorius of Autun said, "They do not recognize God, therefore God rejects them."[4] The goliards, the earliest documented group of wandering entertainers, were unemployed clerics who populated episcopal courts, largely in France, composing secular poetry that dealt with such themes as wine, women, and the stinginess of their patrons. By the thirteenth century, church councils demanded that they shave their heads and canceled their clerical privileges. With the growth of learning in the thirteenth century, the university became a breeding ground for the rootless-

and Female Pinzochere in Tuscany: From Social Marginality to Models of Sanctity," trans. Margery J. Schneider, in *Women and Religion in Medieval and Renaissance Italy*, ed. Daniel Bornstein and Roberto Rusconi (Chicago: University of Chicago Press, 1996), 84–103 passim.

4. Honorius of Autun, *Elucidarium*, 2.18, in Jacques-Paul Migne, ed., *Patrologia Latina. Cursus completus*, 221 vols. (Paris: J. P. Migne, 1844–55), 172: 1148.

ness and purported immorality that had earlier characterized the wandering scholars and goliardic poets. As tonsured lower clergy (and therefore subject to canon law), these students were both free of the restrictions of secular law, and without the responsibilities of the clerical hierarchy. It was therefore claimed that the student population was infiltrated by a criminal class that exploited clerical privilege as a means of subverting justice.

The minstrels or *jongleurs* (a term applied to all manner of secular entertainers, including acrobats, singers, and instrumentalists) were lay entertainers who appeared in Europe's public squares and in the courts of the nobility, composing much of the vernacular poetry of the period. Denied access to the sacraments by some churchmen, their poetry (like that of the thirteenth- century Parisian poet Rutebeuf) sometimes expressed deep criticism of the prevailing social order. One late thirteenth-century observer included them among the hangers-on, the flotsam and jetsam who populated every court. His catalog may be regarded as a good list of some of the marginal groups with which this volume is concerned:

They rush and flock to the courts of princes from every nation, profession, condition which is under heaven, just like vultures to a corpse, and like flies following the sweetness of oil; that is, poor persons, the sick, blind, crippled, maimed, bowlegged, and those otherwise deformed in body; menial servants, minstrels, tumblers, lutists, flutists, lyre-players, trumpeters, horn-blowers, actors, gesticulators, loafers, parasites, mimes, itinerant actors, jesters, rascals, clowns, flatterers, singers, traitors, detractors, mutterers, apostate sons of perdition, washerwomen, prostitutes, who are sweet up until they reach the exit.[5]

The author contrasts all these persons with the "upright and good."

The clearest sign of exclusion among those deemed unworthy of membership in Christian society was excommunication. Those suffering excommunication and interdict (in canon law) and the badge of infamy (in secular law) were branded with the formal, legal signs of social exclusion. In the Old Testament, the Hebrew term *ḥerem* referred to the ban on the common use of an object or contact with a person considered ritually polluted. In rabbinic times it represented a form of discipline in accordance with which a person was labeled with a religious curse which led to the severing of all ties with his or her community, family, and friends, and which in some instances might lead to death. In Christianity, the ceremonial rite of anathema dramatized the transfer of the excommunicate from a state of grace into

---

5. Edmond Faral, *Les jongleurs en France au moyen âge*, 2d ed. (Paris: Champion, 1971), 323.

the hands of the Devil. The canon lawyer Hostiensis (ca. 1250) numbered excommunicates with Saracens, schismatics, and pagans as persecutors of the church. Since excommunication was regarded as a kind of contagious disease, believers were prohibited from exchanging letters with such persons. Denied religious services, in extreme cases they could not even stand outside the church during mass. The secular legal status of the excommunicate derived from his or her position as an infamous person. Beginning in the late thirteenth century, excommunicates were sometimes subject to public humiliation or ridicule, as when political foes, ribalds, prostitutes, Jews, the aged, and others were forced to take part in humiliating races, occasionally in the nude;[6] in the Italian communes, caricatures of criminals were portrayed on the walls of civic buildings in order to expose them to obloquy. Public executions and the use of the pillory were further means of exposing infamous malefactors to shame. A good indication of those rejected by the Christian polity may be found in the numerous visions of the afterlife found in medieval literature, in which the geography of Paradise, Purgatory, and Hell is recorded. A monk of Eynsham in 1196, for example, provides a graphic account of the sufferings experienced in Purgatory by a sodomite, a leper, and a prostitute. Gautier de Coincy listed the following persons among the denizens of Hell: thieves, murderers, traitors, looters, Jews, pagans, *bougres* (a word that could mean Cathars and homosexuals), heretics, the haughty, the wicked, and hypocrites.[7]

But the parameters of marginality here employed are somewhat broader, not simply restricted to those who had undergone a ritualized ceremony of separation and humiliation. In Western Catholicism, the new stress in the central Middle Ages on the Eucharist as the incarnate body and blood of Christ gave sacramental form to Christian unity. This identification of the body of the faithful as those who took part in the Eucharist service (and thereby shared in the divinity) entailed the ceremonial exclusion from the community of those deemed marginal, excommunicated, or ideologically incompatible. The communion service, during which believers partook of the body and blood of Christ, thus effectively defined the boundaries of the Christian polity. And it was precisely when such Christian

6. Richard Trexler, "Correre la terra: Collective Insults in the Later Middle Ages," *Mélanges de l'École Française de Rome: Moyen Âge* 96 (1984), 845–922.
7. Gautier is cited in Peter-Michael Spangenberg, "Judenfeindlichkeit in der alfranzösischen Marienmirakeln. Stereotypen oder Symptome der Veränderung der kollektiven Selbsterfahrung?" in *Die Legende vom Ritualmorde zur Geschichte der Blutbeschuldigung gegen Juden*, ed. Reiner Erb (Berlin: Metropol, 1993), 159; for the Eynsham vision see Herbert Thurston, ed., "Visio monachi de Eynsham," *Analecta Bollandiana* 22 (1903), 225–319.

unity was given public expression, during Easter, Christmas, and the Feast of Corpus Christi, or in the course of a common European enterprise such as the Crusades, that violence against minorities reached its bloodiest height. Excluded from such communion, the largest category of "marginalized persons" were the ideological foes of Christianity, such as Jews, Muslims, heretics, and apostates, who were outside the Christian polity and were denied salvation. They lacked full civil rights, did not share in the dominant religious consensus, could not occupy public office or take part in the public festivities that were a mark of social and ideological unity, and suffered persecution, expulsion, and sometimes even execution because of their faith. Converts (such as Obadiah the Convert, a former Christian, and the former Jews Hermann of Scheda and Sa'id ibn Hasan of Alexandria) occupied a more anomalous status; on the one hand, they were excommunicated and deprived of contact with their former communities; on the other hand, they were not yet fully accepted by their new coreligionists.

Membership in a religious minority was perhaps the most persistent and easily recognizable form of marginality. In the late eleventh and early twelfth centuries, the Gregorian reform movement had clarified the theological foundations of Catholic Christianity, at the same time narrowing the limits of permissible belief and behavior. As a result, the mechanism of defining, identifying, and persecuting minorities gained force in the late twelfth and thirteenth centuries and spawned an ever more intolerant ideology. After both learned polemics and the efforts of the local clergy and older orders such as the Cistercians and Praemonstratensians had proven inadequate to the task, beginning with the council of Verona (1184) the Church undertook a militant program aimed at rooting out heresy. The steps included: (1) legal sanctions and the enlistment of the state in the persecution of heretics; (2) the establishment of the papal Inquisition; (3) the creation of new religious orders, such as the Dominicans, responsible for preaching to wayward believers; and (4) armed conflict against heretics, such as the Albigensian Crusade (referred to in the testimony of Arnauda da Lamotha included in this volume). The ideology of crusade was extended to include not only those who threatened Christendom's geographical periphery — the pagans in Eastern Europe and the Muslims in North Africa, for example — but also the heretical enemy within. This battle produced new Christian martyrs, such as Peter of Castelnau (d. 1208) and Peter Martyr (d. 1254), whose killings became the occasion for heightened persecution of their enemies.

The growing exclusion of religious minorities had a particularly devastating impact on the Jewish community, whose right to religious identity and communal autonomy had been recognized since Roman times. The First Crusade of 1096/99 and the blood libel accusations (the first documented ritual murder charge dates from Norwich in 1144) initiated a series of pogroms, mass suicides, forced conversions, and expulsions that shook the very foundations of European Jewry. The Fourth Lateran Council of 1215 imposed a badge of identification on the Jews, and in the course of the thirteenth century — with some exceptions — they were at best transformed into servants of the crown, as in the Holy Roman Empire, and at worst expelled, as in England and France. Yet the virtual disappearance of the Jews from many areas of Europe by the early fourteenth century did not reduce prejudice against Jews. Anti-Judaism (opposition to the Jewish faith for ideological reasons) was increasingly transformed into anti-Semitism (distrust or hatred of the Jews themselves), often based on economic, racial, or nationalist grounds. This may be explained by the fact that the Jewish faith remained the major intellectual challenge to the triumph of Christianity. Scholastic theologians and preachers continued their unrelenting attack on the "stubborn Jews" through the publication of polemical treatises entitled *Contra judaeos* — sermons which took Jewish perfidy as their theme — and the establishment of cults devoted to the alleged victims of Jewish ritual murder.

If tolerated, Jews continued to perform a necessary economic role and were permitted the kind of communal autonomy described in the epistle Judah ben Yehiel Asheri of Toledo wrote to his son. Nevertheless, social contact or friendship, as noted in the confession of Baruch the German of Languedoc, might continue to exist; sexual contacts between Jew and Christian (including Christian prostitutes), on the other hand, could lead to severe retribution and massacre, a fact documented in trials held in such regions as Aragon, where Jews were still tolerated.

In his study of the blood libel legend, the folklorist and anthropologist Alan Dundes has introduced the notion of projective inversion as a plausible way to explain the stereotypical accusations hurled against the Jews as desecrators of the Eucharistic wafer (i.e., the Host), which was the central element of the Catholic communion service. The wine of the Eucharist is transformed into the blood of Christ, and the bread into his body. Dundes has argued that Christian believers in fact experienced a deep sense of guilt for partaking in the symbolic cannibalism of the Eucharistic service, in which the body and blood of Christ are ceremonially consumed as a way of achieving unity with God and of expressing membership in the community of believers. As Dundes asks, "Where is the guilt for such an act displaced? I submit it is projected wholesale to another group, an ideal group for scapegoating."[8] Although the Jews are explicitly prohibited in their dietary regulations from drinking blood, they were portrayed in the blood libel accusation "doing what the Christian worshipper was doing in fantasy" (in the words of Hyam Maccoby), that is, killing a child and drinking its blood.[9] Similar accusations of ritual cannibalism had been hurled at second-century Christians by their pagan opponents.

The second great ideological foe of Christianity, Islam, was at first largely a military threat. After the earlier practice of executing defeated Muslims had ceased in the eighth century, Muslim prisoners of war were often enslaved (as were their Christian counterparts in Muslim countries). The Muslim population of Spain was, like the Jews, given considerable religious freedom between the twelfth and fifteenth centuries, although subject to increasing liabilities, such as a ban on public worship. This tolerated minority, the Mudéjares, were eventually forced to convert in the sixteenth century. Likewise, the Muslim minority in southern Italy was at first tolerated; but in the 1230s thousands were deported to the town of Lucera (later renamed Città Santa Maria), where they were subject to high taxation and eventually forced to convert. Many of the Muslims of Minorca, conquered in 1287, were enslaved. The account of Ramon Llull comes from such an environment, in which learned Muslims, like the slave who taught him Arabic, represented a gnawing threat to Christian hegemony.

The underlying hatred and resentment of lepers, Jews, and Muslims came together during the brutal violence of the Shepherds' Crusade of 1320 and the Cowherds' Crusade of 1321, which were focused on southern France and northern Spain. Because the Jews were fiscal agents of the crown, this violence may perhaps be seen as an expression of opposition to royal taxation, which was imposed indirectly by means of the high interest on loans extended by the Jews (who in turn passed the monies on to the state). The largely rural Shepherds' Crusade was initiated by a youth's vision calling for a crusade against the Moors, but was eventually suppressed by the French crown. The testimony of Baruch the German of Languedoc before the Inquisition eloquently describes of the desperate position of those Jews caught up in such circumstances, who were given the choice of conversion or execution. The events of 1321 began with accusa-

---

8. Alan Dundes, ed., *The Blood Libel Legend: A Casebook in Anti-Semitic Folklore* (Madison: University of Wisconsin Press, 1991), 354.
9. Hyam Maccoby, *The Sacred Executioner: Human Sacrifice and the Legacy of Guilt* (London: Thames and Hudson, 1982), 154–55.

tions against the lepers for allegedly attempting to spread the moral and physical infection of their disease throughout Christendom by means of magic and poison. Here the French king did little to intervene, although the king of Aragon attempted to redirect the violence.

But such exclusion from the Christian polity was not based solely on intellectual differences. Persons whose physical or mental condition suggested Satanic influence were also increasingly marginalized. The mentally distressed were often identified as possessed by demons and as the prisoners of the Satanic Enemy and were physically isolated and bound. Although modern observers may discern the symptoms of schizophrenia, Tourette's syndrome, multiple personality, or other neurological or psychological disorders in their condition, the partial nature of our documentation and the differing understanding of disease in the Middle Ages demand that we delay judgment. Thomas Aquinas (d. 1274) noted that some people may deny that the Devil exists, saying that the human imagination conjures up fears and attributes them to demons. Nevertheless, belief in the real presence of the Devil and in his attempts to gain control of the weak — infants, suicides, the mentally distressed, and so on — were the common heritage of all believers, both Jew and Christian; as a fallen angel, the Devil possessed the same miraculous powers attributed to God's agents, although his aims were malevolent. Many of the autobiographical accounts (Otloh, Llull, Salimbene, and Celestine V) depict the author's inner turmoil and doubts as a battle between conflicting visions and dreams in which demons, angels, and saints play a central role. The testimonies of Giacomuccio, Yves of Penguennan, and Christina of Stommeln, for example, describe the dual view of the possessed in the Middle Ages: on the one hand, gripped by an alien force; on the other, the objects of therapeutic and familial concern and occasionally a witness to the power of faith. These documents graphically describe the passage from the marginality of mental disorder to the stability of health and social acceptance.

At the same time, a physical disease such as leprosy could be regarded as the outward manifestation of inner sinfulness and likened to heresy in its pernicious effects. Such demonization led to the exclusion of lepers from civil society, their confinement in leprosaries, and the requirement that they wear special garments and carry a bowl and clapper. The accused sodomite and heretic Arnaud of Verniolle, for example, whose face broke out in a rash after a sexual encounter, voiced the fear of being classified among the excluded during a time of persecution, when Muslims, Jews, and lepers were accused of conspiring together to overthrow Christianity.

Others, whose marginality was temporary, voluntarily chose to place themselves outside civil society and reside on the geographical periphery. Forest, sea, mountain, and desert have traditionally been regarded as the sites of both devilish temptation and spiritual opportunity. A figure such as Pope Celestine V, for example, born of a poor family in the Italian Marches, chose the eremitical life in a remote mountain region during his formative years. Some of the leading members of his order (like Angelo of Clareno) were driven into exile and persecuted. The great polymath Ramon Llull, despite his noble background, regarded himself as a man outside the general consensus, whose reform programs and philosophy did not find a ready ear. He continually carps about the unwillingness of the Church to adopt his scheme to convert the nonbelievers and the resistance of the Muslims to his allegedly superior logic and preaching. Llull's life of wandering in France, Spain, North Africa, and Italy was symptomatic of a failure to find full acceptance. In the end, however, his scheme to provide missionaries skilled in Arabic, Greek, Hebrew, and Aramaic was confirmed by the council of Vienne (1312). Another such voluntary "exile" was Clare of Assisi, who, according to the report of her companion Filippa, was rejected by family and friends; devoted to poverty and assistance to the dispossessed, she moved from marginality to widespread popularity and patronage.

Autobiographical Accounts and Personal Testimony

In this volume members of such marginal groups speak in their own words, either by means of spiritual autobiographical accounts, or in court testimony directly based on the statements of the witnesses themselves. Some other sources have been added merely in order to place the first-hand sources within their historical context. The nineteenth-century philosopher Wilhelm Dilthey argued that "autobiographies are the most direct expression of reflection about life." In his history of autobiography, Dilthey's disciple Georg Misch encompassed nearly every scrap of personal testimony, including testaments, letters, chronicles, travel accounts and visions in his catalog of self-revelatory documents. Nevertheless, first-person accounts were relatively rare in the Middle Ages, and almost invariably focused on the transcendental issues of religious conversion and spiritual turmoil. The paradigmatic spiritual autobiography was Augustine's *Confessions*, which portrayed the author's odyssey from disbelief to faith. Therefore, although the sources here collected encompass Jewish, Muslim, Christian, and allegedly heretical examples, they all focus on the confluence between the transcendent and the mundane and confirm a universal hunger for spiritual meaning in medieval society, even among so-called marginal individuals.

The central Middle Ages, the period from about 1050 to 1350, witnessed a flowering of spiritual autobiographical accounts in particular. In the twelfth century, Peter Abelard, Guibert of Nogent, Petrus Alfonsi, and Hermann of Scheda, among others, left a rich legacy of autobiographical literature. In the thirteenth century, the following factors enhanced the self-examination which is a prerequisite to an autobiographical tradition: (1) the Christian stress on penance (also found in Jewish Hassidism and Kabbalism and Muslim Sufism, for example); (2) the post-Fourth Lateran Council (1215) requirement to confess at least once a year, which applied to all believers, whatever their station; (3) the rise of the mendicant and tertiary religious orders, which stressed penance; (4) the intensified campaign against the perceived foes of Christianity, including heretics, Jews, Muslims, and wavering believers, all alleged victims of devilish snares; and (5) the encouragement of local cults and confraternities, through which rural and urban folk became more deeply involved in the Church, and whose confirmation by ecclesiastical authorities demanded direct personal testimony of the sacred. The spiritual quest evident in contemporary theological tracts is likewise reflected in the testimonies of unlettered laypeople, not only learned theologians.

The central Middle Ages witnessed the liberation of the individual from the constraints of family, clan, village, and class, a necessary prerequisite for the "rise of the individual" and the production of autobiographical literature. The new geographical and social mobility may have created the conditions for the rise of the independent personality, free to pursue his or her own intellectual, economic, and spiritual path. In contemporary literature, the young knight-errant found in courtly romance who is forced to undergo a series of trials in pursuit of his fortune and mate has been the emblem of medieval culture. This heroic quest has its parallel in the ideal of the saint who forsakes family, class, and homeland (like Clare of Assisi and Celestine V) and battles with his or her inner demons in pursuit of perfection, going outside the normal bounds of society. Provided the saint followed hagiographical precedent, such marginalization could eventually become institutionalized.

The new emphasis on confession and penance enhanced the process of self-examination. This awareness of the crisis of faith which each believer undergoes lay at the basis of spiritual autobiographical accounts. Such inner conflict was almost invariably resolved through a sense of mission, which permeates most of these testimonies. The confession was regarded as a kind of therapeutic process of contrition, whereby the poison of sin is expelled and spiritual health is restored. Penance was often referred to in medical terms, as sin was cured through the balm of contrition and the believer was made whole again. The writings of Otloh of St. Emmeram, Ramon Llull, and Hermann of Scheda, for example, may be read in this light. The contemporary notion of pilgrimage regarded every believer as a kind of spiritual wanderer (*peregrinus*) who must undergo a series of trials in his or her quest for salvation. Thus every believer was merely a temporary resident and stranger in this world.

Many of these selections were occasioned by religious conversion, personal experience of the miraculous, direct contact with a saint, or an inquiry into heresy. Because God was perceived as the cause of all things, believers were predisposed to seek transcendental explanations for the turning points in their lives. Despite the dominant ideology, all the speakers describe tensions and conflict with a hostile environment: heretics were persecuted by the Church; Jews were forcibly converted or expelled; nascent Christian saints faced the opposition of their peers. Four broad classes of personal testimony are identifiable among these texts: (1) the accounts of those who experienced miraculous healing or other apparent contact with the supernatural; (2) recent apostates, who recorded the events surrounding their conversion to an alien faith; (3) heretics or others on the fringes of orthodoxy; and (4) believers who faced severe obstacles in the fulfillment of their faith. Some are confessional tracts that provide advice to coreligionists or call upon others to experience a similar spiritual rebirth, such as the works of Hermann of Scheda or Pope Celestine V. Others are traditional apologia, intended as a response to questions raised about the author's intellectual position, such as the lengthy autobiographical account Ramon Llull.

But as Bronisław Geremek has noted, the marginal person most characteristically appears in judicial and criminal archives. Therefore, sources for many of the following are the testimonies of witnesses who appeared at the canonical procedures undertaken in support of candidates for sainthood, such as Yves of Tréguier, Nicholas of Tolentino, Thomas of Hereford, Clare of Assisi, and others; or of persons summoned before the Inquisition and charged with heresy, such as Baruch of Languedoc, Flordebellina of Milan, Beatrice of Planisolles, Arnaud of Verniolle, and Arnauda da Lamotha. The Inquisition was organized in the early thirteenth century with the aim of investigating heresy in accordance with the procedures laid down in canon and Roman law. Although the investigators sought evidence concerning heretical belief and practice, those individuals who fell into the net of such an investigation often provide us with much valuable knowledge about the daily lives and beliefs of a broad spectrum of persons. Without the use of such sources, our access to persons other than the nobility and university-trained clerics, whose views are well reflected in contemporary institutional sources, would be severely limited.

The judicial testimony found in this volume passed through several hands. Typically, the witness spoke in the vernacular. For example, during the Montaillou inquiry at which Beatrice of Planisolles, Arnaud of Verniolle, and Baruch the German testified, the witnesses generally spoke Occitan or Gascon; Baruch spoke German. The notaries and scribes then translated this material into Latin (which is the source of many of the texts translated here) for the investigating commission, and then read this Latin version (retranslated again into the vernacular) back to the witnesses in order to verify its contents. The Latin often echoes the peculiarities and phrasing of the original, which cannot always be captured. Some of these witnesses may have corrected their testimony or recanted; if so, this is not reflected in this translation.

The canonization procedure had likewise been established in the late twelfth century. Its aim was to gather reliable testimony concerning the life and miracles of candidates for official recognition by the Church as saints. A commission of inquiry was appointed consisting of high ecclesiastics and theologians, which often heard hundreds of witnesses testifying under oath in accordance with the rules of evidence laid down in canon law. A staff of notaries, canon lawyers, scribes, papal proctors, and translators assisted in the inquiry. Many witnesses were layfolk drawn from all classes, and their testimony represents a rare opportunity to glimpse the daily lives of otherwise anonymous persons caught up in the enthusiasm of a religious cult. While the aim was clearly partisan — to prove the candidate's worthiness for sainthood — we may glean a good deal of indirect evidence from such testimony concerning family structure, economic concerns, and medical problems among the laboring classes. Those witnesses who appeared at a hearing into a putative saint's life and miracles (for example, Thomassa of Montefalco, Giacomuccio Fatteboni, Filippa di Leonardo di Gislerio, and Joan of Marden), or before a court investigating heresy, therefore often speak to us via the filter of notaries, canon lawyers, translators, and investigators.

The fact that such judicial inquiries lay at the foundation of many sources does not necessarily imply that the testimonies herein presented have been tainted by the self-interest of the court authorities and thereby rendered unreliable. The underlying ideological program of the court officials may be distinguished from the responses of the speaker nonetheless, and an adversarial relationship might have existed between the speaker and interlocutor. In heresy trials, the inquiry generally aimed at achieving conviction and demonizing the accused. In canonization trials, which were probably undertaken only if the likelihood of success was great, the aim was to demonstrate the would-be saint's virtuous life and miracles. Nevertheless, those "men of law" (the canon lawyers, proctors, and notaries) involved in such trials had often received a classical education and were highly skilled in the procedures of both Roman law and canon law as taught at Bologna. They were often members of a guild that was jealous of its reputation and status, and they were schooled in the procedures required to draw up legal depositions and guard against forgery of evidence. As first-hand eyewitness testimony about their own lives, the accounts elicited from individuals at such trials may be an imperfect source. Nevertheless, little else is available to us if we wish to reach beyond the governing classes and to hear the voices of persons who have historically remained inarticulate. At the same time, traditional autobiography was likewise apologetic, ideological, and aware of the interests and needs of its audience.

The translations included in this volume are largely autobiographical accounts and personal testimonies from the central Middle Ages (ca. 1050–1350). An attempt has been made to provide a broad range of materials not readily available in English. Monastic and clerical first-person accounts (such as those of Guibert of Nogent and Peter Abelard), the spiritual visions of female mystics (such as Angela of Foligno, Hildegard of Bingen, or Margery Kempe), and epistles and travel accounts (Marco Polo and Benjamin of Tudela, among others) may be found elsewhere and are therefore excluded. Most of the sources have been translated or adapted by me from Latin or Hebrew (one is a French translation of the original Arabic). As these texts are based on printed editions, rather than manuscripts, if the original editor misread the manuscripts on which the edition is based, these errors may be reflected in my translation.

In some cases I have slightly altered the original in order to enhance readability, although I have made every effort to retain the original meaning. I have occasionally inserted the original language for terms whose translation may be imprecise. In other cases, the authors themselves (Obadiah, Ramon Llull, and Celestine V, for example) often move between first-

and third-person narrative in a confusing manner. Furthermore, the considerable use of Biblical citations—the common heritage of Jew, Christian, Muslim, and heretic alike—is found woven throughout these texts (when identified, these verses follow the New English Bible). In many instances, a mere word or phrase could call forth a series of literary, historical, and linguistic associations in the medieval reader or listener, that are not always accessible to a modern audience, no longer so intensely exposed to Scripture. In addition, such citations and specialized religious vocabulary (for example, the terminology found in the mystical tract by Abraham Abulafia's disciple) are not easily traced.

The notes provide further details concerning persons, places, and technical terms which are otherwise not clarified in the text. Secondary readings also have been suggested. Several texts take note of a particular hour of the day by using the canonical hours (nones, vespers, and so on). The time given is therefore merely approximate, since the canonical hours differ over the course of the year.

Furthermore, some may argue with the overall structure of this volume. As in more recent times, the rubrics of marginalization in the Middle Ages might be quite fluid, and many of these testimonies may fall into several categories. Hermann of Scheda, for example, converted from Judaism to Christianity and then became a monastic; Baruch of Languedoc was forced to abandon Judaism for Christianity, voluntarily returned to Judaism, and again returned to his adopted faith. Arnaud of Verniolle was both a sodomite and a heretic. Celestine V may have come from a rural environment and lived most of his life in a remote monastery; however, as pope he achieved the highest office the church can confer. Clare of Assisi was born into a privileged family, which she abandoned, living at first on the margins of the church; eventually her order was given official recognition, and she was canonized shortly after her death. These emotional and physical meanderings indicate the difficulty of satisfactorily categorizing many subjects in this volume.

Although all translations are my own, I would like to thank several people who have provided suggestions or have assisted in the preparation of this material: Alan Bernstein, Brenda Bolton, Urzula Borkowska, George Ferzoco, Ronald Finucane, Avner Gil'adi, Marian Goodich, Ellen Joyce, Ruth Karras, Menachem Kellner, Sean Kinsella, Amalia Levanoni, Caroleigh Neel, Olga Sagi, and an anonymous reader. The staff of the University of Pennsylvania Press has been highly forthcoming in providing the expert advice and assistance necessary to see this volume through to publication:

Jerry Singerman, Kym Silvasy, Alison Anderson, Ellen Fiskett, and Noreen O'Connor. The libraries of the Institute of Historical Research (London), the University of Haifa, the University of California at Los Angeles, Columbia University, York University, the University of Toronto, St. John's University (Collegeville), the Vatican Library, and the Pontifical Institute of Medieval Studies graciously opened their doors to my research on this project. A debt of gratitude is also due to my students, who have often provided perceptive and creative insights into the problems encountered in the reading of such texts.

Chapter 7 is partially based on Michael Goodich, "Battling the Devil in Rural Europe: Late Medieval Miracle Collections," in *La christianisation des campagnes: Actes de colloque du C.I.H.E.C. (25–27 aôut 1994)*, ed. J. P. Massaut and M. E. Henneau, 2 vols. (Brussels: Institut Historique Belge de Rome, 1996), 1: 139–52; the testimony of Arnaud of Verniolle, shortened with slight revisions, is taken from Michael Goodich, *The Unmentionable Vice: Homosexuality in the Later Medieval Period* (Santa Barbara, Calif.: ABC-Clio, 1979; New York: Dorset, 1984), 89–123.

I

The Jews: From Tolerated
Minority to Persecuted Foe

The Jews were often perceived as the chief foes of the Christian faith. Their reasoned rejection of the faith paradoxically became one of the grounds for the scholastics' effort to base Christian belief on a firmer foundation. The Jews' persistent adherence to the old law — the faith of Jesus — was regarded as sufficient grounds for tolerating the practice of their faith and the security of their goods. Their civil status had been recognized under Roman law, which allowed them to own land and occupy public office, although after the ninth century in the Christian west many of these rights began to erode. Under the canon law *Sicut judaeis* their liberty, goods, and tombs were protected. Nevertheless, early scholastics such as Peter the Chanter (d. 1197) defined them as "common serfs of the church" who, as sons of Cain, could in no way expect to be equal to the descendants of Abel.

Although learned contacts between Jew and Christian had been particularly fruitful for Biblical exegesis during the twelfth century, the intellectual climate began to change drastically in the late twelfth century as the stereotypes of anti-Semitism began to appear. Overt hostility to the Jews based on their rejection of the divinity of Jesus and alleged complicity in his Crucifixion began to transform mere rumor of Jewish perfidy into more general hatred, sometimes based on economic grounds, which spawned bloody massacres. The desire to create cultural and political uniformity spawned the increasing marginalization of European Jewry following the rise of a more militant Christianity. Some of the anti-Semitic measures to which the Jews were subjected included prohibition on the employment of Christian servants and joint meals between Jew and Gentile, confiscation of goods, expulsion, and sometimes forced conversion. In many places, most notably the Holy Roman Empire, Jews were transformed into servants of the crown, partially protected against popular resentment and at the same time dependent on the prince's sufferance.

A variety of active steps were taken in the direction of exclusion of the Jews from the body politic, despite traditional recognition of Jewish religious and communal autonomy. The thirteenth century began with the canonical legislation of the Fourth Lateran Council (1215), which enacted a series of rules regarding the Jewish community. By the twelfth century Jews had become increasingly involved in moneylending, which served the needs of a growing economy. The council argued that their alleged dishonesty had led them to impose usurious rates of interest on loans, leading to the impoverishment of their Christian clients. Should they continue in this way, contact with them should cease until proper amends had been made. They were required to compensate the church for the loss of revenue caused by their receipt of property on which tithes had formerly been paid. In order to prevent untoward mixing, both Jews and Muslims were required to wear distinctive garb, although the secular authorities do not appear to have been overzealous in enforcing this recommendation. On the days of Lamentation and Passion Sunday Jews were forbidden to appear in public, on the grounds of blasphemous behavior. Finally, they were prohibited from holding public office.

The demonization of European Jewry gave birth to a series of libels that would eventually lead to their virtual expulsion from Western Europe. In the early eleventh century they had been accused of collusion with the Sultan Al-Hakim in order to destroy the Church of the Holy Sepulcher, the site of Jesus' burial. It was later claimed that the Jews customarily practiced the ritual murder (and even crucifixion) of Christian children as part of their Passover festivities and that they carried out acts of cannibalism, poisoned wells in order to spread disease among Christians, and tried to injure Christ himself by desecrating the Eucharist. The first great wave of anti-Jewish violence had occurred during the disastrous pogroms of the First Crusade in 1096, referred to in the autobiographical account of Obadiah the Convert, when the great Jewish communities of Speyer, Trier, and Worms were decimated. Jews were increasingly regarded as a kind of fifth column who, along with the heretics, were attempting to weaken Christianity from within. The next canard voiced against the Jews was the claim that they had ritually murdered defenseless Jewish children (usually servants) during the Passover season. The number of such documented cases may have reached as high as a hundred and fifty. The first such "blood libel" charge referred to the case of William of Norwich in 1144; it was followed by cases in York and Lincoln and others on the continent. As a result, Jews were often expelled from their communities or killed. Anti-Jewish outbreaks often focused on the major Christian feast-days, such as Corpus Christi, Easter, and Christmas.

In order to avoid forced baptism, some Jewish communities committed mass suicide, which may have strengthened the Christian belief in the hard-heartedness and perversity of the Jews, who were even willing to sacrifice their own children rather than see them experience the joy of Christian salvation. In York, for example, it was reported that a hundred and fifty men, women, and children were martyred on the Sabbath feast before Passover in 1190, perhaps during a mass suicide. This blood libel charge reached its fullest form at Fulda in 1235. A Jewish poet bewailing the Munich massacre of Jews in 1286 quoted these justificatory words uttered by their killers: "These unhappy Jews are sinning, they kill Christian children, they torture them in all their limbs, they take the blood cruelly to drink."[1] Papal bulls issued in 1247, 1259, 1272, 1422, and 1520 totally rejected charges of ritual murder; however, they failed to stem popular stereotyping and its consequences.

The next type of anti-Semitic charge, widely voiced in Germany, concerned Jews' alleged theft and desecration of the consecrated Host in which Christians believed the Lord to be incarnate, as a means of torturing Jesus. The Eucharistic miracle as a foil to such Jewish calumny is first dated from Berlin in 1243. Some secular and religious figures attempted to squelch these charges and to stem the rising tide of anti-Semitic violence. Emperor Frederick II, for example, had extended his protection to all the Jews of the Holy Roman Empire in 1236 as a means of countering the baleful effects of such anti-Semitism. Pope Gregory X (1271–76) condemned such accusations as a "silly pretext" in order to extort money from the Jews and seize their goods. In April 1298, however, a massacre of Jews began in the Franconian town of Röttingen at the instigation of a German knight named Rundfleisch, who accused them of desecration of the Host. In 1336–39 German bands known as Armleder (due to their armbands) slaughtered Jews in Alsace and elsewhere. As a result of such conditions, in the later Middle Ages Jews began migrating into the more welcoming regions of eastern Europe, where their skills were needed by a burgeoning economy. Such anti-Semitic stereotypes nevertheless persisted, even in areas such as England and France, from which Jews had largely disappeared by the fourteenth century.

1. Cited in Yehuda Slutsky, "Blood Libel," in *Encyclopaedia Judaica* (Jerusalem: Keter, 1971), 4: 1122.

Popular violence was accompanied by determined efforts to bring about the conversion of the Jews. A series of theological "dialogues" were conducted in southern France and Spain between Christian theologians and Jewish scholars with the aim of bringing them to the true faith. At the Barcelona disputation of 1263 the convert Pablo Christiani and the great sage Nahmanides (Rabbi Moses Ben Nahman, i.e., Ramban, 1194–1270) took part. Despite the respect in which he was held by King James I of Aragon, Nahmanides was accused of blasphemy and was forced to flee to Palestine. Another result of anti-Semitic agitation was the burning and banning of the Talmud on the grounds of heresy and blasphemy at the order of Pope Gregory IX in 1242 following its examination by a panel of theologians, including former Jews. It was claimed that the Talmud included scandalous and blasphemous remarks about the Virgin Mary and Jesus. Some theologians even argued that the Jews of the first century had recognized Jesus as the Messiah and Son of God, but had killed him out of spite. According to William of Auvergne, their greed had led to a loss of their earlier understanding of the Law. Like the heretic, in art, sermon, and *exempla* the Jew was increasingly viewed as an agent of the Devil, an adherent of the "synagogue of Satan."

At the same time, because of Christianity's own Jewish origins, Christian authorities had a rather conflicted approach to Jewish belief and practice. The basic foundation of discourse between Jew and Christian was the Bible, which engendered a wide range of auditory, visual, and other sensory experiences in which the Jew was depicting in negative terms. Although the portrayal of the Jew in the New Testament was often negative, nevertheless, according to the principle of progressive revelation, Christian sacraments and doctrine were based on Jewish precedents, and both art and sermon familiarized the believer with the figures of the Old Testament. The Merovingian and Carolingian hagiographers in particular had been inspired by similarities between the early history of the Jewish people and their own. Persons and events in the Old Testament often found echo among the Christian saints. Adam (who bore the gifts of Paradise), Abraham (who responded to God's call), Joseph (who was devoted to chastity), and Moses (who led the Children of Israel out of Egypt into the Promised Land) served as models for eremitical and monastic hagiography. The virtues of the Christian saint were personified by their Jewish predecessors: Noah stood for forbearance, Abraham obedience, Moses clemency, Elijah zeal, and Jacob contemplation. Adam and Eve's younger son Abel was regarded as the prototypical martyr, and the early *passiones* of the martyrs were often modeled after the tale of the Maccabee martyrs, who were presented as symbols of constancy, mirroring the torments of those who would die for the Faith. The Old Testament miracles of Elijah, Elisha, and Moses even served as the prototypes of Christian miracles. In the internal discussions surrounding the miracles of Bishop Thomas of Hereford, canonized in 1307, for example, the revival of a drowned child, allegedly due to prayers to the dead bishop, was regarded as authentic since it conformed to the precedent of Elijah. The possibility that one might be cured through a vision is proven with references to Jacob and Solomon. A biographer of Archbishop Louis of Toulouse (d. 1297) likened the bishop-saint to Moses, who had led the Jews out of Egypt by a pillar of fire and clouds (Exodus 13.21–22). Furthermore, just as Isaiah 11.1–3 had prophesied that the Messiah should come from the tree of Jesse, so, as the son of the Angevin King Charles of Sicily, Louis was descended from the Hebrew kings. The wings of the seraphim (Isaiah 6.2) sent to the prophet in a vision were likened to the six kinds of charity displayed by Louis. Louis' pastoral activity was compared to Moses' use of the staff in the victory of the Children of Israel over the Amalekites, the parting of the Red Sea, and the bringing forth of water from the Rock (Exodus 17.8–9, 7.20, 8.13, 9.33). His avoidance of carnal pleasures is akin to Daniel's refusal to partake of Nebuchadnezzar's feast, his learning to King Solomon, and his steadfastness under pressure to Tobias. A second biographer compared Louis to Solomon, John the Baptist, and Daniel. Self-conscious awareness of such precedents is also found in the life of Edmund Rich, archbishop of Canterbury (d. 1240). Avoiding fellow students in his youth, Edmund had come upon a bush that was flourishing out of season. He exclaimed, "God, who figuratively appeared to Moses at Mount Sinai, in the burning bush which was not consumed, reveal to me what this miracle portends." As he prayed, the Infant Jesus appeared.

The pursuit of Jewish sources might even lead to fanciful derivations of a saint's name from the Hebrew words suggested by Isidore's (d. 636) *Etymologiae* and Jerome's treatise on Hebrew names. This indicates at least some superficial knowledge of Hebrew in learned circles, even if it was based on a reading of ancient sources and not direct contact with the Jewish community. It was argued that the name served as a premonition of the saint's virtues. Albert of Trapani's name, for example, was allegedly derived from "alab," meaning milky or sweet in Hebrew, and "thus" incense in Latin. Landgravina Elizabeth of Thuringia's (d. 1231) name allegedly came from the Hebrew for "my God knew," "the fullness of the Lord," or "the seventh part of my God" — referring to the classic seven deeds of mercy.

Hagiography was nevertheless enlisted in the battle against the Jews.

Active persecution of the Jews might be another virtue for which candidates for sainthood were praised, although such earlier saints as Bernard of Clairvaux (d. 1153) had preached religious tolerance. One of the virtuous acts of Bishop Thomas of Hereford (d. 1282) was his advice to King Edward I not to allow a former Jewish knight the power of life and death over his Christian subjects. Thomas argued that the forgery of money and the high interest rates exacted by Jewish moneylenders had led to the impoverishment of many good Christians. On another occasion, Thomas was allegedly offered a bribe by five hundred Jews if he would cease his persecutions. The saint refused, unless they converted, "because they were the enemies of God and rebels against the Faith." Another English saint, Bishop Richard of Chichester (d. 1262), also opposed the building of a synagogue by the Jews at Lewes, an act that was praised by his biographer for his rejection of both their pleas and their money. King Louis IX (St. Louis, d. 1282) of France, while often compared to the just King Hosea, at the same time approved the actions of a knight at Cluny who had objected to the presence of Jews at a debate and had struck one of them who had failed to honor the Virgin. In his youth, Louis had in all likelihood also been present with his mother, Blanche of Castile, at the debates held in 1240 at Paris concerning the allegedly anti-Christian character of the Talmud, and the banning of Talmudic study was vigorously pursued during his reign. The Talmud contains the legislative decisions of the Jewish governing bodies between the second and sixth centuries along with the commentaries of the great jurists; its precedents were often applied to the governance of Jewish civil society in the Middle Ages.

The underlying reasons for this growing animus against the Jews and their eventual marginalization and expulsion have been a subject of some debate. Some have argued that the rise of the nation-state and its centralization inevitably led to the suppression and expulsion of those whose national or religious identity could not conform to these changes. Others have suggested that the Jews were driven out partly as the result of the envy of their economic rivals, the Italian bankers, who sought to replace them as the major moneylenders and sources of capital. Their service as moneylenders, after they had been excluded from the exercise of nearly every other profession, had made them at the same time both indispensable to a dynamic economy and hated by those in their debt. As the classic economic "middlemen" who served the feudal aristocracy and bishops, the Jews were the most immediately perceived objects of popular resentment; and those, like the lesser nobility, who were indebted to Jewish moneylenders and were unable to repay their debts, agitated for their expulsion, as occurred in England in 1294 and France in 1306. The involvement of the new religious orders, the Dominicans and Franciscans, in much of the anti-Semitic agitation further suggests that the messianic and apocalyptic fever which gripped Christianity in the later Middle Ages demanded the purgation of the Jews, who were perceived as the descendants of those who had persecuted and crucified the Savior. The final blow came as the Jews were blamed for the ravages of the Black Death in 1348/49, and were victimized by mobs looking for a scapegoat to hold responsible for the high mortality rate, which did not seem to affect the Jewish community. They were accused of conspiring to poison wells, springs, and drinking water as part of an international conspiracy led by their rabbinical leaders aimed at destroying Christendom. Their heinous activities, often proven through confessions elicited under torture, led to the massacre of many Jews, although in some places roaming beggars were also so victimized. The continuing persecution led to the virtual disappearance of the Jews from much of western and central Europe by about 1500 through a series of royal decrees. For example, in 1288 King Edward I of England had issued the decree *Statutum de judaismo*, aimed at forcing Jews out of moneylending and usury into agriculture and handicrafts, an attempt that failed. In 1294 he finally expelled the Jews from England. Between 1306 and 1394 they were eventually expelled from all of France. As a result of the atrocities committed against them and their gradual expulsion from most of Western Europe, the center of European Jewry moved eastward to Poland-Lithuania.

The Jewish minority represents the best documented marginal group resident in medieval Europe. In addition to the huge number of primary sources produced by the Jews themselves dealing with their status as a barely tolerated minority, both church and secular chanceries produced numerous primary sources dealing with the condition of the Jews. The following selections therefore represent a mere introduction to the condition of members of the Jewish community, largely in their own words. The first selection includes two versions of the childhood conversion of a Jewish girl of Louvain to Christianity in the 1220s, which contains many stereotypical themes of anti-Jewish propaganda. It may be read in conjunction with contemporary accounts of charges of ritual murder and their consequences, along with the considerable polemic literature, which indicate the kind of atmosphere of exclusion and persecution in which the Jewish communities of western Europe increasingly found themselves.

The autobiographical Jewish testamentary will written by Judah ben

Asheri to his son mirrors the concerns of a prominent Jew living under conditions of relative tolerance. This document provides a personal account of the financial and communal arrangements from one of Spain's more prominent Jewish communities just prior to the Black Death and the sharp deterioration of the condition of Spanish Jewry at the end of the fourteenth century. Judah himself speaks of the catastrophes that had befallen German Jewry and regards Spain as an island of tolerance.

The nearly contemporary account of the forced conversion to Christianity of Baruch the German of Languedoc comes from an Inquisition protocol of the 1320s. Although such a text is itself a product of persecution, it provides valuable details about the interaction between the two communities. It illustrates the precarious condition of southern French Jewry during a time of expulsions, forced conversions, and massacres, and how the unsubstantiated charge of collusion between Jews, Muslims, and lepers had disastrous results.

The final selection summarizes the views of a minority within a minority, the Kabbalistic followers of Abraham Abulafia. Abulafia himself claimed to have been denounced to the Church by fellow-Jews, presumably because of his prophetic and messianic claims. The Kabbalists had largely rejected the rational foundations of normative Judaism in favor of mystical contemplation, symbolism, and an esoteric understanding of Scripture. In addition to the selections in this chapter, our understanding of the position of the Jewish community may be expanded by a reading of the autobiographical accounts in Section Two of Obadiah the Convert, Hermann of Scheda, and Sa'id ibn Hasan of Alexandria, who speak of their conversion experiences, the first from Christianity to Judaism, the second from Judaism to Christianity, and the third from Judaism to Islam.

Caesarius of Heisterbach (ca. 1225) and
Thomas of Cantimpré (ca. 1263) on Catherine of Louvain

The life of Catherine of Parc-aux-Dames, née Rachel, who had turned to Christianity at the age of about six to eight despite her parents' appeals to church and state authorities, weaves together contemporary anti-Jewish hagiographical themes with historical events. Her conversion is reported in two sources that were close to the circles involved in the conversion of heretics and Jews, the *Dialogus de miraculis* (ca. 1225) by the Cistercian Caesarius of Heisterbach and the *Bonum universale de apibus* (ca. 1263) by the Dominican Thomas of Cantimpré. A number of hagiographical *topoi* appear in her *legenda*: the superior instinctive intelligence of the child; the theft of table scraps to feed the hungry; a nighttime vision of the Virgin as a bridge to conversion; the parents' attempt to frustrate their daughter's religious urges through offers of marriage; the attempt to woo the nun/novice from the monastic life by means of a handsome youth; and the corruption and stench of the Jew. The life of a young Jewish convert could thus be transformed into a vehicle for the transmission of hagiographical themes. Rachel's case cannot be seen in isolation from other contemporary instances of conflict over the conversion of Jewish children against the will of their parents. In Frankfurt in 1241, as a result of attempts by the community to convert a child, the Jews suffered pogroms, suicide, and forced baptism. In a case referred to by Gregory IX in a letter to Berthold von Tech, bishop of Strasbourg (1223–44), the pope supports a recently converted father's claim to raise his son as a Christian.

At the same time, this tale sheds light on the relations between Jew and Christian by referring to the apparently open social contact at Louvain between members of the two faiths, including their children; the willingness of the duke of Brabant and the bishop of Liège to aid Catherine's parents in retrieving their underage daughter; the ties between Rhenish Jewry and the Jews of Louvain; some of the stereotypes increasingly applied to the Jews, including their alleged stench, stubbornness, greed, and sexual appetite; and the role of the Cistercian order in defending the girl's decision. Nevertheless, the text provides scant evidence concerning childrearing in the Jewish community. Although the sources present Rachel as a tabula rasa at the time she first met the chaplain Rayner, in fact, in keeping with contemporary Jewish tradition, Rachel would have probably already been acquainted with some parts of Jewish Scripture, probably the Pentateuch, daily prayers, Sabbath observance, dietary regulations, and various ceremonies to which Jewish children were exposed at a young age, although the stress would have been placed on domestic skills. It had been remarked by observers (Abelard among them) with some dismay that Jewish girls were often more learned even than their male Christian counterparts, and some examples of learned Jewish women appear in the sources — such as Dolcia, the daughter of Eleazer of Worms, who led women in prayer. The version of Catherine's life that appears here represents a conflation of the two contemporary accounts.

Source: *Acta Sanctorum*, ed. Socii Bollandiani, 69 vols. (Paris: V. Palme, 1863–1940), 4 May I, 532–34. Taken from Caesarius of Heisterbach, *Dialogus de miraculis*, ed. Joseph Strange, 2 vols. (Cologne: J. Heberle, 1851), and Thomas of Cantimpré, *Bonum universale de apibus* (Douai: Baltazar Belleri, 1627).

Bibliography: Aviad Kleinberg, "A XIIIth Century Struggle over Custody: The Case of Catherine of Parc-aux-Dames," *Bulletin of Medieval Canon Law* n.s. 20 (1990): 51–67.

*   *   *

Recently the young daughter of a certain Jew of Louvain converted to the Christian faith in the following way. A priest who was chaplain to the duke of Brabant[1] customarily entered the home of a certain Jew who was a foreigner in that same city and disputed with him concerning the Christian faith. He had a small daughter who listened intently to the disputation in accordance with the capacity of her intelligence, weighing both the priest's word and the father's response. And so she grasped the meaning through divine disposition and was brought to the Catholic faith. So great was the girl's understanding [*discretio*] that, although not yet five years old, in the home of her Jewish parents she began to consider why there was such a difference between the name of the Jew and of the Christian; since the men of both peoples [*gens*] possessed the same appearance and language. She was more attached (as she said afterward) to the Christian than the Jewish name, and she was especially delighted to hear the name of the blessed Mary, which Christians customarily used both in prayer and while swearing. She used to hide bread from her parents' table under her sleeves and secretly gave it to beggar children so that she could hear them thanking her in the name of Mary. In these matters she continued from time to time in a wonderful way, but wisely hid them, so that neither of her parents could learn or hear anything about their daughter's thoughts.

It happened that in the course of time she came with several children to the home of the priest master Rayner. This priest knew her by name, and asked her, "Have you come, dearest Rachel, to become a Christian?" And she said, "I want you to teach me what it is to be a Christian." Then the priest, being a holy man and joyful in spirit, felt that this girl would have a divine future. And starting with the Creation, he began to explain Scripture to her, through which the faith of Christ, or Christ Himself, can be explained or shown. The explanation of these matters (as she reported afterward) was so complete that at the age of six and a half she comprehended by means of such great understanding of the spirit, so that rarely did the priest

---

1. Henry I (1218–35), duke of Brabant, was buried at the church of St. Peter of Louvain.

repeat any explanation. They studied for a year and a half in secret, in the course of meetings during which he taught the excited girl furtively and at the right time. What evidence of wonder! Rachel could never be satisfied, nor did she tire of hearing the word of God. Since both the priest and his assistant Martha, a religious[2] and prudent woman, were often tired, they would teach her in turns.

What more? Soon her parents turned their attention to their daughter, and in consultation with the other Jews agreed that the girl should be sent away from Louvain to the other side of the Rhine in order to be bound in marriage.[3] When the girl found out, she tearfully told the priest that if that very night he did not remove her, and she did not become a Christian, she would be lost and troubled forever. When the priest had heard this, he told her to come to the usual entrance early in the morning. After she had agreed, in the evening she said to her mother, "Mother, I want to sleep by myself tonight." Since she was still a little girl, her mother refused for a long time, but agreed in the end, and ordered her daughter's bed to be prepared as a pillow at her feet. The little girl slept until morning, and since she disregarded what she had promised the priest the previous night, the glorious mother of God appeared to her dressed in a robe as white as snow and offering her a shining staff, saying, "Get up, Catherine, and take the road; a great road awaits you." When she heard these things, Rachel, believing she was grasping the wand, fell out of bed and cried out. Her mother, awakened by the cry, asked why she was crying, and the girl carefully dissimulated. Rachel then got up and went to the agreed-upon spot, where she soon found the priest. He joyfully lifted her up and went to the Cistercian monastery of Parc-aux-Dames, which was situated a league and a half from Louvain. He baptized her in the presence of many onlookers, giving her the name Catherine, which she had first been called by the mother of Christ, and she was baptized while wearing the holy garb of the order.

When her father and his friends heard what had happened, without delay they angrily approached the local duke, the bishop of Liège, and Pope Honorius[4] in order to give them a great deal of money so that the girl would be returned to her parents, since she had been taken away before she had reached the legal age.[5] Should she remain in her parents' home until the

2. Martha may have been a beguine; on the beguines see Christina of Stommeln (Section Four).

3. The center of Jewish life in the region was at Cologne in the Rhineland.

4. Hugh of Pierrepont, bishop of Liège (1220–29), and Pope Honorius III (1216–27).

5. The age of discretion was twelve for girls and fourteen for boys.

age of twelve, and should she remain firm in the faith, then she could rightly take a Christian name. They evilly thought that they could easily change the child's mind should she return to her parents' home. How grievous are the treacherous struggles of our times! Many great and learned men cherish the money that has been given them; which is why the priest was very concerned. He therefore tearfully invoked both Christ and his Mother, as she had been the cause of this event. Because the duke wanted to restore the Jewish daughter to her Jewish father, the priest Rayner stood firm and said, "Oh my lord, if you commit this evil deed against God and his bride, your soul will never be saved." The lord abbot Walter of Villers also approached the duke.

The Jew saw that the hope he had placed in the duke was in vain. He decided to bribe Hugh, the lord bishop of Liège. At the Jew's request, Hugh sent letters to nuns at the convent of Parc, urging that his daughter be restored to him. Finally the Jew came with his friends and relatives to the convent, where Catherine was studying in the cloister. Although she knew nothing whatsoever of their coming, she felt a great warmth, and said openly, "I don't know what it is, but the Jewish stench oppresses me." In the meantime, as the Jews knocked on the window, the abbess spoke to the girl, "My daughter Catherine, your parents want to see you." She replied, "It is their stench I feel, although I don't see them." She refused to go out. The bishop of Liège has recently made an accusation concerning this matter, in the presence of the lord Archbishop Engelbert of Cologne[6] in his synod, and it has been decided that he should no long trouble the convent concerning the baptized girl.

At that time he submitted, but in the end he did not obey. For afterward he summoned the girl to Liège by letter under pain of excommunication in order to respond to her father's objections. She came, but under good protection. The Jewish contention was that she had been taken away as a minor and baptized by force. They said to the girl, "Catherine, we are told that you will willingly return to your father if allowed." She replied, "Who says this?" They replied, "Your father." She then said the following in a clear voice, "My father lies totally through his beard." Oh what a wonderful thing, that up to now, through the centuries, has been unheard of! The girl asked the priest to accompany her to every summons and judge. "Perhaps," she said, "the judges are persuaded by my age and moved by my sacrifice." It happened as she said. She came to Liège, and in the presence of

---

6. Archbishop Engelbert of Cologne, who was consecrated in 1216 and martyred on November 9, 1225, was also the subject of a biography by Caesarius of Heisterbach.

the bishop, clerics, and magnates she confounded and moved various lawyers and judges with constant and truthful reasoning. For a great distance
the voices of persons crying out with tears were heard from the church of
St. Lambert of Liège. Astonished, all clearly saw and said that the wisdom
of the divine spirit had remained strong in one so young. At this point,
when the Jews' lawyer got up, lord Walter, abbot of Villers[7] excitedly said to
him, "Master, you speak against God and your honor. You should surely
know that should you utter anything against the girl, I will go to the pope
and request that you be permanently silenced in all legal proceedings."
Secretly fearful, he answered the abbot, "Lord abbot, who will it harm if I
am able to extort money from the Jews. I will say nothing that will injure
this girl." Since he would soon receive his payment, he said to the Jew, "I
dare not say any more."

Around that time, when lord Guy, abbot of Clairvaux, visited the
monasteries of his order in the diocese of Liège, he conferred with the
bishop, admonishing and asking him how long, in God's honor, he would
continue harassing a girl already consecrated to Christ. The bishop answered him, "Good lord abbot, why is this case important to you?" The
abbot replied, "It is important for two reasons: firstly because I am a Christian; and secondly because the house where she lives belongs to the line of
Clairvaux." And he added, "I decree that the girl and her case should be
under the pope's protection, and I appeal those letters sent by you against
her." He did what he said, and sent to the prior of Parc those letters sent by
the pope against the bishop, lest the bishop try to disturb the convent
because of the girl, and so that they could defend themselves with those
letters.

After two years the matter came to an end by legal judgment. A decep-
tive snare was then prepared by the Jews, using a handsome Jewish youth
for the purpose. He came to the convent where the girl lived, pretending
that he wanted to be baptized. When he had represented himself in that
way, he asked to speak to his cousin Catherine because of her learning. He
said the following, "The word of my cousin will be more effective to me
than the speech of others." Catherine perceived the youth's falsehood in
coming to the Faith, and neither imprecations nor money or any obedience
could persuade her to speak even a single word with the youth. When the
Jews saw this, they left her alone, and the Jew returned to his vomit.

After the above, much grace flourished in the person of the most elect
Catherine, who was loved by all; no one was more serene than she.

---

7. Abbot Walter (1214–21) of Villers, one of the largest Cistercian monasteries.

Meir ben Isaac, *Purim* (1236)

Beginning in the twelfth century, the most frequent and destructive canard hurled against the Jews was the ritual murder of Christian children. At least a hundred and fifty examples have been catalogued, and there are considerable variations on the theme. It was generally claimed that during the Passover season, which celebrates the Exodus of the Jews from Egypt and closely coincides in date to Easter, the Jews would customarily ritually slaughter a Christian child (often a servant in the employ of the Jews), in order to make use of his blood. This charge led to gruesome reprisals against the Jews and frequently to their expulsion from communities in which they had lived for years. Often, their increasingly important role in society as moneylenders and the dependence of the local authorities on them as a source of revenue lay behind popular anger. During these and other anti-Semitic outbreaks, lay and ecclesiastical rulers sometimes did their best to protect the local Jewish community, as illustrated in the following eyewitness account. In 1236, the Jews of Narbonne, one of Europe's oldest and most respected Jewish communities and often a refuge from persecution elsewhere, were the victim of popular violence, whose genesis is not entirely clear. This rather incomplete account appears in a contemporary Hebrew chronicle.

Source: Adolf Neubauer, ed., *Mediaeval Jewish Chronicles and Chronological Notes* (Oxford, 1895; rpt. Amsterdam: North-Holland, 1970), 251.

Bibliography: William C. Jordan, *The French Monarchy and the Jews: From Philip Augustus to the Last Capetians* (Philadelphia: University of Pennsylvania Press, 1989).

*   *   *

On 20 Adar 4996 [March 8, 1236] from the creation of the world, the entire population of the city of Narbonne gathered together in order to destroy us. They were about to enter our homes and bedrooms. Nevertheless, none of our people were wounded and none were delivered into their hands because God didn't allow it. In fact, before the people could break down the doors of the house, God took pity on those who were inside. The assailants were gripped with a great fear. Thanks to our master, viscount Aimeri, long may he live! He suddenly arrived with the police and his advisers in order to change the evil thoughts they had against us. All the notables of the city also came to our aid and opposed the aims of the attackers. In my home, the riot-ers had already entered and broken the gates. They had pillaged a commen-tary on the Torah along with other books, but whatever had been taken was returned to me afterward. May the holy name of the all-seeing God be blessed forever! . . . This miracle had happened because a French Jew had gotten into a quarrel with a sinner [a Christian] who was a fisherman and hit him on the head with a wooden tool. The people were aroused and brought him to a Christian physician, who had let him die. In this they followed the advice of another sinner who hated the Jews and is named Paulivina. The others then joined said Paulivina and did what is described above. . . .

Rabbi Judah ben Yehiel Asheri of Toledo (d. 1349), *Testament*

In the central Middle Ages, Spain was divided into several Christian king-doms, including Navarre, Portugal, Castile-León, and Aragon, with the remnants of the Muslim states concentrated in the south. As a people of the Book, the Jews in Muslim Spain were relatively secure, and with the recon-quest of Spain by the Christians, which began in the mid-eleventh century, they largely continued to enjoy these privileges until the late fourteenth century. Classified as *servi Regis curie* (servants of the crown), they were guaranteed freedom of worship and forced conversion was prohibited, al-though one could not build a new synagogue or expand an older structure without permission. Jews were barred from holding public office, yet this rule was often relaxed due to their considerable administrative, financial and linguistic skills. In the kingdom of Castile and León, the victory of Henry of Trastámare (King of Castile, 1333–79) led to a worsening of conditions for Jews, but this was largely the result of their backing of his unsuccessful rival to the throne, Peter IV (1376–87, in Catalonia known as Peter III), rather than any overt increase in anti-Semitism. In Aragon, the condition of the Jews began to worsen, partly due to the influx of colonists into regions recently conquered from the Muslims, and the Jews tended to reside within self-contained communities, the *juderia*. In Majorca, despite its relative affluence and security, in 1309, they were forced to pay the considerable fine of ninety-five thousand pounds as a result of a charge of ritual murder.

The following document provides a good glimpse of the Jewish com-munity during the late thirteenth and early fourteenth centuries. It is writ-ten in the form of an ethical will aimed at providing practical examples of the application of theological and ethical principles to everyday life. Often addressed by a father to his son, the earliest example in Hebrew (translated from Arabic) was perhaps written by Solomon ibn Gebirol, and others were composed by Judah ibn Tibbon, Nahmanides, and Eleazer of Mainz. Similar testamentary advice also appears in James of Aragon's *Libre de saviesa o doctrina*. The father of the author of the following epistle, Asheri ben Yehiel (ca. 1250–1327), known as Asheri or Rosh, had been the leader of German Jewry after the death of Meir of Rothenburg. This didactic letter contains considerable detail concerning learning, financial arrangements, affectional ties, and communal organization among Spanish Jewry during a period of relative religious tolerance. The will is filled with Biblical and Talmudic citations (which is common to other such sources).

Source: The source and an earlier translation are to be found in Israel Abrahams, ed., *Hebrew Ethical Wills*, 2 vols., 2d ed. (Philadelphia: Jewish Publication Society, 1948), 2: 164–200 passim (Hebrew).

Bibliography: Yitzhak Baer, *A History of the Jews in Christian Spain*, trans. Hillel Halkin and Louis Schoffman, 2 vols. (Philadelphia: Jewish Publication Society, 1966), 1: 306–78.

*   *   *

He ordered them to keep to the way of God their master, not because they are not as good as their contemporaries, but to train them in the ways of the ancients. Those who are called "friends of God" maintain the deeds of their fathers. About that I say "open reproof is better than love concealed" [Proverbs 27.5], for then their hearts will be bound and the rebukers will be pleased, knowing that those who listen will be protected as "the apple of the eye" [Deuteronomy 32.10]. "Take a man to task and in the end win more thanks than the man with a flattering tongue" [Proverbs 28.23]. I will open with the voice of thanks, first of all to Judah, the awe-inspiring Rock of Ages, to whom belongs the glory and the power, and transcends all in blessing and glory; and who, before I was born, remembered me for the good. When my mother, my teacher, was still pregnant with me, she was told in a dream that she would give birth to a son. Would she want him to be intelligent or rich? She replied that she would want him to be intelligent. This proves that dreams speak vainly, since I was not intelligent; although in a kind of lying way the world may think that I am learned and "put forth lovely boughs" [speak well, Genesis 49.21]. God also gave me wealth more than others of my age. May it be that "He provided me only with the food I need" [Proverbs 30.8], for I am contented with my portion.

When I was three months old my eyes became diseased, and I was not cured. When I was three years old a woman tried to cure me, but she worsened my condition, so that I remained indoors at home for a year, since I could not see where I was walking, until a Jewish woman came who knew how to cure eye disorders. She tried for two months and died. If she had tried one more month, I would perhaps have been able to see as at the beginning. And if it weren't for these two months when she made the attempt, I would probably have never been able to see at all. Blessed be He who granted me grace and opened my eyes to the deeds of His hands.

Afterward, I studied the Talmudic tractates which my father taught me in the yeshiva to the best of my ability without arguments and answers. When I was thirteen years old I was taken out of the land of persecution. "He will shake you out, shake you as a man is shaken out" [Isaiah 22.17].[1] Although I had spent years studying in Ashkenaz,[2] I did not enter into years of study in France, since exile confuses the mind. I had neither the hand-writing nor the language to study their books or understand their rhetoric. Nor could I work day and night because of the weakness of my eyes, since they were clouded. I therefore couldn't write books or compose essays. When I was twenty-eight years old my father of blessed memory sent me to the city of Toledo to find a position, and I did so. The community of Toledo sent for him and wouldn't allow him to leave; they sent messengers after I had left. On my return I was waylaid by evil Gentiles who wanted to kill me, but the God of my father stood beside me, and I was surrounded by angels, returning safely to my father's house. Twenty-three years later my father died. Although there were greater and wiser men than I in the city, God's grace shone upon me and I was appointed to my father's place. But I did not try to follow the others, nor was I wise enough to do so. For I am a foreign resident and regarded as of no value, and my knowledge very limited, and "I had not made my fortune" [Hosea 12.8].

One day I sat thinking and "my heart is dazed with despair" [Psalms 143.4]. I was holding a book of Writings,[3] which indicated what my fate would be. Opening the book, I came upon the following verse, "And

1. A variant translation is "But Yahweh will throw you away, strong as you are, will grasp you in his grip."

2. Medieval Germany, including parts of eastern France.

3. One of the three parts of the Old Testament, which also includes the Pentateuch (Genesis, Exodus, Leviticus, Numbers, and Deuteronomy), the Writings, and the books of the Prophets.

Nathan answered David, 'Do whatever is in your heart, for the Lord is with you'" [1 Chronicles 17.2]. I regarded it as an omen. When I had accidentally come upon this verse I rejoiced, and I said, "Although there has been no divination, there is a sign." Thanks to the merciful and loyal God I have carried out my affairs well and thus far God has helped me.

My desire for children was not because of my love for them or to be honored by them; only in order to carry out the commandment, and so that I would have a seed to replace my ancestors in Torah in fulfillment of the commandments. Such was my prayer throughout my life on the graves of the innocent righteous [*Tzaddik*] ones. God in his mercy granted me five sons, and I considered myself alive among them, among my people and my brothers. But because of my sins my "middle bar" [son, cf. Exodus 26.28] was taken from me, on whom I thought my house depended. "A smoking brazier and flaming torch passed between the divided pieces" [Genesis 15.17] and placed a living man beside me. I confess to the God of heaven and earth that I owe this to God and even more, for I knew that His judgments are just. "The Lord did indeed chasten me, but He did not surrender me to death" [Psalms 118.18]. I was consoled by the fact that he will not be punished in heaven because of his own sin. The few years he lived were spent in the faith of his ancestors. When my turn comes I will go and see him and "find him in Beth-el" [Hosea 12.5].[4] I depend on the mercy of heaven to give me a replacement for him, and the pleasure of my heart will be renewed. "And the original . . . and its substitute shall be holy to the Lord" [Leviticus 27.10].

Now my heart is filled with a desire to write them [i.e., to his children] this epistle of rebuke and to provide ethical advice. I command them to read it once a month.[5] . . .

I left Ashkenaz at the age of thirteen and at the age of fifteen came to Toledo on the first day of the month of Iyar in the year sixty-five.[6] When I was thirteen I clearly had nothing. When I married the daughters of both R. Yehiel and R. Solomon, may they rest in peace, I did not receive enough to cover the cost of the clothes and the wedding. And from my father I only inherited a small number of his books, since all that he had at his death including his house was not enough to fulfill the terms of his will. I have never taken gifts from anyone, with the exception of fourteen hundred gold

4. In Hebrew the place-name Bethel means "the house of God."
5. This is followed by a long series of ethical principles, a program of study, and suggestions for proper behavior and the kinds of people to avoid.
6. In the year 5065, according to the Jewish calendar, which was April 26, 1305.

pieces which I asked from three people as a loan, which in the end they gave to me as a gift. And because of their importance and position I could not refuse. I used this money for the marriage of my sister. I lost money because of people who did business for me, and the capital wasn't my own.[7] . . .

The terms of the contract given to me by the community were not given because I asked for them, since I knew I was unworthy. It was rather because of their grace and love for my father of blessed memory. After ten years the community heard that I wanted to seek a resting-place [presumably a job] elsewhere. They decided to give me fifteen hundred gold pieces a year. If I had wanted more they would have given it to me, as is documented in a letter to me which I have dated 1341. When Mordecai [the Frenchman] ran away, I lost more than six thousand. When the leaders of the community heard that I wanted to move to Seville, they asked me to remain and they increased my contractual salary to three thousand a year. I knew it wasn't because of me, but rather because of God the merciful and loyal and because of my fathers, "the rebuilders of broken walls" [Isaiah 58.12], the holy ones who were on the earth. . . .

One of the good ideas I had was to marry my daughters to the sons of my father's family. I have many reasons for this. One reason is that one receives good grapes when one pairs grapes from the same vineyard. It is also a great *Mitzvah*,[8] as our wise men say, to love one's kindred, to marry off one's sister's daughter, and lend money to a poor person in distress. Concerning such a person it is written [Isaiah 58.9], "if you cry to Him, He will say, 'Here I am.'" Furthermore, the women of our family have become accustomed to men who study the Torah. The love of the Torah has already entered their hearts, and they will help their husbands to continue their studies. They also haven't gotten used to unnecessary expenses and will not ask their husbands for luxuries. Demands for luxuries keep men away from study. Generally speaking, children [sons?] resemble the mother's family. If in the course of time a man seeks his fortune in another city there will be no one who will keep the wife from following her husband.

My second idea was that I should write a bit about the history of my sacred ancestors on this earth for the benefit of those who come after us. Since the Lord blessed be He "who shakes you out" drove us to the great

---

7. This remark is followed by a discussion of his financial affairs and his contractual obligations to the Toledo Jewish community, including salary, pension scheme, arrangements for his children, and provisions for his heirs.

8. According to Maimonides, there are 613 *Mitzvoth* or sacred Biblical injunctions. The term may also in a general sense refer to charitable deeds.

and glorious city of Toledo [cf. Isaiah 22.17],[9] and shortly thereafter the Jews were driven out of France, perhaps someone might think that we were driven from our country or that we left because of some kind of calumny or suspicion. When our descendants are acquainted with the honest ways of our ancestors, they will be very much ashamed if they don't follow their path. In whatever they do they should try to maintain the path of their ancestors. If they do so they will find favor in God's eyes. If not, it would have been better if they had strangled at birth, as babies who have never seen the light of day. Since I left Germany when I was thirteen years old I didn't manage to hear about their upright and righteous deeds, except for the little which I heard from my father of blessed memory, and from his sister and my grandmother of blessed memory who told me about their ancestors of blessed memory. Whatever I heard about the deeds of our first ancestors I report here.

My grandfather R. Yehiel Bar Asher was born in the year 4970 [1210]. When he was twelve years old he had a loyal friend named R. Solomon Hacohen of blessed memory. They agreed that each should have a part in the deeds of the other, both in *Mitzvoth* and in other matters. They kept this pact all their lives. They were pious men [Hassidim] and "men of action" unique in their generation. On Yom Kippur eve in the year 5024 [September 5, 1263] early in the evening the candle belonging to my grandfather of blessed memory went out while he was in synagogue. For it was customary for every male to light a wax candle for himself in the synagogue on Yom Kippur eve which would burn day and night. During Hol ha-Moed of Succoth[10] my grandfather of blessed memory died and they honored him greatly at his death. They came from neighboring areas for his funeral. It is the custom among people of Germany to place the coffin on a special stone near the cemetery and to open it to see if the dead person's limbs have moved because the coffin has been shaken about. When they did this to him, R. Solomon Hacohen approached, and four cubits away said loudly in the community's presence, "I ask you to remember the agreement you made with me." He then began to laugh from within the coffin so that the entire community could see. I testify that the fact that they saw him laugh was told to me by my father and grandmother of blessed memory. One day R. Solomon Hacohen of blessed memory was studying in his school during the day and suddenly saw my grandfather of blessed memory sitting beside him. He was very surprised and asked how he was doing. He replied that he

9. A play on the words *Toledo* and *letaltal*, "to shake out."
10. The intermediate days of the harvest Feast of Tabernacles, which occurs in September or October.

was doing very well. R. Solomon said, "I am surprised that you are allowed to be seen by mortals." He replied, "I can visit my own home as in the past, but I don't want them to say how much prouder this pious man [*Hassid*] is than the other righteous ones."

Six months after his death at midnight on Saturday night he appeared to his wife and said to her, "Hurry and get up. Take your sons and daughters and take them away from here, because tomorrow the Jews who are living here will be killed. This has been decreed concerning the entire region. We prayed and our prayers were received, except regarding this place." She got up and did as she was told, but returned to save her belongings and was killed along with the community.[11] . . .

The cause of the departure of my father of blessed memory from Germany was the capture by the governor of Rabbi Meir of Rothenburg[12] of blessed memory. He was ransomed by the German communities for a great fortune. The governor refused to take anyone as a guarantor except my father of blessed memory, who became a guarantor for a huge sum of money. But before the costs were divided among the various communities R. Meir died in prison. The governor slandered my father by saying that since he had died in prison my father was still responsible. The communities and my father were still required to pay the ransom. My father escaped to another city, but out of fear of the authorities he left Germany and came to the great city of Toledo. During the first year he was there they sent him a letter from the *consejo* [town council] where he had lived to return home; they would send fifty officers to greet him at the German border and would give him a safe-conduct from the king. Since they knew his wisdom and status, they were willing to follow his advice in all matters. That was the reason that my father of blessed memory came to this country. As a result of this God provided my father with many students in Spain.[13]

Baruch the German of Languedoc (1320)

The condition of French Jewry was often dependent on the crown's need for ready funds or the willingness of a local lord to protect his Jewish

11. The author here discusses various members of the family, some of whom his grandmother rescued.

12. Meir of Rothenburg (ca. 1215–93) was a leading scholar and Talmudic authority, often consulted on points of Jewish law, who died in prison.

13. The author next speaks of his father's writings, and how he replaced him as leader of the community. He continues to further discuss various financial matters and the disposition of his property.

population. Established in Gaul since Roman times, hundreds (perhaps even thousands) of small Jewish communities had characterized France until the twelfth century. Although first officially expelled from the royal domain by Philip Augustus in 1181/82 (and recalled in 1198), the Jews had managed to reestablish themselves in urban communities, generally dwelling in specific districts or streets. But despite the imposition of heavy fines, expulsion, and execution during this period, Jews continued to live in such peripheral regions of France as Provence, Burgundy, and the Comtat Venaissin (under papal protection).

The following report comes from the testimony of Baruch the German of Languedoc, who was tried as a heretic by Bishop Jacques Fournier of Pamiers (ca. 1280–1342, later elected Pope Benedict XII), on the grounds that, after having been baptized, he attempted to return to his former faith. Baruch's forced conversion had taken place during the popular uprising and massacre of the Jews associated with the shepherds (the *Pastoureaux*) of southern France, who believed that lepers, Jews, and Muslims had conspired to overthrow Christianity. The Pastoureaux had first appeared in the Île de France with the aim of conquering the Holy Land, and had freed one of their number from prison and had attacked the royal provost. Further south, they began by forcibly baptizing Jews, pillaging their goods, and burning evidence of debts. Despite efforts to control the movement, including its condemnation by Pope John XXII, the authorities were largely powerless to curb its violence (one of whose victims was Baruch) prior to its dispersal in autumn 1320. After a series of trials and attempts to convince him of the truth of Christianity, Baruch changed his name to Jean, rejected the Mosaic law, and accepted the sacraments of the Church during a ceremony at Pamiers on September 25, 1320 in the presence of ecclesiastical and secular officials and local residents.

Despite their re-expulsion from France in 1306 by King Philip IV, the following report confirms the continuing existence of a Jewish community consisting of both local and German Jews who were involved in trade in Agen, Grenade, Ondes, and the region of Toulouse and who sometimes served as royal agents on both sides of the Pyrenees. The attempts made to protect Baruch further suggest that at least some Christians maintained amicable ties with the Jews, despite their precarious position. Nevertheless, the Jewish community of Toulouse and its environs suffered a sharp decline in the fourteenth century in the wake of the crisis of 1320/21, as its property was taxed or sold and its members killed or expelled. This document contains an accurate picture of the ceremony required to readmit a Jew back to his faith. The kind of forced conversion herein described had been the common fear of European Jewry at least since the First Crusade in 1096, when perhaps several thousand Jews, largely from the Rhine region, had been massacred rather than undergo baptism. These events were repeated in 1320/21 at Montclus, where 337 Jews were killed; although more widespread and bloodier pogroms were to occur during the period of the Black Death in 1348/49, when Jews were blamed for the spread of the plague, by allegedly having poisoned the wells and streams of Europe.

Source: Jean Duvernoy, ed., *Le registre de d'inquisition de Jacques Fournier (Évêque de Pamiers), 1318–1325*, 3 vols. (Toulouse: Edouard Privat, 1965), 3: 177–90.

Bibliography: Malcolm Barber, "Lepers, Jews, and Moslems: The Plot to Overthrow Christendom in 1321," *History* 66 (1981): 1–17.

*   *   *

Baruch the German, a former Jew, having put aside Jewish blindness and perfidy and after having converted to the faith of Christ and received the sacrament of baptism in the city of Toulouse during the time of the persecution of the shepherds [Pastoureaux or Pastorelli], but returning "to the vomit like a dog," that is, to the Jewish faith and rite, was captured while living with the Jews of the city of Pamiers. . . .

He confessed that . . . on June 12, 1320 the Pastoureaux arrived carrying a flag, traveling from Bergerac to Grenade, and threatened to exterminate the Jews. The Jews Salomon of Ondes and his scribe, Eleazer, sought out the bailiff[1] of Grenade, as he told the speaker afterward, in order to receive refuge from the Pastoureaux. The bailiff replied that he would help, but when a great crowd appeared he told Salomon that he could not hold him safely and that he ought to take a boat up the Garonne to Verdun, where there is a strong royal fortress.[2] Salomon then took a boat and started out for Verdun, but the Pastoureaux, hearing and seeing them, also arrived by boat, drove him ashore, and took him by river to Grenade. They told him that if he did not accept baptism, they would kill him. The bailiff, who was present, said that if they killed Salomon they should also kill him. Hearing this, the Jew said he didn't want the bailiff to suffer on his account

---

1. A low-ranking local official, who often purchased his office, was responsible for the royal fort, and probably protected the Jews because they were regarded as the property of the crown. Jews themselves sometimes filled this office in France.

2. Le Mas-Grenier (Tarn-et-Garonne).

and asked the Pastoureaux what they wanted of him. They told him that he must either be baptized or be killed. Salomon said he preferred baptism to death, and he was baptized along with his scribe Eleazer. The next day they both came to the speaker in Toulouse, told him what had happened to them, reporting that they had been baptized, although not out of faith, and that they would willingly return to Judaism. The speaker told them that, while he knew the Jewish law well, he didn't know Christian law, and didn't know what advice to give them as to whether they could return fully to Judaism. But he would ask friar Raimond de Jumac,[3] a suppliant of the inquisitor of Toulouse, to find out if this was possible.

The speaker went with Bonnet, a Jew of Agen, to friar Raimond de Jumac and master Jacques, the notary of the inquisitor of Toulouse, and told them about Salomon's experience, asking whether a baptism that had been undertaken unwillingly and without desire, but out of fear, was valid. The friar told the speaker that such a baptism is not valid, or so he understood his reply, that is, that a baptism undertaken in this way was not a baptism. He immediately returned to Salomon and Eleazer, telling them that friar Raimond and master Jacques had told him that it had not been a true baptism and that they could definitely return to Judaism. Afterward he heard that Salomon had surrendered himself into the hands of the seneschal[4] of Toulouse until such time as it could be determined at the Roman curia if such a baptism was a true baptism. . . .

The speaker said that baptized Jews who returned to Judaism did so in the following way according to the teaching of the Talmud: they cut the nails on the hands and feet, the hair on their head is shaven, their bodies washed in running water, in the same way that according to the Law one purifies a foreign woman who marries a Jew. They believe that baptism renders those who receive it impure.

The following Sunday [June 15], Alodet, the sub-vicar[5] of Toulouse, brought to the town twenty-four wagonloads of Pastoureaux, who had been captured for killing a hundred and fifty-two Jews at Castelsarassin and environs.[6] When the Pastoureaux reached Château Narbonnais and about twenty wagons had entered the château, a large crowd of Toulousains gathered. The Pastoureaux who were in the last wagons asked for help as they

---

3. Perhaps Junac near Foix.
4. In France, a royal representative, who fulfills both military and judicial functions.
5. A local official of the court of Toulouse. The vicar was head of the local royal administrative unit, responsible for defense.
6. Castelsarassin was royal property.

had been captured and imprisoned because they wanted to avenge Christ's death. Some of the Toulouse crowd broke the ropes holding the wagons, and, once the Pastoureaux were freed, they jumped out and called out along with the crowd, "Death, death, let's kill all the Jews!" Baruch heard this reported everywhere in Toulouse, although he himself was not a witness.

These Pastoureaux invaded the Jewish quarter along with a great crowd. Baruch was in his room, studying and writing, when a large number of people came into his room crying aloud at him, "Death! Death! Either be baptized or we'll kill you immediately." Having seen the people's anger and having witnessed the murder of other Jews who had refused baptism, he replied that he'd rather be baptized than killed. They then grabbed him and immediately forced him out of the house, without allowing him to take any clothes aside from what he was already wearing, taking him to the church of St. Etienne de Toulouse. When he got there, two clerks showed him some Jewish corpses in front of the church, saying, "If you aren't baptized, you'll have to die like those you see here." He was then badly beaten by some bystanders, and replied that he preferred to be baptized. He told them that he had a friend, a preaching friar[7] at the city's friary named John the German, whom he wanted to be his godfather. He had said this because he thought that if he could reach the friar, who was his great friend, he could then avoid death without being baptized.

The two clerks then made him leave the church and wanted to take him to the Dominican friary. But when they were outside, Asser, a Jew of Tarascon in Provence, along with someone else, was killed before his eyes, and the crowd asked whether Baruch had been baptized. They replied that he hadn't, although he had asked them to say that he had. He was then knocked on the head, but he did not bleed and the swelling quickly healed without the aid of a doctor, a bandage, or other treatment. But he thought that the blow made the eyes pop out of his head. He saw that other Jews who did not want to be baptized were killed, and since the two clerks told him they could not protect him or get him to the Dominicans' house, for he would be killed before he could reach the street, he asked what he could do to avoid being killed. They told him, "You surely see that you should be immediately baptized or you'll be killed!"

The speaker responded, "Let's go back to the church. I'd rather be baptized than killed."

They returned to the church. He told the clerks to wait a bit to see if his

---

7. The Dominicans were known as the preaching friars.

sons had arrived. They waited, but since his sons did not come, they said they could wait no longer, and that he could either be immediately baptized or leave the church and go to where the other Jews had been massacred.

He said that he wanted the sub-vicar of Toulouse to be his godfather, because he hoped that a sergeant named Pierre de Saverdun,[8] a friend of his, was with the sub-vicar and would save him from death without being baptized. But he was told that the sub-vicar couldn't come because on that day he had accompanied the Pastoureaux to Castelsarrasin, and was now resting from fatigue.

Shortly afterward, the clerks instructed the speaker to step on the stone near the baptismal font. He agreed, while pronouncing the word "sub-vicar," implying that the vicar should be his godfather, but also that, should he arrive after the baptism, the vicar would say that a baptism undertaken out of fear of death is not valid, and therefore his baptism would be invalid. If, on the contrary, he said that such a baptism was valid, the speaker's would be.

He then voluntarily went up to the stone on which others had been baptized and stood before the curate, who did to him what is generally done to anyone about to be baptized, so he believed. However, before the curate began to read and do what is done at a baptism, the clerks told the speaker to tell the curate that he had voluntarily come to be baptized, and that if he didn't say this, he would be killed. He did so, although he thought otherwise.

He was then placed on the stone near the water and was baptized, and what is generally done in such cases was done to him. He was given the name Jean.

When this was done, he told the clerks to accompany him to see if any of his property had been left. They told him they wouldn't do so, since they were tired and exhausted, but he did go with him to their house, and he drank wine with them. They eventually accompanied him to his home to see if anything remained, and they found that all the speaker's books had been torn to bits, that his money had been stolen, while only six pieces of cloth, some of which he had taken as a pledge, and some of which were his own, including a silk coverlet, remained. The clerk who had served as his godfather put them in a sack to be taken along. As they were about to leave, they met an officer of the municipal council of Toulouse whom his godfather knew. The officer was armed in order to protect the Jews. The speaker's godfather told him, "This man has been baptized and is a good Christian."

8. Saverdun is situated near Pamiers.

The man winked at him and took him aside, saying, "Do you want to be a good Jew?"

He replied in the affirmative, so that he then said, "Do you have any money?"

"No, but take this," said the speaker, giving him the sack containing the items noted earlier. The officer said, "Do not fear. Say that you are a Christian, and in that way you'll escape."

When they were outside, the clerk who was his godfather, along with the speaker, found ten council members with armed guards. A councilman asked him in a low voice, "Are you a Jew?"

He replied in the affirmative in such a way that the clerk couldn't hear him. The council official told the clerk to leave the speaker alone and handed him over to the sergeant, ordering him to guard him as he would his own person, in the name of the council, the sub-vicar, and the seneschal. When they were near the city hall, the speaker admitted to being a Jew; but when they were on dangerous streets and when the sergeant was asked if he was a Jew, on the speaker's instructions he said that he had been baptized and was a Christian.

As he said, the murder and pillage of the Jews lasted until evening. That night he told the sergeant that they should go to the sub-vicar of Toulouse in order to inquire if a baptism undertaken out of fear of death is indeed valid. When they were at his place, he was eating, and the sergeant said to him, "Lord sub-vicar, here is the Jew who wants to be baptized by you."

He responded, "We are eating. Come to the table." Since the speaker didn't want to eat, he glanced around, and saw Pierre de Saverdun. Taking him aside, he said he didn't want to be baptized, and that he should tell the sub-vicar not to force him to receive baptism, since such a baptism would not be valid, as he had said.

Pierre told the sergeant to leave, for he would guard the speaker, and handed him over to another sergeant with whom the speaker walked to Château Narbonnais. When the sub-vicar finished eating, they went back to his residence. He then said, "Do you want to be baptized now, or wait until tomorrow?" Pierre de Saverdun, however, took the sub-vicar aside and conferred with him; the speaker didn't know what he said, but the sub-vicar said, "I certainly won't forcibly baptize this Jew or anyone else." The speaker gathered from this that his baptism had been invalid. He believed that, if the sub-vicar had so desired, it would have been considered a true baptism, and if not, it would not.

After this, he consulted Pierre de Saverdun as to whether or not he should stay at Château Narbonnais. Because Pierre reported that those Jews who remained at Château Narbonnais would be either baptized or killed, they decided that he should leave Toulouse. Pierre gave him three sterling and accompanied him to the fork in the road that leads on the right to Montgiscard,[9] advising him to make haste and to speak German on the way.

The speaker hurried to Montgiscard. When he got there an armed crowd fell upon him, asking if he was a Jew or a Christian. He asked who they were, and they replied, "Pastoureaux! If you are a Jew, we want to kill you unless you are baptized."

The speaker told them he wasn't a Jew, and they said they were going to imprison him. He responded, "Do you have the power to imprison people?"

They said they had, because the local bailiff and his men were present. Thinking he wouldn't be harmed if he said he was a Jew, he allowed them to lead him to a house in which the bailiff, master Bendit Loup, his daughter Bonne, and several other Jews were to be found. He spent the night and the following day with them. The next night they went with the bailiff to Mazères,[10] and from Mazères to Pamiers. He was asked whether in Pamiers or elsewhere he was returned to Judaism in accordance with the method noted above. He replied in the negative, since according to the teaching of the Talmud, if someone has been totally baptized willingly and wants to return to Judaism, this is accomplished in the way noted, since such a person is regarded as having been polluted. But if he has not been fully baptized but was forced to accept baptism, he is not returned to Judaism in this way, since such a baptism is not regarded as binding.

He was asked if he had told anyone, or particularly anyone who had been baptized out of fear of death, that they weren't in fact baptized and could return to Judaism without punishment and sin. He replied in the negative, aside from what he had already testified concerning Salomon and Eleazer. When asked if he had told a Jew or Jews that they should temporarily accept baptism in order to escape death and should then return to Judaism, he replied in the negative. Asked if he had ever been present at a ceremony in which a converted Jew had returned to Judaism, he said that he had not. He was asked if he knew any Jew who had been baptized in this way and had then returned to Judaism, and he replied that he did not.

His testimony was given on the year and day noted above in the

9. Montgiscard is situated near Villefranche in the Haute-Garonne. The term *sterling* was applied to a variety of both English and continental currencies. It is not clear here which currency is meant.

10. Near Pamiers.

presence of the persons noted above and in my presence, Guillaume Petri Barta, notary of the lord bishop. I wrote these things down and kept them.

Afterward in the same year, on the fourteenth day of the month [July 14, 1320], when Baruch was brought to judgment in the apostolic chamber before the aforesaid bishop, the testimony he had given on the previous day was read to him in the vernacular. He was asked by the lord bishop whether he wished to stick to this confession or wanted to add something or to change or correct it. He said he would stick by what he had said, but wished to add that when the baptized Jews Salomon and Eleazer came from Grenade to him at Toulouse (as mentioned in his confession), they met Salvatus, a Jew from the district of Tarascon.

He also added that after he had told Salomon and Eleazer that the baptism they had undergone was not binding and that they could return to Judaism, he had said this was so because such a baptism is not a true baptism, and they could return to Judaism.

He also added that the number of Jews killed on that day in Toulouse was about one hundred and fifty.

He was asked by the lord bishop whether when he stood before the chaplain and the baptism ceremony was carried out or when they placed him in the baptismal font, he had expressed any resistance in either word or deed or indicated that he refused to be baptized (or indicated any unwillingness or opposition to the baptism). He answered that he did not, since he was afraid that if he did so he would be killed. His godfathers also told him to tell the chaplain that he had come willingly, otherwise he would be killed. He believed that the chaplain heard this, which his oath will attest. He begged them to ask the chaplain whether it was true that he would have been killed if he had shown resistance in word or deed.

He was asked if according to the Law, the Talmud, or in his opinion a Jew can be saved only through keeping the Law and not in Christianity or paganism; and that such a Jew should prefer to be killed and should not join the Christian religion or paganism. He replied that if without the order of a ruler someone should want to kill him or any believing Jew that can be saved, unless he become a Christian or pagan, then it is preferable to become a Christian or pagan than allow himself to be killed, since this is only temporary and immediately afterward he will be able to return repentant to Judaism. If something like that should happen because of an order of the ruler, then the Jew should be killed rather than convert to Christianity or paganism, since the ruler's decision may last a long time.

He was asked if he believed that it is a greater sin for a Jew (who believes that he can only be saved within the Jewish faith) to be baptized in order not to be killed, or rather to be killed so as not to be baptized. He answered that it is a greater sin for a Jew to be baptized than to be killed. Asked if he believed that a Jew (who believes he will be saved in Judaism) who is killed rather than become a pagan has sinned in any way, he said no, but rather that such a Jew has done the right thing.

He was asked the following: since he believed that the Jew who has been killed because he did not want to become a Christian or pagan did the right thing, as he said; and, as he had testified, one who becomes a Christian or pagan has sinned, why did he himself prefer to be baptized? He replied that he did not believe that his own baptism was complete, since it was only short-lived. He believed in his heart that should the sub-vicar of Toulouse confirm the baptism it would be considered legitimate, otherwise it would not be. He was convinced that he would return to his faith in repentance for having been baptized; because of this he preferred to be baptized than to be killed.

He was asked whether from now on he would like to be a Jew or a Christian. He replied that he would rather be a Jew and not a Christian, since he didn't consider himself a Christian.

Asked if when he was baptized he thought it would be a legitimate baptism or wanted it to be so, he replied that he never believed that it was legitimate, and he would never have been baptized if it weren't for the particular circumstances. . . .

The witnesses were Pierre de Viridario, archdeacon of Majorca, master David (a Jew), and I, Guillaume Petri Barta, aforementioned notary, who received and recorded the aforesaid.

The lord bishop immediately warned him and made it clear to master Baruch that since he was baptized in this way, as he said, not completely by force, according to both law and reason he must keep and believe the Christian faith. The same conditions that brought him to the Faith did so for good and not for evil so that from now on he should believe and keep the Christian faith. Otherwise, he ought to know that should he stubbornly maintain that he is a Jew, he would definitely be brought to trial, as is customarily done against a stubborn heretic in accordance with the full force of the law.

Master Baruch replied that he didn't know what the Christians believe and why they believe what they believe. In contrast, he knows the Law and its beliefs, and why the Jews believe what they believe, because their belief is confirmed by the Law and the Prophets, which he had read for twenty-five years as a teacher. Therefore, unless it can be proven to him that, according to the Law and the Prophets, Christian belief conforms to the Law and the Prophets, he will refuse to believe and keep the Christian faith, and would prefer death rather than abandonment of Judaism, since he is not considered an authority among the Jews of the region. Yet, if the lord bishop or someone else should prove to him or show him according to the Torah and the Prophets that what the Christians believe and keep is in accordance with the commandments of the Law and their Prophets, and that the Jewish religion and cult no longer provides salvation, it would be right to abandon the religion and cult of the Jews and transfer to the religion and faith of the Christians. The lord bishop promised to do so with God's aid, in the presence of the aforementioned master David the Jew and newly baptized persons who could translate Baruch's words and the Law to the bishop, since he could not speak the local language well.

The bishop began a disputation concerning the articles of the Christian faith against Baruch, who, with all his heart, tried to resist by making use of those very things written in the Old Testament which were said by the lord bishop in support of the Christian faith.

First, they argued about the principle of the Trinity, the unity of the divine substance, and the special names of the persons of the Trinity and their origin. This argument lasted for almost two full weeks, and Baruch was defeated on every issue, and he had nothing more to say. He admitted that the Trinity and the unity of the substance or nature of God are to be found in the person of God. According to him, he believed this as a result of the authority of Holy Scripture, that is, the Law and the Prophets. He admitted that the names of God—the Father, the Son, and the Holy Spirit— are the proper names of the person of God and are to be found in Holy Scripture.

The argument then turned to proving that it is suitable that the Messiah, or Christ, who is promised in both the Law and the Prophets, should be both God and man. As a consequence, due to His true divinity and humanity, He must be one entity, namely, both God and man. This argument lasted almost eight days. The Jew, who could muster no argument against this from Holy Scripture, was surprised that he had not reached this conclusion earlier through a reading of Holy Scripture, since it claims that the Messiah is supposed to come as a real man like other men. Baruch admitted that he believed this principle in accordance with Holy Scripture.

The argument then turned to proving that the Messiah promised in the Law has already come. That was the most difficult of all the arguments, and the discussion lasted more than three weeks. The Jew was defeated and accepted this principle. Among the subjects raised in the discussion was the attempt to show by means of the Law and Prophets that Christ was conceived and born of the Virgin, suffered death for our sakes and for our salvation, descended to Hell, and on the third day was resurrected, rose up to heaven, and will return to judge the living and the dead, and that the sacraments of the church bring forgiveness of sins and grant divine grace. Although he was stubborn concerning the Eucharist, he agreed afterward, but it was difficult to prove to him that human bodies are eternal after the resurrection; that these bodies don't need food and the other needs of life; that growth and corruption come to an end in these bodies; that cursed bodies may exist forever in fire but will not be consumed, but must suffer incalculable pain. In the end, the Jew agreed to all the above.

He asked afterward why the commandments of the Old Testament are not kept by Christians, who in everything else keep the faith and belief of the Prophets. They proved to him by means of the Law and the Prophets that the commandments come to an end with the coming of Christ. After he maintained these beliefs for almost two weeks, he refused to continue being called Baruch, but wanted to be called Jean, no longer a Jew but a Christian, and wanted to learn more through his reading of the Law and the prophets. Nevertheless, the lord bishop was told that he had begun to raise doubts about the Christian religion and told someone that he did not believe in what Christianity believes. As a result the last investigation, which follows, was undertaken by the lord bishop.

The lord bishop again taught Baruch and solved the problems that had led him to raise doubts, claiming that he had found them through a reading of the Law and the Prophets. Baruch said he wanted to be a Christian and to reject Judaism.

In the aforesaid year on August 16 Baruch was brought to judgment before the lord bishop and his assistant, friar Gaillard de Pomiès, in the court of the bishop of Pamiers. He was asked if after his confession the bishop had proven to him by means of the Old Testament that the Divinity consists of the Trinity (namely, the Father, Son, and Holy Ghost), that there is unity in the Divinity, and that these are the same thing. Baruch answered in the affirmative, but afterward had found that there are conflicting views in the Old Testament. . . .

He was asked how long he held the view that the Trinity is to be found in the nature of the Divinity and that there is unity in its substance. Baruch said that he read the Old Testament for eight days and did not find otherwise. He therefore believed this for a certain length of time. But he afterward found the opposite in Holy Scripture and ever since has had doubts and continues to have doubts.

He was asked which verses in the Old Testament led him to doubt whether the Trinity constitutes the persons of the Divinity. He said that his doubts first arose from the fifth book of the Law. "Hear O Israel, the Lord thy God, the Lord is One" [Deuteronomy 5.45]. He cited this verse in order to deny the Trinity, since it says "The Lord our God," and this verse states the unity of the substance or nature [of God]. The phrase "is One" indicates the uniqueness and unity of the person of God.

Second, another verse in the same book led him to raise doubts: "See now that I, I am He, and there is no god beside me" [Deuteronomy 32.39].[11] He explained this verse in the following way in the vernacular: "Veiatz ara que yeu yeu so. Enoya Dieu ammy; yeu aucire et yeu vivre fare."[12] He cited this verse as "I, I am He," which excludes any multiple natures, since the person is twice called "I," and the next part of the verse further explains this. As it says, "and there is no god beside me."

Third, he was led to doubt by the verse in the same book that begins, "You have had sure proof that the Lord [Adonai] is God [Elohim]; there is no other" [Deuteronomy 4.35].[13] He explained the meaning of this verse in the following way in the vernacular: "Tu garda per saber que Adonay es Habelhoym, mes plus ses lu ses lu." This same verse appears as, "Ut scires quoniam Dominus ipse est Deus, et non est preter eum." He understood this verse in this way: those Jews who say that the Father and the Son also appear in the Divinity as two separate persons claim that the name Adonai refers to the Father and that the name Elohim refers to the Son. Since in Holy Scripture both names frequently appear separately and often appear next to each other, they therefore claim that God the Father should be distinguished in its person from the Son. But in his opinion, their view is disproved by the aforementioned verse, since it says that "Adonai is Elohim," and the "He" referred to here is "He Himself." Therefore God the Father is in every way the same as God the Son. From this he drew the conclusion that the Father is not distinguishable from the person of the Son.

Fourth, he was led to doubt by the fact that in the books of Moses it is frequently written, "I am Adonai," when speaking of God; while it does not say, "I am Adonai Elohim," which would appear if the Father and Son were God.

11. Deuteronomy 32.39. This verse is cited in Hebrew transliterated into Latin and is filled with numerous errors in the original protocol.
12. A translation into Provençal of the original Biblical text.
13. Cited in transliterated Hebrew.

Fifth, the following verse in Isaiah led him to raise doubts: "Thus says the Lord, Israel's King, the Lord of Hosts, his ransomer: I am the first and I am the last, and there is no God [Elohim] but me" [Isaiah 44.6].[14] This same verse appears as "Hec dicit Dominus rex Israel et redemptor eius Dominus: ego primus et ego novissimus et absque me non est Deus." He understood that this verse leads to rejection of the view that the Son is a separate person from the Father, but that He is rather the same. In Hebrew the first verse says, "Lord of Hosts," which is understood to be God the Father; and in the second verse, "I am the first and I am the last," is followed by "and there is no God but me," which means that Elohim is the Lord of Hosts, so that the Son is the same as the Father.

Sixth, he was led to doubt by what the people say in the third book of Kings[15] following the sacrifice of Elijah, "The Lord [Adonai] is God [Elohim], the Lord is God" [1 Kings 18.39]. This same verse appears as "Dominus ipse est Deus, Dominus ipse est Deus," which he understood as follows: since the people did not say "Adonai Elohim" but rather said "Adonai is Elohim," it is to be understood that there is no Father and Son in the Divinity. Otherwise it would have read "Adonai Elohim". But since the word "He" [in the Hebrew original] appears in the middle [i.e., between "the Lord" and "God"], the people did not distinguish the person of Adonai from Elohim (that is, the Father from the Son), so that the Father and the Son are the same.[16] At the moment he didn't remember what other additional things led him to doubt whether the Father and the Son are one person or several persons.

Anonymous Disciple of Abraham Abulafia,
Shaarei Tzedek (*The Gates of Justice*) (ca. 1290/95)

The following autobiographical account (perhaps by Rabbi Shem Tov of Spain) was written in Upper Galilee or Hebron in 1290 or 1295 by a follower of the Kabbalist Abraham Abulafia (1240–92?). The word "Kabbalah" derives from the Hebrew root "to receive" or "to accept" and refers to a school of Jewish mysticism which flourished in the thirteenth century and which includes practices of a meditative, magical, and devotional nature known only to a select group of initiates and allegedly based on a secret

14. Cited in transliterated Hebrew.
15. In Christian (especially Roman Catholic) editions of Scripture, the two Books of Samuel are often included with the Books of Kings, resulting in four books under the rubric Kings. The Jewish and Christian numeration may therefore differ.
16. The Hebrew original may be literally translated as "The Lord, He is God."

oral tradition. Its adherents claim to possess a higher understanding of Scripture, the Creation, the soul, and divinity. The following text describes the various paths of spiritual development encountered by the author in his odyssey in search of truth — the popular (i.e., Muslim asceticism or Sufism), the philosophical, and the Kabbalistic.

The Kabbalistic categories discussed in this selection suggest that the author was a disciple of Abraham Abulafia, much of whose work survives. Abulafia was born in Saragossa in 1240 but spent much of his career in Italy. Abulafia, like many other mystics, makes some autobiographical remarks. In a work written in 1285 he reports his birth in Saragossa and subsequent journeys to Tudela (where he was raised), the Holy Land, Greece, Capua, Rome, Barcelona, Messina, and elsewhere. He complains that most of his students were not capable of understanding higher principles. Abulafia reports that his first great revelations occurred at Barcelona when he was thirty-one, although he was plagued by both divine and Satanic visions. But only when he was forty-five did all the confusing images to which he had been subjected become clear.

He developed his own peculiar form of messianic Kabbalism, which anticipated the imminent coming of the Messiah (he was born in the year 5000 of the Jewish calendar, seen by some as an important turning point in history) and reportedly sought unsuccessfully to meet the pope in 1285. Speculative, esoteric, mystical Kabbalism was looked on with suspicion by normative Judaism. Abulafia believed that the Hebrew alphabet itself was divine in character, and he made use of combinations and permutations of Hebrew letters as a meditative tool. The precise translation depended on the specific context in which these terms appear, and the author of this text assumes prior knowledge of the Kabbalist frame of thought, a situation that considerably hampers clear translation.

Source: Gershom O. Scholem, ed., " 'Shaarei Tzedek': Maamar be-Kabbalah Me-Ascolat R. Avraham Abulafia meyoohas le-R. Shem-Tov (Ibn Gaon?)," *Kiryat-Sefer* 1 (1924): 127–39 (Hebrew). For another translation see Gershom O. Scholem, *Major Trends in Jewish Mysticism* (New York: Schocken, 1974), 147–55.

Bibliography: Moshe Idel, *Studies in Ecstatic Kabbalah* (Albany: State University of New York Press, 1988), 91–101.

*   *   *

I, a youthful anonymous soul, walk "in the footprints of horses" [Genesis 49.17; Judges 5.22], and in my room I am looking into "the holes of the crescent" [Isaiah 3.19], that is, into my heart, in order to find "the words of truth" [Ecclesiastes 12.10] through abstraction and other means of illumination; that is, in three possible ways, the popular,[1] the philosophical, and the Kabbalistic. The popular method of illumination is the way practiced by Muslim ascetics. They lay aside the external forms of the soul, namely, "the natural forms," in various ways, until they say that if some spiritual form enters their soul, it is isolated in their imagination, and strengthens it, so that they can foresee what will happen to us before we do. I inquired about the matter and learned that they recall the name of God in their language, namely, Allah. I inquired further and understood that after they recall the letters of this name and direct their thoughts away from consideration of all natural forms, the letters of Allah's name will act in accordance with their own characteristics; and through the multiplication of this action, they enter a kind of trance without understanding why, because they haven't studied Kabbalah. The removal of all natural forms from the soul is termed *Mekhikah*, Erasure.

The second method is philosophy, which is difficult to banish, because of its attraction to the human mind; it achieves completeness, allowing the student to visualize a mathematical form through example, and through analogy to understand a form in both natural science and theology. One continues to contemplate this because of the sweetness attendant upon such understanding. This sweetness is so attractive that the student can find no gate or door through which to escape the views he has already formed. He may be so entwined in contemplating such notions that he isolates himself so as to avoid having his thoughts fouled by contact with others, until his thoughts are disturbed like the image of "a sword whirling and flashing" [Genesis 3.24]. The reason for this minimal understanding is the apprehension of the letters out of which his thoughts are formed. Whatever he may understand through the agency of human reason grows stronger, and his understanding of all the sciences improves, since it is in his nature. And he will say that understanding of this or that subject is understood as if in a prophetic way, but he won't comprehend the real reason and will mistakenly believe that it is merely a consequence of ordinary human understanding. I discovered in the writings of Avicenna, one of the great philosophers of his generation, that he used to isolate himself when he wrote his great works. When he encountered difficulty, he would try to define and limit his subject, continue to contemplate it, and if the problem persisted,

---

1. The author is here referring to Sufism, a popular form of Muslim mysticism.

he continued to think about it.[2] He would drink some strong wine in order to fall asleep, and his train of thought continued even stronger, but passed from being merely superficial to internal, and the problem was solved. But this is in fact also the form of the letters of his imaginary thoughts, which he had intended to continue contemplating with respect to these problems, which may have had an effect on him as a consequence of his movements, although he did not know.

But should you pose questions, and ask why we recall the letters and try to produce effects with them without noticing any results, I will try to provide an answer with the help of Shaddai,[3] and I, the youth, will tell you about my experiences in this matter. You ought to know that at first I wanted to learn the Torah and learned something from it and from the rest of Scripture. Nevertheless, I could find no one to guide me in Talmudic studies, not so much because of the teachers themselves, but because of homesickness and affection for my father and mother, until God planted within me the power to search for the Law [the Torah]. I had left my native land for many years in order to discover and study the Talmud. But the fire of the Torah continued to burn within me without my realizing it. I returned to my native land and God brought me into contact with a Jewish philosopher with whom I studied a bit of the *Guide to the Perplexed*[4] and my appetite continued to grow. I learned some logic and natural science and was very much attracted to these disciplines, since, as you know, "like attracts like." God is my witness, if it weren't for the little bit of learning I had already acquired from the Torah and Talmud, my desire to keep many of the commandments would have been completely extinguished, even though the fire of intention continued to burn within me. What I learned from my teacher about the method of study was insufficient until God brought me into contact with a man of God, learned in the Kabbalah, who taught me the way of the Kabbalah in its broad outline. Nevertheless, the bit of philosophy I had already learned limited me, and the path or way of the Kabbalah seemed blocked.

My teacher answered me, saying, "My son, why do you deny some-

2. Avicenna (980–1037), whose Arabic name was Abu Ali al-Hussain Ibn Abdallah Ibn Sinâ, was a physician, encyclopedist, philosopher, and mathematician whose *Canon* of medicine became the standard textbook of the Middle Ages. For the episode reported here see William E. Gohlman, ed. and trans, *The Life of Ibn Sina* (Albany: State University of New York Press, 1974), 29–31.

3. One of the names of God that appear in Scripture.

4. The *Guide* was written ca. 1185/90 by Maimonides (1135/38–1204) in Judaeo-Arabic and was later translated into Hebrew. In this work Maimonides tries to adapt philosophy to Judaism. His *Mishnah Torah* (ca. 1178) is the standard codification of Jewish law.

thing you haven't as yet tried? You should at least try it; and should you find
that you can't blame your lack of understanding on yourself, then you may
say it's worthless." I was limited in whatever he taught me by my interest in
nature. He would therefore make the subject more attractive until my reason grasped it, and I acquired some interest. I clearly understood and drew
the conclusion that in this matter there would be only gain, and no loss. I
would see whether I would find anything in it. If so, I would profit. If not, I
would still possess what I had. I applied myself, and he taught me the
method of permutations and combinations and numerology[5] [*Gematria*]
and the other methods found in *The Book of Creation*.[6] He allowed me to
wander about and explore every method he taught me for two weeks, until I
grasped it clearly. He guided me in this way for four months and then
ordered me to erase everything, saying, "My son, the aim is not to remain
attached to one limited form, even though it be of the very highest order.
Rather, the aim is 'the Method of the Names,' whose very value rests on its
incomprehensibility, until you reach the activity of that power which is not
under your control; and your reasoning and thoughts are under its control."

I answered him, "Why do you write books linking the natural sciences
to the 'Method of the Names'?"

He replied, "For you and those like you among the philosophers, in
order to attract their human reasoning by natural methods. Perhaps this
attraction will be the means whereby they will come to appreciate God." He
took out for me those books containing letters, names, and mystic numerology, which no one can understand since they are not composed in a com-
prehensible fashion. He said, "This is the 'Method of the Names.'" I didn't
want to see it because my reasoning didn't comprehend it. He said, "I did a
foolish thing in showing them to you."

In the end, after two months my thoughts became clearer and I understood higher matters. For three nights I studied and wrote the letters,
making a small change by means of the philosophical method without
telling him. But on the third night, after midnight, I dozed off with pen in
hand and paper on my knee. I saw the candle about to go out. I got up in
order to fix it, as often happens when one wakes up. I saw that the light

5. Gematria is a method of Biblical interpretation in which each letter of the alphabet is
granted a numerical value. Words or phrases are thereby understood in accordance with
peculiar numerical calculations and systems.
6. *The Book of Creation* (*Sefer Yetsirah*) is a third- to sixth-century cosmological text
whose authorship was ascribed to Abraham and Rabbi Akiba. It focuses on the mysteries of
Creation, in which the twenty-two letters of the Hebrew alphabet are presented as the foundation stones of the Creation. This work was highly regarded in mystical and Kabbalistic circles.
See Benzion Bokser, ed., *The Jewish Mystical Tradition* (New York: Pilgrim Books, 1981), 65ff.

remained, and was astonished to see that it issued from me. I did not believe, and walked about the house accompanied by the light. I covered myself with a sheet as I lay in bed, and the light continued to accompany me. I said that what I have seen is no doubt a great and new sign.

In the morning I reported to my teacher what had happened and brought him what I had written. He praised me and said, "My son, if you devote yourself to the construction of names, you will experience something even greater than this. Now, my son, admit that you cannot bear not writing [creating combinations in the Kabbalistic way]. I suggest that you divide the night into two parts. During half the night you will write; and during the other half you will do permutations."

This is what I did for about a week. The next week my power of writing increased to such an extent that even ten men couldn't write what I was able to write in the course of this experience in accordance with the new method. On the third night, possessing this power, after midnight, when the power had grown stronger and my body had weakened, I decided to combine and permute the Name of God, which consists of seventy-two names. As I permuted it for a while, the letters grew in size and appeared to be as high as mountains (in accordance with this method of contemplation). I began to shake, taking hold of myself, unable to stand, my hair on end, I felt as though I were out of this world. I immediately fell down, feeling as though none of my limbs had any strength. Suddenly a kind of speech issued forth from my heart and reached my lips, forcing them to move, and I said, "Perhaps, God forbid, a foolish spirit has entered into me."

But, behold, it spoke words of wisdom. I said, "This is undoubtedly the spirit of wisdom." Shortly thereafter much of my natural strength returned to me, and I got up, although I was very weak. I still did not believe myself, but continued as before to make permutations of the Name. In fact, the same power continued to act upon me. Nevertheless, I didn't believe it until I had tried four or five times.

When I awoke in the morning, I reported to my teacher, who said to me, "Who allowed you to touch the Name? I told you not to permute numbers alone. You have no doubt achieved a high degree of prophetic power." He wanted to free me of it since he saw that my face had changed.

I said to him, "In God's name, perhaps you can give me some power which will allow me to bear that force which emanates from my heart so that I may draw some benefit from it. It appears to be a kind of great blessed spring filled with water. If it opens up, a man may drown in its waters and his soul may separate from him."

He said, "God will grant you the necessary power, since such power is ordinarily not in man's possession."

It again acted within me on the Sabbath eve as it had done before. Two signs appeared which indicated that I was able to receive this power. Following two sleepless nights, I had practiced the permutations day and night and had studied learned principles aimed at understanding the true reality and banishing irrelevant subjects. The first sign which appeared was that my thoughts concerning learned principles were strengthened in a natural way. As I sat in contemplation, my body became weaker, and my soul was so strong that I felt as if I were enveloped in my soul. The second sign was that my imaginative power had become so strong that my brow appeared to explode. I then knew that I was ready to receive God [the Name]. That Saturday night I tried the great ineffable Name [of God, *YHWH*]. The moment I touched it, I felt very weak and a voice issued forth from me, saying, "You will surely die, and you will cease to exist. Who allows you to touch the Name?"

I suddenly fell down and beseeched God, saying, "Master of the Universe! I only entered into this for the sake of heaven, as Your Honor knows. What is my crime and sin? I entered into this only in order to know You. Even David said to Solomon, 'Acknowledge your father's God and serve Him' [1 Chronicles 28.9]. Moses, blessed be he, told us in the Torah, 'Teach me to know Thy way, so that I can know Thee and continue in favor with Thee' [Exodus 33.13]."

And I, in the course of this speech, felt as though I were covered from head to foot with anointing oil, and I jumped with an indescribable joy, which was both spiritual and pleasurable. All of this was experienced at the very beginning by Your servant. I do not report this, God forbid, out of self-aggrandizement. I know that popularity is a fault and a form of inferiority among true seekers after the highest truth, and that it differs in both genus and species as light differs from darkness. If our own Jewish philosophizers, who are drawn to natural science and whose power of comprehending the secrets of the Torah is weak, will look into the matter, they will no doubt laugh at me and say, "See how he wants to attract our attention to what he says with the ridiculous and imaginary tales he tells, which have utterly confused him and which he takes to be true because of his poor understanding of natural science."

But if the Kabbalists, who have acquired some knowledge, and, even better, those who have had some personal experience of the matter, should see these things, they will rejoice and will be pleased by all that I report.

They will only be distressed by the fact that I have clearly publicized all of this. But God is my witness that my aim is the glory of God, and my only wish is that all of the Jewish people would be more praiseworthy and purer that I am, so that I could then reveal to them those things which I don't as yet know. For this is true knowledge. . . . This knowledge is available to all creatures who are willing to receive it, each according to his own abilities and according to the virtues he may possess. I could not bear not to influence others to achieve what God has given me. This kind of wisdom possesses no natural proofs [demonstrative arguments], and its spiritual premises are similar to its derived principles [or theorems]. It was therefore necessary for me to tell of my own experiments, since the only demonstrative arguments of this wisdom are through experiment. One who has not had such an experience is similar to one who has, in the same way that one who comprehends one principle with the aid of many demonstrative arguments and inferences [derived principles] is similar to one who comprehends merely the first inference. This will appear, compared to the latter, in the form of a kind of deepening underderstanding, such that it brings the knower [one who has achieved the higher knowledge] to the knowledge of the many consequences which were demonstratively verified for me. I say to anyone who rejects this method: I will give him a demonstrative argument from my own experiments; that is to say, I will provide testimony from the knowledge of the letters in accordance with the method of the *Book of Creation*, which I undertook through spiritual exercises which I tried. I did not, however, attempt to achieve the corporeal goals, because, although this may be possible, I did not want to do so, since such an attempt is shameful, and my aim is the perfection of the soul. Rather, it seems to me that such things desecrate God, a fact which our teachers imply when they say, "But when lawless men became many, etc."[7] For one who attempts this method should be concerned about necessary physical matters, since he (himself) is composed of them, and connected to them, especially when he is seeking the advantages of "the perfect knowledge" [Job 37.16] of God.

I therefore correct the knowledge of anyone who wants to undertake this method. He should do so for the glory of heaven, and should not reject anything until he has tried it. He should know that if the effort does not succeed, he should blame himself for not having been properly prepared.

---

7. *Talmud Kiddushin*, trans. Jacob Neusner, 2 vols. (Atlanta: Scholar's Press, 1992), 1: 128.

And if he is lacking, he should compare himself to a person who possesses the hidden truth, but does not have the sharp sense to enter into the secret and rejects it.

Besides, the Truth is utterly true, for it is at the very core of its existence; and even though he does not know it until God causes a knower to extend his intellect upon it, and to enjoy its existence, as it says, "the whole world was created for it." In other words, God has opened the eyes of whole world before the intellect of the knower for its own pleasure and has granted it as its own heart's desire in order to receive what is true.

The third way is the path of the Kabbalah, which consists of combining in the soul of a man the sources of learned and natural wisdom after he has already studied the principles of the Torah and of the Faith. In this way his reason becomes used to sharp sense and he will not easily believe everything, and will not be in need of all these skills, since he has been properly trained. For it is unsuitable for a learned person who is held prisoner not to examine his cell and look for a way of escaping by means of a hole or some small crack. If we possessed a prophet today who could show us the tools capable of piercing natural reason and of discovering the narrow tunnels whereby we could escape, we would not be in need of those natural sciences in addition to the Kabbalistic knowledge, which has its roots in what are known as "chapter headings" in the *Book of Creation*, and of the letters. This is the very wide path whereby are revealed to us the wonderful secrets of nature, of the divine means of the transmigrations or permutations [*gilgulim*], conjugations [or declensions, *netiyoth*] and direct vowels [*tenuoth*], and the numbers or emanations [*sefirot*] according to the transformation of the letters. The prophet would show us the secrets of combining the letters, and would combine their *tenuoth* with the vowels, and the means of undertaking such combinations, and the paths which derive from the hidden powers and their circumstances, and the reasons whereby they are occasionally prevented from on high.

II

Apostates and Converts

In Christian theology, the first apostates were regarded as those fallen angels who through the sin of pride had been led to reject God and set up a rival kingdom, and the Antichrist, who followed in Satan's footsteps. Thomas Aquinas equated heresy and disbelief with apostasy as expressions of human pride. The canon lawyer Hostiensis (ca. 1250) in his *Summa aurea* distinguished three forms of apostasy. *Apostasia a perfidia* is rejection of one's faith and conversion to another, like the much maligned Emperor Julian the Apostate (361/63), who had canceled the privileges granted to the Christian faith in the Roman Empire. Hostiensis regarded leaving the true faith after one has experienced its grace as a greater evil than never having known this faith. The apostate who converts to another faith was treated as a traitor and branded with the label of infamy, which would entail loss of property and even life. The second form of apostasy, *apostasia inobedientiae*, represented voluntary transgression of one of the major commandments. Such disobedience had been displayed by Adam and Eve, who had eaten of the tree of the knowledge of good and evil, and as a result had been expelled from Eden and had lost the promise of eternal life. The third form of apostasy, *apostasia irregularitatis*, refers to priests and professed monks and nuns who have gone back on their sacred vows. Those who denied their religious vows became renegades, and were expelled from their homes and imprisoned.

Jewish law displayed a special interest in the subject of apostasy because of the large number of communicants who had converted to either Christianity or Islam, and the aggressive efforts made by the Church through polemics, preaching, and the imposition of legal pressure to bring about Jewish conversion. Jewish law generally regarded birth to a Jewish mother as the irreversible grounds of Jewish identity. The twelfth-century theologian and philosopher Maimonides (d. 1202) therefore viewed the Jewish convert to another faith as a great sinner and transgressor of the

Law, but nevertheless a Jew, who remained bound by the obligations of
the Faith. Special prayers were reserved for forced converts (*anusim*) and
the community was encouraged to seek their return to the fold. Those who
returned to the faith after having converted to another were expected to
undergo a ritual purification ceremony and to express heartfelt repentance.
A fifteenth-century letter refers to the following factors as the presumed
grounds for abandoning Judaism: the material gains to be made as a result
of conversion; philosophical doubts about religion; despair concerning the
possibility of Jewish survival; and the discovery of new theological principles in one's newfound faith. Proselytes to Judaism, like the Biblical Ruth
the Moabite (ancestor of both King David and Jesus) and Obadiah the
Convert, because of their willingness to undertake the heavy obligations of
the Law, were looked on with special reverence and solicitude.

In his 1268 bull *Turbato corde*, Pope Clement IV complained that Jewish converts to Christianity had relapsed and that "many Christians, turning
their backs on the Christian faith, have, to the damnation of their souls,
become Jews." There is, however, little evidence of any such substantial
conversion to Judaism in the Middle Ages. Clement's fears appear to be
rather for recent Jewish converts to Christianity who sought to return to the
faith of their forebears, probably in southern Italy and Spain. Urban IV
therefore assisted former Jews financially in order to lessen the danger of
return to Judaism, and Nicholas III issued legislation encouraging conversion efforts, while renewing ties with Christians in North Africa and Ethi-
opia. The pope perhaps most active in attempts to convert the infidel was
the canonist Innocent IV (d. 1254), whose efforts were directed at Muslims
(known as Saracens), Mongols or Tartars (animists, who had not yet converted to Islam), Jews, and the pagans of northeastern Europe, such as
Lithuanians and Prussians. The earlier treatment of the Jews served as a
precedent. Innocent also claimed the right to interfere in the religious practices of those nonbelievers who fell under the Church's control. They had
been allowed to maintain their faith, but were forbidden to make any
changes from the Old Testament version of Judaism as interpreted by Christian theologians. In the same way, the pope claimed the right to punish
pagans who transgressed the law of nature that applied to them.

Gregory IX's bull *Cum hora undecima* (1235) had defined the missionary responsibilities of the Church, which were largely taken up by the
Dominicans and Franciscans, the new mendicant orders founded in the first
quarter of the thirteenth century. Francis of Assisi had himself taken part in
the Fifth Crusade (1218), whose aim was to recapture the Holy Land by

means of encirclement from the west. Francis had allegedly preached before the sultan at Damietta in Egypt. In addition to attempting the conversion of the small Moroccan kingdom of Sale, Pope Innocent IV sent bishops and missionaries to care for the Christian populations of Tunis, Ceuta, and Bougie in North Africa (also with the aim of converting the nonbelievers) and initiated the policy of sending emissaries to Persia, India, China, and elsewhere in order to spread the faith. The renowned travels of the Venetian merchants Marco Polo, his father, and his uncle date from this brief period of opening to the east during the late thirteenth century. Ramon Llull's missionary journeys to North Africa and Cyprus must therefore be seen in the wider context of the aggressive campaign to convert nonbelievers which characterized the late thirteenth and early fourteenth centuries.

Probably in answer to Innocent IV's call, the Dominican minister-general Humbert of Romans laid down rules to govern the conversion of "barbarian peoples, pagans, Saracens, Jews, heretics, schismatics, and others outside the Church." Ramon Llull, whose autobiographical account details his own efforts to spread the faith, published the *Regulae generales* and *Tractatus de modo convertendi infideles* as a program of conversion. Roger Bacon in his *Opus maius* (1267/68) recommended knowledge of foreign languages as the basis for conversion of the infidel, but also suggested the existence of a kind of natural religion that lay at the foundation of all the faiths. In *De statu sarracenorum* (1273), William of Tripoli went so far as to suggest that knowledge of the Koran and of Muslim belief were essential for successful conversion activity and claimed to have baptized more than one thousand Saracens. Generally speaking, it was suggested that effective polemic employed arguments drawn from the common beliefs of both the Christian faith and its rival and the example of the saints and the miracles of Jesus. On a practical level, both the Dominican and Franciscan orders established branches specifically involved with mission among the infidels. Arabic was taught at the Dominican houses of Tunis, Valencia, and Murcia, and Llull established a Franciscan monastery at Miramar in 1276 where the friars learned Arabic.

Within Europe, the major effort at conversion was directed at the Jews. In the early Middle Ages they had been described as potential objects of conversion, theological adversaries and competitors, persecutors, and witnesses to the truths of Christianity. Among the themes found in miracle stories, for example, were the blindness of the Jew, the link between cure of his soul and his body, and the Jew's role as a necessary witness to the truth of Christianity. It was argued that Jewish complicity in the slaying of the

Messiah had been punished by such disasters as the destruction of the
Second Temple at Jerusalem in 72 A.D., the failure to achieve its reconstruction, the defeat of the revolt of Bar Kochba in 135, the exile from the
Promised Land, and the subsequent dispersion and humiliation of the Jewish people. In such literature, the Jews occasionally serve as a means of
confirming the value of Christian ceremonies (such as baptism), practices
(the sign of the cross, the laying on of hands), and relics (such as the holy
shroud). Nevertheless, they were also often perceived as traitorous allies of
Satan, and a large number of martyrs were portrayed as victims of the Jews.

A stereotypical theological view stressed their blindness and ignorance
in rejecting Christianity and their collaboration at the Crucifixion. Continuing "superficial" adherence to the literal interpretation of Scripture
allegedly kept the Jews from understanding its deeper meaning (a view
stressed in Hermann of Scheda's apologia, the second selection in this
chapter); as a result, the miracle was viewed as the most effective means of
bringing the Jews to the faith. Many of the anecdotes concerning Jewish
greed and disdain for the faith are found in Jacobus of Voragine's *Legenda
aurea* (ca. 1260), which became a vehicle for the dissemination of anti-
Semitic stereotypes in art and sermon. The curse of the Jews is probably
most graphically illustrated in the allegedly incestuous life of Judas Iscariot,
the betrayer of Jesus (inserted into the life of St. Matthew). James's portrait
of St. Sylvester also contains a prototypical dialogue between Judaism and
Christianity of the kind so common in the later Middle Ages. According to
the legend, Helena, the mother of Emperor Constantine (d. 337), had
organized a dialogue in the emperor's presence in which Pope Sylvester led
the Christian disputants and two pagans presided. Twelve Jewish spokes-
men presented twelve arguments against Christianity, all of which were
successfully rebutted. The Jews argued, among other things, that: (1) the
doctrine of the Trinity contradicts the First Commandment; (2) miracle-
working is not necessarily proof of Saviorship; (3) if Jesus were in fact God,
He could not suffer during the Crucifixion; (4) the prophetic citations of
the Old Testament do not necessarily refer to Jesus; (5) if Christ is indeed
from the seed of David, he does not require the sanctification of baptism;
(6) the virgin birth is inexplicable; (7) the temptations Jesus underwent
contradict his alleged status as the Son of God; (8) Jesus was clearly not
perfect, as God should be; and, (9) Jesus' birth outside marriage contradicts God's praise of matrimony. In the end, both Helena and the pagan
judges were converted to Christianity by witnessing a miracle performed by
Sylvester. His Jewish opponent had slain a bull by speaking in its ear, while

Sylvester successfully revived the beast. This episode highlights the view that miracle rather than rational argument is the best proof of the truths of the faith against its heretical, Jewish, and other opponents.

Although Judaism was regarded as the foundation of Christianity, by the late twelfth and thirteenth centuries rabbinic Judaism was increasingly regarded as a kind of heretical misunderstanding of Scripture, and such new mendicant orders as the Dominicans and Carmelites adapted many methods learned in the war against the heretics in their attempt to convert the Jews. Despite the traditional papal and secular opposition to forced conversion, the great scholastic philosopher Duns Scotus, for example, even advocated the baptism of Jewish children against the will of their parents. The Jews were increasingly portrayed as secretive, clannish, greedy, spiteful, and Satanic.

Some of the leading spiritual figures of the period took part in the battle to convert the Jews and other non-Christians. Such activity found voice in such polemical tracts as Ramon Llull's *De modo convertendi infideles*. A leading Dominican, the great canon lawyer Raymund of Penyaforte (d. 1275), had also devoted much of his energy to the establishment of colleges for the teaching of Hebrew and Arabic in order to assist in the conversion effort. But despite the efforts to convert the Jews by means of reasoned argument, witnessing a miracle remained the most potent agency of conversion. It was reported, for example, that a rabbi had converted after seeing the cure of an insane sixteen-year-old boy at Queen Cunegunda's tomb in Bamberg sometime before 1202. Cunegunda's biographer cites Paul's claim [1 Corinthians 1.22] that "the Jews call for miracles" in order to convert.[1] To cite one lesser known effort at conversion, in about 1275 the Carmelite Albert of Trapani encountered a young Jew in the village of Sacca in Sicily in the throes of an uncontrollable epileptic fit.[2] As his parents prayed vainly for help, they turned to Albert in desperation. He asked the youth, "Do you believe in the Lord Jesus Christ and His Mother Mary, who was a virgin at His birth and remained so afterward?" He proceeded to explain the articles of the faith, while the parents said, "We will believe if in His name you restore health to our son. You will be able to do so if you speak the truth." Albert then made the sign of the cross, saying, "May the disease leave you, if what I said about Jesus the Nazarene is true." The youth was cured and converted to Christianity. On another occasion, Albert encountered some

---

1. *Vita Cunegundis*, in Jacques-Paul Migne, ed., *Patrologia Latina. Cursus completus*, 221 vols. (Paris: J. P. Migne, 1844–55), 140: 217–18.
2. "*Vita Alberti confessoris*," *Analecta Bollandiana* 17 (1898): 327 for quotations.

Jews attempting to cross a river near Agrigento during a storm. They asked him to beseech the aid of Jesus. The river became still, and as a result they accepted baptism. Because of such benefactions, it was reported that Jews honored the saint's body as it lay at Messina after his death.

As a Carmelite, Albert could be expected to display a special interest in the Jewish community. One of the order's founders, Angelo of Jerusalem (1185–1220?), was the son of Jewish residents of Crusader Jerusalem who had allegedly discussed the possibility of conversion with Patriarch Nicodemus. On March 24, 1184, around Passover, they had a vision of the Virgin admonishing them to convert and prophesying the birth of twin boys, one of whom, Angelo, would become a martyr. The other, Johannes, would become a patriarch. The highly unreliable biography of Angelo suggests that within four years of his parents' conversion (in 1188, shortly after the fall of Jerusalem to Saladin), forty Jews had found the true faith.

Since the Dominican order (established in 1215) had in particular been entrusted with the conversion of nonbelievers and heretics, its leading figures showed a special concern for the "Jewish problem." On August 4, 1278 a bull issued by Pope Nicholas III ordered the Dominicans to preach to the Jews.[3] The dissemination of this bull, it should be noted, was followed shortly thereafter in Germany by blood-libel agitation. It was reported that Raymund of Penyaforte had experienced a vision in which God revealed to him that the Dominicans should attempt to convert the infidels and wayward Christians to the true faith. He therefore received permission from the kings of Castile and Aragon to have twenty or more Dominican preachers study Hebrew in order to refute the Jewish interpretation of Scripture. As a result, it was said that many converted in Spain and North Africa. In 1263, Raymund convinced James I of Aragon to require Jewish attendance at Christian sermons and disputations.

The biographers of the Dominican Thomas Aquinas likewise stressed such service in the polemical battle against the Jews by means of his intellectual activities, a theme that was to reappear in the sermons dedicated to him. It was reported that Thomas had successfully converted two learned Jews at Molaria near Rome who had come to debate the great theologian concerning Biblical prophecies pertaining to the Savior. Thomas's role as a polemicist was further emphasized by Pope John XXII's words opening the consistory held in the saint's honor in 1318, "He has illuminated the church

---

3. James Muldoon, *Popes, Lawyers, and Infidels: The Church and the Non-Christian World, 1250–1550* (Philadelphia: University of Pennsylvania Press, 1979), 51.

more than all other doctors, in whose books a man may profit more in a
year, than in the doctrine of others one may profit in a lifetime."[4] The
Franciscans were no less devoted to missionary efforts. Many visions of
the Tertiary Franciscan Margaret of Cortona as reported by her confessor
Juncta of Bevagna, for example, include Jesus detailing the various perfidies
committed by the Jews against Him. At the same time, she prayed for their
conversion to the faith, along with heretics, Saracens, and Tartars. Although the events are undocumented, Louis of Toulouse also allegedly
disputed with Jews and Saracens, softening their harshness with citations
from Scripture.

Despite the methods of persuasion advocated by the Church and the
theoretical policy of controlled tolerance of religious minorities generally
advocated in the Mediterranean world, the attitude of the various faiths
toward each other was largely one of hostile acceptance or armed conflict in
the form of the Crusades. Those apostates who abandoned the faith into
which they were born in favor of that of the enemy were looked upon as
traitors who posed a special danger to their former coreligionists. The
Jewish community was particularly sensitive to the role which such former
Jews as Pablo Christiani played in the mechanism of persecution. For example, it was reported that Archbishop William of Bourges (d. 1209) converted a Jew who himself adopted the name of William, served as a deacon,
and wrote a tract against Jews and heretics.

The following documents illustrate, under differing conditions, contemporary attitudes toward the apostate and convert, who occupied a liminal territory, despised and rejected by his former community, but not yet
fully integrated in his new faith. Obadiah the Convert describes how his
conversion to Judaism some time in the late eleventh century at the time
of the First Crusade (1096–99) forced him to abandon his homeland in
southern Italy and to wander from one Jewish community to another in
Syria, Iraq, Palestine, and Egypt. Hermann the Jew's conversion to Christianity occurred shortly after the First Crusade, which had wreaked physical
and emotional havoc on the Jews of northern Europe, who had lived a
relatively peaceful existence since the days of the Carolingian Empire in the
ninth century. The role of interfaith polemics is evident in this autobiographical account, in which the allegedly more spiritual Christian interpretation of Scripture is contrasted with the Jewish version. Hermann's

4. R. Jaquin, "Thomas d'Aquin: Le saint," *Revue des Sciences Religieuses* 50, 1 (1976):
25–37.

childhood dream is presented with two interpretations, one Jewish and one Christian, and represents an unusual chapter in the history of hermeneutics. In many ways the life may be read as a theological tract *Contra iudaeos* rather than a purely biographical text. Hermann's conversion was regarded by Rhenish Jewry as a good illustration of the dangers inherent in too close social and economic contact with Christians, and could justify the increasing isolation of European Jewry, which was in any case imposed by the Christian community. Hermann's act of conversion should be seen in the context of the great losses which the Jews of the Rhineland had recently suffered. The conversion testimony of Sa'id ibn Hasan of Alexandria, on the other hand, is purely theological, and addresses none of the complicated social issues with which European Jewry was forced to wrestle.

While the first three sources were written by apostates themselves, the lengthy report of Ramon Llull provides a graphic account of the rather intrusive religious fervor that gripped those involved in conversion propaganda. The peculiar environment of Llull's birthplace, Majorca, which had only recently been conquered from the Saracens, afforded opportunities for the kind of direct personal contact with Jews and Muslims which was rare for other polemicists. Llull was both instructed by a Muslim slave and influenced in his philosophical work by Arabic authors. Nevertheless, a tone of self-righteous arrogance remains, which even infected his relations with fellow Christians. At this time, Christians' growing demonization of their ideological foes had led to a blurring of the distinction among Jew, Muslim, and heretic, all of whom were lumped together rather indiscriminately as agents of Satan. The sources gathered together in this chapter may be complemented by a reading of both the introductory remarks and selections in Chapter I, which deals with the Jewish community and the issues of conversion and its consequences.

Obadiah the Convert (ca. 1100), *Epistle*

The following autobiographical letter, written in the third person, was given by Obadiah, a Norman convert from Christianity, to the Jewish community of Fustat, with a undated commending letter from Rabbi Baruch Bar Yitzhak of Aleppo. It has been reconstructed by Norman Golb from fragments found at the Cairo Genizah (a storehouse of old documents belonging to the Jewish community), which were later dispersed to libraries at Budapest, Cambridge, and Oxford. Much of the epistle remains obscure, the order of its reconstruction remains tentative, and scholars may differ concerning its reading; the identification of persons and places is not always clear. I have therefore eliminated those lines which are particularly difficult to comprehend.

Obadiah's conversion to Judaism was highly unusual, especially in light of the severe restrictions and persecution suffered by the Jews in the Christian world beginning in the late eleventh century. Obadiah came from a region of southern Italy near Bari, a former Byzantine city conquered in 1070/71 by the Norman Robert Guiscard; his family was Norman. Because it had only recently been conquered for the pope by the Normans, in the eleventh century southern Italy contained a unique mixture of Jews, Byzantine Greek Orthodox Christians, Roman Catholics, and Muslims. Obadiah's odyssey from southern Italy to Egypt during the late eleventh and early twelfth centuries provides graphic testimony of the turmoil faced by the Jewish communities during the Crusades and the apparent rise of Jewish apocalypticism in response to persecution, expulsion, and massacre. Obadiah has also left us one of the earliest examples of synagogal chant notation.

During the ancient period the kind of conversion to Judaism described in the text was often gradual and informal; the procedure became more formalized in the Middle Ages, requiring both a purification ceremony and circumcision in accordance with norms of Jewish law. Despite widely-shared doubts about the advisability of accepting converts, such conversion was regarded as a public celebration of the truth of the Jewish faith. Moses of Coincy, who regarded 1240 as the messianic year, believed that the multiplication of converts would be a sign of the coming redemption. The available documentation provides no way of reliably estimating the number of Christian converts to Judaism, but the phenomenon must have been relatively marginal, given the severe penalties it entailed. Obadiah himself alludes to the conversion of a certain archbishop of Bari. The special intercommunal conditions prevalent in southern Italy are perhaps evident in the fact that during the twelfth century, Bishop Gerland of Agrigento was credited with having converted many of "the best and wisest Jews" to the Christian faith.

The text is written in the third person, a common characteristic of contemporary autobiographical accounts, also found in the life of Otloh of St. Emmeram. The main lines of the narrative are as follows. Obadiah was apparently of Norman parentage, born in southern Italy in the region of Bari, one of twin brothers, one of whom became a soldier. Sometime in adolescence, around the time of the First Crusade (1096–99), he converted to Judaism and was therefore forced to begin a life of wandering in the Middle East, which led him to visit the Jewish communities of present-day Iraq, Syria, the Holy Land, and Egypt. Obadiah was dependent on the charity of his new coreligionists, who were themselves both subject to the liabilities imposed by the Muslim states in which they lived and fearful of the depredations of the threatening Christian armies. Some of the messianic fervor of the Crusaders seems to have affected the Jews themselves, as is evident from Obadiah's encounters in the Holy Land. Despite its sometimes confusing and fragmentary content, this epistle is perhaps unique in its description of the life of a doubly-marginalized person, expelled from his Christian homeland, roaming about within the minority communities of the East. The following epistle begins with an account of Obadiah's father Dreux.

Source: Norman Golb, "Megillat Ovadia ha-Ger," in *Mehkarei Adoth ve-Genizah*, ed. Shelomo Morag and Issachar Ben-Ami (Jerusalem: Y. L. Magnes, 1981), 78–107 (Hebrew).

Bibliography: Joshua Prawer, "The Autobiography of Obadyah the Norman, A Convert to Judaism at the Time of the First Crusade," in *Studies in Medieval Jewish History and Literature*, ed. Isadore Twersky (Cambridge, Mass.: Harvard University Press, 1979), 110–34.

*   *   *

It is called Appidi.[1] He [Dreux, Obadiah's father] married a woman named Maria, who was purified and she bore two sons by Dreux in one day. The first was named Rogerius, or Regier. The second one, born with great pain, was named Johannes, or Jean. Rogerius grew up to love the sword and wars, and Johannes loved the knowledge and wisdom found in books. At that time Archbishop Andreas of Bari[2] conceived in his heart a love of the Law of Moses. He therefore left his country, position, and honor and went to Constantinople. He was circumcised [cf. Genesis 17.13] and suffered great tribulations. He left and fled in the face of the nonbelievers.[3]

Many rose after him and saw what he had done. Others followed in his footsteps and joined the covenant with the living God. He then went to Egypt and remained there until he died. The king of Egypt at that time was

1. Perhaps Oppido Lucano, presumably the author's home town.
2. This may refer to the Greek archbishop.
3. A note in the margin reads: "They wanted to kill him, but God helped him escape unharmed. May the Lord bless and protect converts forever."

al-Mustanṣir. His vizier's name was al-Jamali. The rumor of Archbishop Andreas's deed reached Lombardy and the wise men of Greece and of Rome, which is the seat of the kingdom of Edom.[4] The wise men of Greece and all the wise men of Edom also heard the news and were embarrassed and put to shame. Johannes heard his words while still a youth in the home of his father, Dreux. . . . These are the names of the countries which surround the birthplace of Johannes, son of Dreux. To the west are Rome, Salerno, Potenza, Petrogalli,[5] and Anzio. To the east is Bari. . . . In the first year that Johannes was polluted [puberty?] he experienced a nocturnal emission in his father's house. That year Johannes dreamed that he was serving on the great podium at Appidi . . . and he saw a man standing before the altar on his right. And he [that man] said to Johannes[6] . . . "The sun shall be turned into darkness and the moon into blood before the great and terrible day of the Lord comes" [Joel 2.3].[7] . . . On the way to Jerusalem, one said to another, why are we going to fight our enemy, while here in our own country . . . our enemies [the Jews] reside in our midst . . . and we leave them with their wives.[8] . . . He journeyed to Shinar [Babylon, or southern Mesopotamia]. Afterward, Obadiah the Convert came to al-Raḥba, which is situated on the Tigris River, to the city of Adina, which is called Baghdad, the capital of the Ishmaelite state.[9] He suffered hardships, for the Gentiles wished to kill him, but God saved him. Obadiah the Convert stood before the door of the synagogue.

Obadiah was a beggar at the synagogue where the Jews prayed and they gave him alms. Afterward, Isaac, the head of the yeshiva, suggested that Obadiah join the young orphans in order to learn the Law of Moses, the words of the Prophets in the writings of God in the Hebrew language. Before this the king of Adina, named al-Muqtadî, through his vizier Abû al-Shujâ', who hated the Jews, ordered that the Jews who lived in Adina should be killed, but God prevented it and hid them from his anger. All the

4. The Holy Roman Empire and the papacy.

5. This site has not been identified.

6. The next section is garbled, but clearly refers to the First Crusade in 1095/96 and the ensuing massacres perpetrated on the Jews of Europe, particularly in the Rhineland.

7. In 1096 there was in fact an eclipse of the sun. Obadiah further describes how the Franks, namely the Crusaders (who were mostly French), put the sign of the cross on their garments.

8. Obadiah/Johannes appears to describe next dreams and miracles, and the battles that raged, perhaps involving the Saljuks. He then appears to have decided to convert to Judaism, perhaps in about 1102, after being unable to solve some conundrum or prophecies.

9. The descendants of Ishmael, the son of Abraham by his concubine Hagar. This term is often applied to all Muslims or Arabs.

Jews were required to wear flashing emblems, one on their heads and another on their necks; those which hung around the necks of every Jew were like a weight of gold, made out of lead. On this piece of lead was engraved the amount of tax the Jew had paid. And every Jew was required to wear a belt on his waist. Abû al-Shujâ' required that the Jewish women were to wear two signs. They were to wear one black and one red sandal; and every woman was to wear a copper bell that rang as she moved in order to distinguish between the Jewish and Gentile women. The Jewish men were put under the charge of cruel Gentile men, and the Jewish women placed under cruel Gentile women in order to torture them with every curse and humiliation. They made fun of the Jews, and the people and their children beat them throughout the entire city of Adina. This was the tax that the king of Adina exacted of the Jews every year. Every rich and powerful Jew was to pay four and a half dirhems a year. The Jews of middling wealth were to pay two dirhems, while the very poor Jews paid one and a half. If a Jew who hadn't paid the tax died and left a small amount of property, the Gentiles would not allow him to be buried until they took whatever he had left. Should a destitute Jew die, the Gentiles asked the other Jews to ransom their dead; otherwise they would burn the body.

Such was the law of the Gentiles of Adina in the days of the officer named al-Afḍal. In those days the sons of the leading Jews arose and believed in a prophesy which failed. In the mountains of Assur in the land of Kazaria[10] there arose a Jew named Solomon ben Rogi [of Alroy or Syria], whose son was named Menachem. Along with them was a preacher named Ephraim Ber Azariya the Jerusalemite, known as "ben Paldon." They wrote to all the Jews, both near and far, in all the countries in the area, and rumors of their letters reached a very long distance. They announced to all the Jews in the world wherever they may be that the time had come for God to gather all the Jews together to the Holy city of Jerusalem and that Solomon ben Rogi was the Messiah [*melekh hamashiach*]. When the Jews throughout the world heard this news they rejoiced very much. But days, months and even years passed, and nothing happened. Many of the Jews were penitent, fasted and prayed in anticipation of God's salvation, as His servants the Prophets had said. When nothing happened, they were broken, and much embarrassed before the Gentiles. All the Gentiles and uncircumcised people [Christians] heard about this and made fun of the Jews, say-

---

10. Kazaria is situated in the Caucasus. The Turkic Khazars may have converted to Judaism in the eighth or ninth century. This was reported in *The Book of the Khazars* by Judah Halevi of Toledo.

ing, "The Jews wanted to flee to their country and they have no feet with which to do so." They continued to mock, scorn, and curse the Jews, and said that everything the Jews say is vain lies.

In those days in the city of Baqûba, which is a day's journey from Adina a man known as "ben Shadad" arose among the Jews. He considered himself to be very wise, and decided to prophesy, but failed and spread many lies. As a result the king of Adina jailed the Jews, and I was among them, and "ben Shadad" prayed in my presence.

Obadiah the Convert went from there to Aleppo. At that time the Franks were in Aleppo and the Ishmaelites were suffering tribulations. Ruḍwân, the king of Aleppo, died [in 1113] and his son [alf-Arslan] did honor to Lu'lu', his father's eunuch, falling under his power. One of Ruḍ-wân's servants killed Lu'lu' [in 1117], and Aleppo had no king, because Ruḍwân's sons were minors and none was strong enough to oppose the Franks. The people of Aleppo therefore took an important [Saljuk] Turk named Il-Ghâzi ibn Urtuq [1117–21] to rule over them along with Ruḍ-wân's sons. But Aleppo was in great distress under pressure from the forces of Sirager(?), the king of Antioch and the Turks.

Many of the Jews of Aleppo died, and those who survived were impoverished. The poor were much burdened and begged for bread from the Gentiles of Aleppo and from their brethren. They took pity on Obadiah the Convert, and he blessed them. Obadiah then went to the city of Kalna [al-Raqqa?] and stayed there a while. And God saved the people of Aleppo by means of Il-Ghâzi ibn Urtuq from the Turks, and the evils of the Franks grew.

The Jews of Damascus set up a fund for Obadiah the Convert in his name, and every week made a collection for him . . . when Obadiah was in Damascus. He rejoiced in them and blessed them. . . . Obadiah then left Damascus and journeyed to Dan in the Land of Israel and spent his time there with poverty-stricken Jews. In those days in the month of Elul,[11] a priest from among the Jews, named Solomon,[12] who was learned in Scripture, came to Dan and told Obadiah the Convert and the Jews in Dan that within two and a half months God would gather together His people of Israel from all the countries to Jerusalem the holy city. Obadiah the Convert said to him, "Sir, how do you know this?"

11. Elul may fall in late August to early October, depending on the year.
12. Solomon ha-Kohen, Karaite sectarian. The Karaites are a Jewish sect, founded in the eighth century, which accepts only the authority of written Scripture and rejects rabbinical interpretation.

Solomon said, "I am the man that Israel is waiting for."

Obadiah replied, "I've heard that you are from the seed of Aaron.[13] It is nineteen years since I have joined the covenant of the God of Israel and I have not heard that Israel seeks its salvation through a priest or a Levite, but rather through Elijah the Prophet and the Messiah from the seed of David, the King of Israel. I will praise your words."

Solomon said, ". . . I will not eat bread nor drink water."[14]

Obadiah the Convert said to him, "What do you eat and drink?"

Solomon said, "Pomegranates, dates, almonds, nuts, mulberries, figs, and apples from branches and trees, and I will drink milk."

Obadiah the Convert told him that he was a convert. Solomon rejoiced and said to him, "Don't go to Egypt because within two and a half months we and all the Jews living in exile will be gathered in Jerusalem."

Obadiah the Convert said to Solomon, "I will go to Egypt and return to Jerusalem with our brethren the children of Israel who are in Egypt." Solomon was embarrassed and went to Tyre, and afterward Obadiah the Convert went to Tyre.

Hermann of Scheda (ca. 1107–70), *Opusculum de conversione sua*

The following is the most complete autobiographical account of conversion from Judaism to Christianity during a period of concerted effort to convert European Jewry by either force or persuasion. This work was written by Judah ha-Levi of Cologne, later known as Hermann the Jew or Hermann of Scheda (after the Praemonstratensian abbey he later joined), perhaps ten years after his conversion (the chronology of his life has not been fully established). It belongs to a venerable list of polemical tracts aimed at countering Jewish arguments against the faith; like other medieval autobiographies, the text occasionally moves between first and third person narrative. Hermann was well trained in disputation, presumably as a result of the thorough grounding in Talmudic study with which any male Jew, especially of Hermann's class, was equipped; however, the absence of any reference to Jewish sources and its clearly polemical aim raise may questions about the authenticity of the document. During a visit to Münster, Hermann debated with one of the leading theologians of the period, Rupert of

13. The descendants of Aaron, Moses' brother, served as high priests in the Temple at Jerusalem and continue to perform some special ceremonial duties within Jewish law.

14. The text is corrupted here.

Deutz (1120/29), whose *Anulus sive Dialogus inter Christianum et Judaeum* was written between 1126 and 1128.

On the eve of his conversion to Christianity, probably in 1128 or 1129, Hermann took part in a synagogue disputation in support of Christianity, but later disavowed his own remarks, perhaps indicating the difficult and painful character of his final decision. In the end, he regarded love and example, rather than intellectual arguments, as the surest means of winning the Jew to Christianity. He attributes his own conversion to three factors: the kindness of Bishop Ekbert of Münster (1127–32), the positive reception he received at the Praemonstratensian canonry of Cappenberg, and, the prayers of two women, Bertha and Glismut. The account stresses a childhood dream that occurred when he was thirteen as the precursor of his conversion. The bar mitzvah ceremony takes place at the age of thirteen, but it was not regularized until the fourteenth century, so it is not clear if this played a role in his narrative. This ceremony marks the transition of the Jewish male into full membership in the community, and may thus lie behind Judah/Hermann's crisis. The two interpretations — one Jewish, the other Christian — illustrate the differing approaches of the two faiths to Scripture and indicate the importance of vision/dream in much autobiographical literature.

The persecutions, expulsions, murder, and forced conversion accompanying the First Crusade (1096/99) initiated some of the most gruesome aspects that have come to characterize modern anti-Semitism, and created considerable turmoil among the Jews of Ashkenaz (Germany and Northern France). Emperor Henry V (1106–25), who appears as a benefactor in Hermann's dream, allowed those who had been forcibly baptized to return to their ancestral faith, despite the Church's disapproval. Contemporary Jewish scholars tended to view converts to another faith as sinners, although they remained Jews in the eyes of religious authorities. The wife of a convert such as Hermann remained married, and could not remarry, although his former coreligionists might try to convince the convert to divorce his Jewish wife, even to the extent of asking the authorities to intervene. There was general agreement, however, that such a convert should not be allowed to inherit the property of his Jewish relatives. Despite such rabbinical views, public opinion did not regard such persons as Jews, and required ritual purification should they wish to return to the fold. The Jewish community nevertheless regarded the return of forced converts to the faith as a great Mitzvah (sacred duty or good deed), and a prayer recited every Monday and Thursday following the reading of the Scripture asked

God for their safety. Hermann is regarded as a minor saint, and in 1628 his bones were elevated and treated as sacred relics.

Source: Hermannus Judaeus, *Opusculum de conversione sua*, ed. Gerlinde Niemeyer, in *Monumenta germaniae historica. Quellen zur Geistesgeschichte*, 4 (Weimar: Bohlau, 1963), passim. Another translation may be found in Karl F. Morrison, ed. and trans., *Conversion and Text: The Cases of Augustine of Hippo, Hermann Judah, and Constantine Tsatsos* (Charlottesville: University Press of Virginia, 1992), 76–113.

Bibliography: Aviad Kleinberg, "Hermannus Judaeus's *Opusculum*: In Defense of Its Authenticity," *Revue des Études Juives* 151, 3–4 (1992): 337–53.

*   *   *

Hermann's letter

To my dearest brother Henry, Hermann, who is what he is by the grace of God, warmest greetings in Christ. Many religious, both men and woman, customarily ask me when I converted from Judaism to the grace of Jesus Christ, and to tell them about the first temptations of the evil enemy at the time of my conversion. Recently, in your presence, I was forced by the devout petition of certain religious women, in the course of a holy discussion, to retell those events. I did not indeed convert with ease, as we see many nonbelievers, Jews, or pagans convert unexpectedly out of repentance. Just as yesterday we grieved over their perfidy, today we rejoice that they have become faithful co-inheritors in Christ. For rather, at the moment of my conversion a great storm of temptation grew, and I was attacked by the many snares of the old enemy, and for a long time I was delayed, enslaved by many burdens. It is a pleasure for pious ears to hear how I was miraculously extricated from this state of affairs with great difficulty. Therefore, driven by the devotion of many persons, and especially by you, dear brother, encouraged by pious exhortations, I was led to compose this work, and with the aid of His inestimable grace, "who has called me out of darkness into His marvelous light" [1 Peter 2.9], so that future and present generations of the faithful forever may announce his praise and glory. End of the epistle.

In the name of the Lord, here begins the little work of brother Hermann, of blessed memory, a former Jew, concerning his conversion

1. On the vision he had as a boy

I, Hermann, an unworthy priest and sinner, formerly named Judah, of Israelite origin of the tribe of Levi, whose father was named David and whose mother was Zipporah, was born in the great city of Cologne. When I was still in the grip of the Jewish faith, God graciously granted me a portent, in the form of a vision. At the age of thirteen [ca. 1120/21] I had a vision of the Roman Emperor Henry [V], who ruled after the great King Lothair [III]. When a certain powerful prince had died suddenly, Henry acquired his considerable wealth. The king came to me in this dream and gave me a great horse as white as snow wearing a golden belt from which hung a silken purse, which contained seven large coins. All this he gave to me. "I know," he said, "that the dukes and princes will be indignant that I have given you such a gift. Nevertheles, I will grant you even more benefices, including this dead prince's inheritance as your legal possession in perpetuity." I thanked him for his royal munificence and put on the noble's belt. After mounting the horse, I went to his palace at the king's side. I then dined splendidly with his friends, reclining at his side, and ate out of a bowl filled with herbs and roots. I awoke happily from that vision with childish levity. Although still a boy, realizing that these things were unusual, I did not believe them to be vain and thought they might portend something great. I therefore reported the dream to a kinsman named Isaac, a man of great authority among the Jews. I asked him to interpret it to me as best he could. Such a person, "who lives according to his lower nature" [Romans 8.5], gave me an explanation which is pleasing to the flesh. He said that the great white horse indicates that I would marry a noble and beautiful woman; the money in the purse indicates that I will be very wealthy; the meal celebrated in the emperor's company indicates that I will achieve great honor among the Jews. Much later, after I was filled with the gift of divine grace, the true interpretation of this dream was to be given to me, as future events were to bear witness. I will now explain the circumstances of my conversion and how it began.

2. On his first experience with Christians and how he came into their company

Seven years later [ca. 1127/28] I came with several merchants to do business at Mainz; for, indeed, all of the Jews are involved in trade. At that time the glorious King Lothair was counseled by a venerable man, Bishop Ekbert of Münster. Since the king detained the bishop concerning matters pertaining to the kingdom longer than expected, all his money had been used up. He was therefore forced to come to me in order to borrow money. Contrary to normal Jewish practice, I refused to accept a pledge from him, that is, a precious pawn, in light of the man's trustworthy character. When this became known to my friends and parents, they fiercely attacked me, saying that I had been very negligent for providing money to someone without a pledge, especially that of a man involved in so many affairs. In such a case, it is customary among the Jews (as I well knew) even to ask for a pledge of more than twice the amount of the loan. I was counseled to remain at his side and to remind him, until I should get the debt back. Fearing that, by remaining with the Christians, through the instinct of imitation, I might turn my back on my ancestral faith, they committed me for study to a certain aged, learned Jew named Baruch, who had acquired a name for himself in business.

Giving in to the counsel of my parents and friends, I journeyed to Münster, where the episcopal see is situated. When I found the bishop there, I reminded him of his debt, saying that I dare not go back to my parents until it had been repaid. Because he couldn't repay me at the moment, he detained me for almost twenty weeks. In the course of this time, as was his custom, this good pastor provided his flock with the food of God's word. With the curiosity of the adolescent, I was seduced to mix myself with the flock of sheep, with a certain thoughtless presumption, because, as a result of the foulness of error, I still deserved to be counted among the goats rather than the sheep. There I heard "a scribe learned in the Kingdom of Heaven bringing forth new and old from his treasure" [Matthew 13.52]. He proved by very satisfactory explanations that the Old Testament refers to the New, and the New derives from the Old.[1] The laws, namely, "Thou shalt not commit adultery, thou shalt not bear false witness, honor thy father and thy mother" [Exodus 29.11, 15, 16, 12], each have a literal, superficial meaning. In others cases, such as "Thou shalt not plough with an ass and an ox yoked together" [Deuteronomy 22.10] and "Thou shalt not boil a kid in its mother's milk" [Exodus 23.19], the superficial, literal meaning is superfluous. It is far better to apply the allegorical explanation. Making use of this kind of distinction, the bishop argued that the Jews, like brute beasts, are satisfied with the chaff, namely, with the literal interpretation in this case; whereas the Christians, making use of the spiritual intel-

---

1. Hermann's use of the terms Old and New Testament indicates acceptance of the Christian view of the two dispensations, with the second succeeding and replacing the first. The Jews did not and do not accept this designation.

ligence in their reasoning, are refreshed by the pith of the chaff. I heard the bishop declaring avidly such things to the people with pleasure. I took note of what he knew concerning the Old Testament, recalling the Hebrew interpretations of these texts. Knowing that animals which do not chew their cud are regarded in Jewish law as unclean, I was pleased by whatever he said. I frequently ruminated in the stomach of my memory everything that was said to me by the Christians, listening very attentively to whatever they said.

When I was asked whether I was pleased by the bishop's sermons, I replied that sometimes more so and sometimes less so. While praising me for my curiosity, they at the same time deplored my errors with pious love. They urged me to attach myself to the Catholic faith, arguing that Jesus is most merciful and rejects no one who comes to Him. This fact is noted in the Gospel, which says, "The man who comes to me I will not turn away" [John 6.37]. In order to commend to me the munificence of this grace, they told me about the case of his apostle Paul, in whose honor the small church of the city had been built and dedicated. They told me that he had been a Pharisee and had followed their law. He had persecuted those faithful to Christ's authority with insatiable cruelty. Nevertheless, in the course of his evil, due to celestial action, he was thrown to the ground by a flash of light. After he was forbidden by Christ from continuing such savagery, he changed his name from Saul to Paul, turned from being a wolf into a lamb, changed from being a persecutor into a preacher through the clemency of God. The Christians thus struck me with these and similar sermons, as I have said, urging me to lay aside the heavy burden of the Mosaic law and undertake the sweet burden of Christ [Matthew 11.30]. As a result of their frequent conversations, in the course of time I entered the church not so much as a believer, but rather out of curiosity, in order to learn at closer range about the sacraments of the Church, although I had formerly been terrified of this place, as though it were a pagan temple. Peering at everything with interest, I saw a particularly monstrous idol there among the artful varieties of statues and pictures. I saw a man wretchedly hanging by his back on a cross, both humiliated and raised on high, both despised and exalted, hated and glorified. He was portrayed above in a lying way as if beautiful and deified. I must confess that I was astonished, believing that such effigies were symbols whereby the Gentile is accustomed to recall his foolish errors to himself. The Pharisaical doctrine which was once my own, convinced me that was the case. My Jewish teacher, however, whom I have mentioned above, cleverly analyzed what I felt, when he caught me frequenting Christian gatherings as often as I could and hanging around the precincts of churches. He warned me sharply to deliver myself up to his care, warning me that he would report every instance of illicit curiosity to my parents' ears. When I boldly turned a deaf ear to such threats and arguments, I continued to devote myself to such pursuits every day; even more so as I was living under the bishop's care, because I was freed of all other business. When I entered the clerical school, I would take books from them, in which I read about the characteristics of single grammatical elements and studied the words in detail. Much to the astonishment of my listeners, without being taught, I quickly turned letters into syllables and syllables into words. I thus soon understood the science of reading Scripture. Lest this should by chance seem surprising to anyone, this should be ascribed not to me, but to God, for whom nothing is impossible.

3. On the disputation held with Abbot Rupert of Deutz

At that time the abbot of the monastery of Deutz was in Münster, a man of subtle intelligence and eloquence, learned in both divine and human literature. I was moved to take part in a disputation with him. As the Apostle says, he was "always ready with a defense of the hope and faith you possess" [1 Peter 3.15], as one who possesses Christ should be. He undertook, at whatever time and place I wanted, to discuss every subject with me with the aid of reason and the authority of Scripture, with God's help. I thus began to address him in this way: "You Christians harbor great prejudice against the Jews. You spit abuse and hatred at them as if they were dead dogs, although they were chosen from ancient times by God 'among all the nations to be His special possession' [Deuteronomy 7.6]. He led them alone to knowledge of his sacred name. To them alone was granted the most perfect rule of justice, whereby they live as holy persons [Leviticus 11.44–45, 19.2]. Just as He is holy, they are made holy by observing this law, which he deigned to inscribe with his own hand on stone tablets [1 Peter 1.16]. I say that to them alone, as you yourselves daily repeat, the Scriptural remark applies, 'To Jacob he makes his word known, his statutes and desires to Israel: he has not done this for any other nature, nor taught them his decrees' [Psalms 147.19–20]. You, however, blinded by your hatred for us, detest us more than all other mortals, despite the divine blessing, although you know that we are loved and honored by God more than all men, as you have read. Nevertheless, with patience and loathing we bear the hatred and contempt of men, persevering faithfully in God's law and ceremonies. For it is better to incite a man's anger against us than to disobey God's law [Daniel 13.23]. What is more fearful than to suffer the anger of man or of God? Is it better to be despised by men or damned by God? In the divine law, so it is written, 'A curse is on all who do not persevere in doing everything that is written in the Book of the Law' [Galatians 3.10]. Our justice, which is based on the law, is in all of these words defended by the very highest authority against all of your niggling remarks. And so your pride, whereby you foolishly claim to observe the law to us and denigrate us, who follow our ancestors by keeping the law, is clearly proven to be impious behavior. For it is written, 'A curse upon all who do not fulfill this law by doing all that it prescribes' [Deuteronomy 27.26]. Nothing is therefore to be taken away, nothing is to be removed. You do not, as you say, practice the law, but nevertheless judge it [James 4.11]. But this is a ridiculous statement, since you correct it at will, while at the same time accepting certain things. Other things you reject as superstitious or as 'occult.' On the other hand, if it pleases you, you say that what is accepted are the depraved falsehoods of foolish old men and women. It is foolish temerity and a fatuousness to be derided on every occasion, for men to want to correct those things which God has established and has ordered to be observed under pain of a terrible curse to men. You Christians regard this curse as obnoxious, while you presume to judge the Law, although you are proven to be wrongheaded prevaricators. In the meantime, one case out of many may be provided, which would suffice to justify your damnation: why do you, who extol the observances of the law, at the same through time impiety defy it through acts of obvious idolatry? For I have seen with my own eyes the great painted and sculpted images found in your pagan temples which you have skillfully adorned in order to worship. Would that you would decorate it with another witness, rather than with the image of a crucified man, as a sign of your damnation. Since the authority of the Law says, 'A curse on everyone who is hanged on a gibbet' [Galatians 3.13; Deuteronomy 21.23]. How can you be more accursed than to worship someone who is hanging on a gibbet? Furthermore, if it says elsewhere in Scripture, 'A curse on the man who trusts in man and leans for support on humankind' [Jeremiah 17.5], how much worse are you who fall under a sentence of malediction by putting your hope in a crucified man? You don't even hide the foolishness of your superstition; this is not only a great evil, but you even preach it, glorying in your sin as did the Sodomites. Select one of the two options, whichever pleases you: either explain to me the authority of this abominable worship, if you know it; or surely, which is the result, if you cannot, because you clearly cannot, confess and be ashamed by the fact that this error is damnable and in every way contrary to the holy law."[2] . . .

4. Response

. . . Rupert answered all my objections with beautiful and correct arguments drawn from Scriptural authorities. Like the mist from a dark night, he banished away these objections with the clearest rays of his answers. But wretch that I am, "like a deaf asp which stops its ears and will not listen to the sound of the charmer" [Psalms 56.5], I did not hear the words of his sweet speech with the ears of my heart, and I could not see the light of truth with the eyes of my mind, since the mist of Jewish blindness darkened them. . . .

7. How, after he returned to his parents, his Jewish guardian made accusations against him

After these things had occurred, the Easter holiday passed, and the debt having been repaid to me by the bishop, I returned to the metropolitan of Cologne, where I remained, with my Jewish rival.[3] Just as he had threatened to do a while ago, he weakened the affection of parents and friends for me with many accusations. He asserted that contrary to what was allowed, I had attached myself to Christians with such perseverance and familiarity that I was no longer a Jew, but could be considered a Christian. It was only out of a kind of fake piety that I had feigned, purely out of habit, to follow my paternal faith. "God, the Lord of vengeance" [Psalms 94.1] soon repaid him for his evil accusation; for, in the prophet's words [Jeremiah 17.18], a double punishment was imposed on him. For he was immediately gripped with a severe fever and died within fifteen days, and passed from the pains of the world to the eternal suffering of Hell. In this way, "the all-just Judge" [2 Timothy 4.8] in this same act demonstrated both mercy and truth. He displayed the truth by repaying him with the punishments which were justly his, and mercy by freeing me from the snares and accusations he thrust at me. . . .

2. This is followed by Rupert of Deutz's reply to Hermann the Jew's contentions. Rupert argued that: Christians are not idolaters, but worship one God; the image of the cross is not a form of idolatry, but rather a devotional and mnemonic tool; and, Christian ritual has its foundation in the Old Testament.

3. The Jewish teacher who had threatened to denounce him.

10. How, against his will and desire, he was forced to marry and through his love remained ensnared in his original error

The Devil, author of evil, held me entrapped up to that point in the embrace of lack of faith. He observed that I hastened daily to church to zealously hear the word of God, who strengthened me against the tricks of every tyranny. He was very envious over the progress I had made, and attacked armed with his old tricks. Indeed, he gave to the first parent the taste of death by means of a woman [cf. Genesis 3.1], which he reserved for the most holy Job not as a consolation among all his goods, but rather as a subversion. He joined me in marriage in order to encompass my ruin. A certain Jew named Alexander came to me, so that I might become betrothed to his young daughter. He then began to insist that I fix the day, urging, exhorting, and asking me to do so. Up to that point I was still unsure whether I would persevere in the Jewish faith or become a Christian. I cautiously considered that should I bind myself more to a wife I would have to devote myself to domestic matters rather than daily disputations, as I had become accustomed. I thought that in the meantime it would be more convenient if I could delay the marriage for some reason, while, with God's mercy, I would discover some sign what I would have to do in order to bring about a remedy for my soul.[4] . . . Without any further hesitation, obeying the universal will of the Jews, I set for them the date on which the marriage couch was to be celebrated. They were so excited by my marriage, the joy shown toward me by everyone was so great, that the general support of all attracted me more than the fear it had formerly aroused had driven me away. When the day of the marriage approached, not only many Jews but also my Christian friends came there. The Jews took pleasure in my false happiness. The Christians, on the other hand, grieving with Christian affection at my fatal circumstances, prayed on high for some consolation of piety. "How," they asked, "oh wretched Jew, did you lapse so quickly from your good intentions into such an abyss of perdition?"[5] . . . Soon, when I had experienced the corruption of the flesh, so affected by the slippery pleasure and love of the wife who had been joined to me, my mind was so blinded that I was unable to feel the very heavy sluggishness of my soul. . . . Thus said the Apostle concerning married persons: "The married man cares

4. After various delaying tactics, including suggestions that he go to France for further religious training, Hermann remained a Jew. He was presented with the option of either marrying or being expelled from the Jewish community. At this stage he preferred marriage.
5. This is followed by the warnings of his Christian friends.

for worldly things, his aim is to please his wife, and he has a divided mind"
[1 Corinthians 7.33]. I began to decline, due to the various cares of the
world, not searching for those things which are of God, but rather devoting
myself to those things which would be pleasing in my wife's eyes.⁶ . . .

14. How he withdrew his brother from Judaism and how the Jews conspired against him

. . . When it was discovered that I intended to go Mainz, "conspiring together," as it is written, making "plans that could not be made firm" [cf.
Psalms 2.2, 20.12], they [the Jews, who noted that he had ceased attending
synagogue] sent letters to the Jews of Mainz via a certain Wolkwin, chaplain
to Queen Richenza.⁷ The contents of those letters were that they had decided that I was an evil apostate and that they would impose a suitable punishment on me in accordance with the rigor of divine censure. But, as the
Apostle says, "If God is on our side, who is against us?" [Romans 8.31].
Therefore, "He dissipates the plans of the Gentiles and condemns the plans
of the princes" [Psalms 32.10], dissipating their plan at His command, pow-
erfully freeing me from their snares, and mercifully aiding the accomplish-
ment of the plan I had conceived in order to gain my brother (for the faith).⁸

18. On a vision which he had before his baptism

After three weeks had passed and after I had become a catechumen,⁹ on the
Wednesday before the Sunday when I was baptized [November 26, 1128 or
November 20, 1129], I had a dream which is extremely sweet both to see
and report. I saw the sky open up [cf. Acts 7.55] in the east. The structure
which I imagined appeared to be adorned completely with the purest gold.
There I saw the Lord Jesus seated on the highest throne, with the most honored and powerful majesty of the Father, holding in place of a scepter the tri-
umphal sign of his cross over his right shoulder. It appeared to me that I sat

---

6. Nevertheless, Hermann remained haunted by doubts, and, restraining his lust, he
continued his conversations with Christians. This revived his reservations about Judaism, as he
frequented churches. The example of two celibate women of Cologne, Glismut and Bertha,
especially impressed him, bringing him to Christianity. As a result, he decided that his seven-
year-old half-brother, who was then living in Mainz, should be baptized.
7. Wife of Emperor Lothair and daughter of Heinrich of Nordheim, d. 1141.
8. Hermann subsequently managed to burn letters written by the Jews against him; to
preach the Christian faith at the synagogue at Worms; and to kidnap his brother from Mainz,
escaping to the monastery of Flonheim.
9. *Catechumen* is a term generally applied in the early church to a neophyte Christian,
admitted to instruction in the faith prior to full membership.

beside him with his very best friends. I took pleasure in the ineffable contemplation of his inestimable sweetness. I saw my aunt's two sons, Nathan
and Isaac, moving about behind my back with nimble steps. From their
limpid movements it could be understood by observant persons that this
blessedness was not shown to them as a solace, but rather as a punishment,
so that they should be deeply tormented in their souls, since they were not
worthy of experiencing the glory of the saints, which they saw.[10] . . .

*21. He then understood the first dream he had seen in childhood concerning his
future grace in Christ and how it is to be interpreted*

This is the interpretation of the vision. The worldly emperor which appeared to me signifies the heavenly king, concerning whom the Psalmist
says, "The Lord of virtues is the king of glory" [Psalms 24.10]. He had a
great prince, i.e., an angel, who, at the beginning of creation, He made
more noble than all the other angelic spirits and placed him before all the
other orders of angels. But he then truly died from the moment that he
proudly rose up against God. His glory stripped of its dignity, he was
transformed from an archangel into a devil. So the king of kings deigned to
visit me with His grace, giving me a white horse, which is the grace of holy
baptism, whereby I was bleached "whiter than snow" [Psalms 51.7]. He
gave me the bridle which provides me with the virtue of restraining the
changing desires of my flesh. The seven heavy coins are to be properly
understood as the seven gifts of the seven-formed spirit, which fill whoever
is endowed with a grave nature. When the purity of life begins to shine as
does tested gold, by means of the Holy Spirit, such a person (from the love
of God and eternal life), begins to ring sweetly, which the sound of the gold
truly signifies. Lest they be easily lost, these seven coins are deposited in a
purse, which I believe signifies the *carismata* [the spiritual gifts] of the Holy
Spirit, which mercifully will not abandon me, but will remain with me until
the very end in order to defeat all the tricks of temptations and bring me to
the kingdom of heaven. But the princes were indignant at my happy advancement, because the evil spirits whom the Apostle calls "potentates of
the world" [Ephesians 6.12], namely, the Jews, who because of the law
received from God usurp for themselves preeminence among all other nations, envied me for the grace that Christ had granted me, of which they
themselves were unworthy. But I, constrained by the sacred belt, that is,

10. After being baptized and joining the canons regular (clergy living under a rule) at
Cappenberg, he understood the dream he had experienced in his youth.

bound by the power of continence, sat upon the royal horse because the grace of baptism "had not been given to me in vain" [1 Corinthians 15.10]. The use of the horse indicates that I had labored to perfect it with God's help by spiritual training and to provide it with a good use. I pursued the kingdom of Christ, condemning the "world and all that is in it" [1 John 2.15], rejecting not only my own things, but even my own self for His love, carrying out what he says about Himself, saying, "I have come . . . not to do my own will, but the will of him who sent me" [John 6.38]. Well seated on the white horse, I accompanied the king, since no one will be worthy of following in the footsteps of Christ unless he has received the grace of baptism, which we have noted above, is signified by the white horse. The palace into which I followed him, I believe designates the site of my own conversion. What do these monasteries of clerics and religious who live according to a rule throughout the world suggest, if not the palaces of the high king? In them, because of the chastity of their lives and their religious character, Christ is believed to dwell as if at home like a member of the family, by grace as a king in his palace. I then attended the king's meal when, although unworthy, I approached the holy mystery of the altar. To attend the meal is to humbly approach the altar of Christ. But it is not possible to explain in words how sweet are the delights of the heavenly banquet. But it is known only to those who by the grace of God are worthy of expressing it. Such, I say, is the banquet of the faithful soul, that no one can understand it unless he approaches the meal of the altar with complete faith, with true humility and contrition of the heart, with sincere devotion of the mind, in which he is fed by the flesh of the immaculate lamb Jesus Christ, and is made drunk by the cup of the holy blood. The salad which I seemed to eat at the royal table, I believe designates the Gospel of Christ. For just as the salad is prepared out of various herbs, so the Gospel of Christ consists of various precepts relating to the eternal life. To eat a salad at a royal banquet is like a priest assisting at the Lord's altar. He skillfully and subtly considers the precepts of the Gospel, as though weighing it in the mouth of his heart, and thinking how humble, devout, shining with chastity, and burning with charity anyone ought to be who desires to celebrate the mystery of such a sacrament in a way that is worthy and acceptable to God. Christ the King dined with us because he is fed by the sweetness of our spiritual progress. He testified in the Apocalypse that the sweet food for him is the pious heart devoted to divine services, saying, "Here I stand knocking at the door; if anyone hears my voice and opens the door, I will come in and sit down to supper with him and he with me" [Revelations 3.20]. . . . And you, whoever may read or hear, praise me and "rejoice with me" [Luke 15.6, 9], because I was dead and am reborn, I was lost and I am found. "Glorify the Lord with me" [Psalms 34.3], who lives and reigns throughout the ages. Amen.

Sa'id ibn Hasan of Alexandria, *Masâlik al-Naẓar* (*The Ways of Understanding*) (1298)

Among the leading Jewish converts to Islam may be numbered the poet Isaac ibn Ezra, the philosopher Hibat Allah Abû al-Barâkat, and the physician-mathematician Samaul ibn Judah ibn Abbas. Like Sa'id ibn Hasan (and unlike converts to Christianity), they tended to stress logical arguments rather than vision, miracle, or a spiritual crisis as the cause of conversion, and sought confirmatory references to Ishmael and Moham-med in Scripture. Hasan's conversion occurred during a turbulent period following the conversion of the Mongols to Islam in 1295, an event which aroused messianic expectations.

Source: Ignaz Goldziher, "Sa'id b. Hasan d'Alexandrie," *Revue des Études Juives* 30 (1895): 1–23 (Arabic and French).

Bibliography: Hava Lazarus-Yafeh, *Entwined Worlds: Medieval Islam and Bible Crit-icism* (Princeton, N.J.: Princeton University Press, 1992).

* * *

Know, may God direct you to obey Him! Know, that I had formerly been a religious scholar among the Jews and that God granted the favor of convert-ing me to Islam! This is how and why:

I had fallen ill, the doctor visited me, and my funeral shroud was al-ready prepared, when, in a dream, I heard a voice calling out to me, "Recite *Surat al-ḥamd*[1] and you will escape death." When I had awakened from my dream, I instantly asked to see a neighbor who was a Muslim whose judicial judgment was approved, took his hand, and said, "I admit that there is no other God but Allah, Who has no partner. I proclaim that Mohammed is His servant and messenger with the goal of directing man to the right path and with the religion of truth, so that he will make it triumph over every other religion." I repeated this confession and said, "You who sustain the hearts [of the believers], sustain me in the faith." When I later entered a

---

1. The first Sura or chapter of the Koran.

mosque one Friday and saw the Muslims standing in rows like the rows of
angels, I heard a voice in my heart, speaking to me, saying, "This is the community whose appearance I had announced to the prophets." When the
preacher dressed in black[2] stepped forward, I was gripped by a respectful
fear, and when he struck the pulpit with his sword all my members shook.
The preacher who spoke at that time at Alexandria was Ibn al-Muwaffaq.
He finished his sermon with these words: "Verily Allah commandeth justice, and the doing of good, and giving unto kindred what shall be necessary; and He forbiddeth wickedness and iniquity and oppression; He ad-
monisheth you that you may remember" [Sura XVI.92]. After the prayer
began, I was gripped with spiritual excitement. The rows of believers looked
to me like rows of angels, and it seemed to me that God was about to reveal
Himself in the midst of their genuflections and bowing, and an interior
voice spoke to me, saying, "If God had revealed Himself twice to the Jews in
the course of the ages, He reveals Himself to this community in the course
of every prayer." I was then convinced that I was born to be a Muslim.

I converted to Islam early in the month of Sha'bân 697 [May 1298].
When I began to study the Koran during the month of Ramadan [June
1298], I was convinced of its attractive eloquence and of the impossibility of
achieving such perfect expression; so much so that the narrative which in the
Pentateuch occupies two quires, is condensed into two verses in the Koran.
That is the inimitable perfection of the book. No human is capable of
producing even a single verse of this kind. Thus it is written in the Koran:
"Moses said unto his people, O my people, remember the favor of Allah toward you, since He hath appointed prophets among you, and constituted
kings, and bestowed on you what he hath given to no other nation of the
world. O my people, enter the Holy Land which Allah hath decreed you,
and turn not your backs, lest ye be subverted and perish" [Sura V.23,24].
This narrative occupies two quires in the Torah. And when Moses ordered
them to enter the Holy Land, they demanded that he send spies. He agreed,
and they selected the men according to the tribes. Each candidate is named
in the Torah, and among them were Joshua and Caleb. These are the "two
men" whom God mentions in his sublime book [Sura V.26]. The Pentateuch next describes their entrance into the Holy Land and what happened
to them concerning the local fruits and the Amalekites.[3] The Jews wanted to
stone Moses and a heavy cloud separated them from him. The verse reports

2. The official color of the Abbasid Empire.
3. The Amalekites are the hereditary enemies of the Jews, to whom other foes were
assimilated, as noted in Exodus 17.8–16.

this event, "The land shall be forbidden them for forty years" [Sura V.29].
But they resisted Moses and marched toward [Greater] Syria. The Amalekites blocked their path and vanquished the Children of Israel. Moses then
interceded before God in their favor in the name of Mohammed.

Ramon Llull, *De vita sua* (1311/12)

The great polymath Ramon Llull (1232/35–1315) spent his early years as
an official and author of lyric poetry and romances at the Majorcan court,
living the secular life of a knight. In 1257 he married, but later he experienced a religious transformation, left his wife, Blanche Picany, and his
children Dominic and Magdalena, and devoted the rest of his life to the
composition of apologetical theological and philosophical treatises aimed
at converting nonbelievers to the faith. His works reveal the influence of
Jewish and Muslim philosophers, especially al-Farabi (d. 950), perhaps the
result of contacts in Majorca and Barcelona, which still had sizable non-
Christian populations. The *Vita* may have been taken down from Llull's
own recollections by a monk at the Charterhouse of Vauvert (situated
in what is today the Jardin de Luxembourg in Paris), probably in late August or early September 1311, prior to Llull's attendance at the council of
Vienne. Schemes similar to those of Llull were also proposed by Pierre
Dubois, who had publicized a plan to reconquer the Holy Land under the
leadership of the French king, and were partially adopted at the council.

Source: Baudouin de Gaiffier, ed., "Vita Beati Raimundi Lulli," *Analecta Bollandiana* 48 (1930): 146–75. Also, Raimundus Lullus, *Opera latina*, 8, ed. Her-
mogenses Harada, *Corpus christianorum. Continuatio mediaevalis*, 34 (Turnhout:
Brepols, 1980), 259–309.

Bibliography: Benjamin Z. Kedar, *Crusade and Mission: European Approaches Toward
the Muslims* (Princeton, N.J.: Princeton University Press, 1986), 189–99.

*   *   *

For the sake of the honor, praise, and love of the only Lord our God Jesus
Christ, Ramon, conquered by the requests of certain monastic friends, told
of his penitential conversion and of some of his other accomplishments,
and had the following things written down.

When Ramon was acting as seneschal[1] at the table of the king of
Majorca and was still a young man, he utterly devoted himself to the composition of vain songs and poems and to the pursuit of worldly vanities.
One night he sat down beside his bed in order to compose and write in his
own language a song concerning a certain woman whom he loved with a
foolish passion. When he started to write the song, gazing to the right, he
saw the Lord Jesus Christ hanging from the cross; this vision frightened
him, and, putting aside his task, he went to bed and fell asleep.

The next day, when he got up, he returned to his customary vanities
with no thought of the vision. But about eight days later, he again turned
his attention to finishing the same song, sitting down at the same hour in
the same place. The Lord again appeared to him on the cross. But this time
he was more frightened than before; he nevertheless again fell asleep. The
next day, paying no heed to the vision, he did not abandon his foolish ways.
A short time afterward, while Ramon was trying to complete his composition, the Savior nevertheless appeared to him in the same way a third and
fourth time with several days intervening, just as before.

The fourth or fifth time, deeply frightened by the same apparition, he
went to bed. But all night long he pondered and asked himself what could
be the meaning of these oft-repeated visions. On the one hand his conscience told him that these visions demanded that he immediately abandon
the world in order to devote himself totally to the service of the Lord Jesus
Christ. On the other hand, his conscience told him that for a long time he
had been guilty and unworthy to serve Christ. Therefore, alternately debat-
ing these matters with himself and praying to God, he passed an anxious,
sleepless night. Finally, thanks to the Father of lights, he considered the
gentleness, patience, and mercy which Christ has displayed and displays
toward some sinners. He thus knew for certain that God wanted Ramon to
abandon the world and serve Christ with all his heart.

He therefore began to consider what service he could perform which
would be particularly pleasing to God, and it seemed that no one could
perform a greater service to Christ than to devote his heart and soul, for the
honor and love of God, to converting the Saracens to that cult and service
which has already been embraced everywhere by so many Christians. But as
he considered this, he realized that he didn't possess the knowledge to
undertake such a task, inasmuch as his knowledge of Latin grammar was
limited.

---

1. In 1265/70; in Majorca the seneschal was a household official. The kingdom of
Majorca included Rousillon and Montpellier in southern France and the Belearics, i.e., Ibiza
and Majorca. Minorca was also conquered from the Muslims in 1287.

He contemplated all this with a heavy heart. But suddenly a strong impulse entered his mind — he didn't know how, only God knows — directing him to compose one of the best books in the world against the errors of the infidels. He was quite surprised, since he didn't know how to accomplish this task, nor even what form the book should take. Nevertheless, the more surprised he became, the clearer and stronger became the impulse to produce such a book.

Considering this matter again, he realized that even if the Lord should give him time to complete such a book, he could not do so himself, especially since he had no knowledge of the Arabic language, which the Saracens speak. But the idea came to him of going to the pope, to the kings and princes of Christendom, in order to encourage them and impress on them the need to set up monasteries in various kingdoms and provinces suitable for this purpose, wherein certain monks and other suitable persons would learn the Saracen tongue and the languages of the other non-believers. Such persons would thus be instructed and equipped to preach and demonstrate to the aforesaid Saracens and other infidels the holy Catholic faith, which is the truth of Christ.

After having firmly conceived these three goals in his mind (namely, to undergo death for Christ by converting the non-believers to His faith, to produce the aforesaid book, God willing, and to set up monasteries for the instruction of various languages, as noted above), early the next day he visited a nearby church. He tearfully prayed to the Lord Jesus Christ in order to effectively achieve those goals which had gripped his heart.

Afterward, he returned home; but since he was living a very secular life, he was very tepid and remiss in undertaking the above three projects during the next three months, until the feast of St. Francis [October 4]. On that same feast day, when a certain bishop was preaching among the Franciscans in Ramon's presence, he heard how Francis had abandoned all in order to follow Christ alone, and so forth. Excited by the example of St. Francis, Ramon sold his worldly possessions, laying a bit aside in order to support his wife and children, and committed himself to Christ. With the aim of never returning home, he undertook a pilgrimage to St. Mary of Rocamadour, St. James of Compostella [in 1263/65], and to other holy sites, in order to pray to God and his saints concerning the direction in which God would lead him in order to achieve the aforementioned goals.[2]

Having completed his pilgrimage, he prepared to go to Paris to study

2. Rocamadour in southern France is the site of a chapel devoted to the Virgin, allegedly founded by the legendary St. Amadour. Santiago de Compostella in northwestern Spain is the alleged site of the tomb of the Apostle James.

the arts and acquire other useful knowledge. But his parents, friends, and especially the Dominican friar Raymund of Penyaforte, who had compiled the *Decretals* of Gregory IX, persuaded him not to go, and made him return to his home city in Majorca.

When he returned home, laying aside the clothes he customarily wore, he dressed himself in the coarsest garments he could find; and in that same city he learned the Arabic language from a certain Saracen slave. Nine years later, when Ramon was not present, that same Saracen blasphemed the name of Christ; when Ramon returned, he heard about it from others who had heard his blasphemy. Moved by his faith, Ramon struck the Saracen on the mouth, forehead, and face. The Saracen was so filled with anger that he began to plan how he could kill his master.

He secretly acquired a sword, and while his master was seated alone, suddenly attacked and wounded him. He shouted out, "You are dead." But Ramon repelled the arm in which the Saracen grasped his sword, as it pleased God. He suffered a serious, although non-lethal wound to his stomach. He overcame the Saracen and violently grabbed the sword from him. When the members of his household arrived, Ramon prohibited them from killing the Saracen, but allowed them to tie him up and to imprison him while he considered what to do. For he knew that it would be difficult for him to kill someone who had taught him Arabic, which he had wanted to learn so much. On the other hand, he weighed the matter for a long time, aware that the Saracen would henceforth not cease planning his death.

After pondering the matter for a long time, Ramon visited a nearby abbey, praying to God for three days regarding this matter. In the end, seeing that he remained undecided, since God had not answered his prayers, he returned home. When he went to prison in order to take a look at his prisoner, he found that the Saracen had strangled himself with the same rope with which he had been bound. Ramon gave joyful thanks to God, who had kept his innocent hands from slaying the Arab, and had freed him from a heavy problem, which had plagued him for so long.

After this [1274], Ramon ascended a certain mountain,[3] located not far from his home in order to contemplate God in greater tranquillity. After he had been there for less than eight days, as he looked deeply at the Heavens, the Lord suddenly illuminated his mind, showing him how to write the book against the infidels referred to above. Ramon gave great thanks to God for this, descended from the mountain, returned to the

---

3. Mt. Randa, situated about fifteen miles from Palma de Majorca.

aforesaid monastery, and began to plan and write that book, at first calling it the *Ars maior*, afterward renaming it the *Ars generalis*. After this book, he wrote many others, as noted above, in which he explained general principles from specific cases in layman's terms, as experience had already taught him. Ramon remained in the monastery composing his book, and again ascended the mountain and had a hermitage built at the same spot on the mountain where he had stood when God had revealed how to write the *Ars*. He lived there for four months or more, praying to God day and night that he would successfully complete that *Ars* to which he had dedicated himself in order to honor God and for the profit of the church.

While he was in the hermitage a shepherd came to him, a happy and handsome youth, with whom for some time he exchanged some good [ideas] concerning God, the heavens, angels and other matters. It seemed to Ramon that in one hour he told him what another man would take two days to say. When the shepherd saw Ramon's books, he kissed them on bended knee, moistening them with his tears. He told Ramon that much good would come to the church of Christ through these books. The shepherd heaped many prophetic blessings on Ramon, making the sign of the cross on his head and body, and then departed. Considering all these things, Ramon was surprised. For he had never seen the shepherd before, nor had anyone to whom he spoke ever heard of him.

After this, the king of Majorca [James II of Aragon], hearing that Ramon had written many books, ordered him to come to Montpellier, where he was staying. When Ramon got there, the king had his books examined by a certain Franciscan, especially his *Meditationes*, which he had written as a kind of devotion for each day of the year, providing thirty special paragraphs for each day. This friar found, not without admiration, that these meditations were full of prophecy and Catholic devotion. Ramon therefore had a book made in that city on the mountain in accordance with the *Ars*, calling it the *Ars demonstrativa*, which was publicly read out. He also wrote a lecture on this work in which he declared how the first form and first substance created the elemental chaos, and how the five universals from that chaos produced the ten categories[4] and are therein contained according to true Catholic theology.

At that time, Ramon convinced the king of Majorca to have a monastery built in his kingdom sufficiently endowed and populated with thirty Franciscan friars who would learn Arabic in order to convert the infidels (as

4. These are the *praedicamenta* of Aristotle.

stated above).[5] In order to provide permanent support for the monastery, for them and their successors, five hundred florins were provided per year.

After this, Ramon went to the Roman curia in order to convince the lord pope and the cardinals, if possible, to have similar monasteries built throughout the world in order to teach various languages. But when he reached Rome he found that Pope Honorius [IV, 1285–87] had just died. He therefore left the curia and went to Paris in order to inform the world of the art which God had given him.

Ramon came to Paris during the time of chancellor Berthold [1288/89], and he provided an explanation [or commentary] of his *Ars generalis* at the chancellor's special request in his palace. After reading the commentary at Paris and seeing the reaction of the students, he went back to Montpellier, where he wrote and lectured on the *Ars inventiva veritatis*. In this book and in others he was to write, he placed merely four figures, removing (or rather dissimulating them because of the weakness of the human intellect which he had learned about at Paris) twelve out of the sixteen figures which were in the *Ars*. When all of this had been done, he journeyed to Genoa, where the *Ars inventiva* was translated into Arabic. He returned to Rome, hoping, as above, to have monasteries built all over the world to teach various languages. But because of certain impediments placed in his path by the curia, he decided to return to Genoa in order to travel to the land of the Saracens, as he alone could carry out his project among them. His aim was to hold discussions with their learned men in order to demonstrate, in accordance with his art (which had been given to him by the Son of God) that the Holy Trinity made incarnate, is in essence the highest unity of the divine Persons. The Saracens believe that we Christians worship three gods.

Since it was quickly reported among the Genoese that Ramon had already arrived in order to travel to the Saracen land to convert them to the faith of Christ, people encouraged him to do so if he could. They hoped that through him God would accomplish something notable among the Saracens. The Genoese had heard that following his penitential conversion, inspired by God, Ramon had received a certain knowledge on that mountain which would enable him to convert the infidels. While the people showed great enthusiasm, at dawn God visited him [but also] began to tempt him with the greatest temptation. For when everyone was ready to board ship and his books along with other provisions had been loaded on board, his mind was often filled with the notion that if he should reach the

---

5. This is Miramar, established in 1275/6.

Saracens, they would expel him as soon as he arrived, or they might even imprison him forever. Fearing for his skin, as the apostle Paul had done during the Lord's Passion, he forgot his aforesaid decision, that is, that he would rather die for the sake of Christ than submit to converting to the faith of the infidels. He therefore remained at Genoa alone, held back by an inherent fear created by God's permission or dispensation, perhaps in order to keep him from becoming overly vain. As a result, he was filled with a great sadness and even became physically ill due to the scandal suffered by the faith as a result of his not leaving, and he languished in Genoa for a long time. He could reveal the cause of his sadness to no one, lest he be reduced to nothing.

Finally, when Pentecost [May 17, 1293] drew near, he had himself taken or was led to the Dominican church, where he heard the friars singing the hymn *Veni Creator*. He moaned to himself, "Can't the Holy Spirit save me?" In his weakened state he was taken to the friars' dormitory, where he lay in bed. There, gazing upward, he saw a light on the ceiling, similar to a pale star, and heard a voice speak to him from the star. "In this order he may be saved." Ramon asked the friars to have him dressed in their habit. They refused to do so because of the prior's absence.

When he had returned to his hospice, Ramon remembered that the Franciscans had been more receptive than the Dominicans to the *Ars*, which God had revealed to him on the mountain. Considering that the Franciscans would be more likely to make use of the art in order to honor the Lord Jesus Christ and aid His church, he thought that he ought to join the Franciscans rather than the Dominicans. As he contemplated this possibility, a belt or rope of the kind worn by the Franciscans appeared to him as if hanging on the wall nearby. When this vision appeared briefly to him after an hour, he saw a light or pale star of the kind he had seen earlier when he had lain in bed in the Dominican house, and a threatening voice came out of the star, saying, "I never told you that you could be saved only in the Dominican order; be careful therefore what you do."[6]

Ramon thought that he would be damned if he didn't join the Dominican order, while the *Ars* and the books he had written would be lost if he didn't join the Franciscans. He chose (what could be more admirable) his own damnation over the loss of his art, which he knew he had received from God in order to lead many to salvation and honor God. Notwithstanding

---

6. This would presumably allow him also to join the Franciscans. It is not certain that he did so, although the Franciscan Tertiaries claim Ramon as their own.

the reappearance of said star, he sent for the Franciscan guardian from whom he requested their habit [1292/93]. The guardian agreed to fulfill his request, when Ramon would be closer to death.

Despairing of God's desire to save him, and so as not to be considered a heretic by either the people or the Franciscans, Ramon wanted to make a superficial confession and compose a will. When in his presence, the priest lifted up the body of Christ, and as the priest stood upright before him in order to confer the sacrament, Ramon felt as if a man's arm had twisted his face in the direction of his right arm. At that moment it seemed as if the body of Christ was lifted up in the opposite direction, toward his left arm, and he was told the following: "You will suffer condign punishment if you now accept me in this way." But Ramon steadfastly persevered in what he had already decided, namely, that he would rather be eternally damned than that the *Ars*, which had been revealed in order to honor God and save many persons, should perish. He again felt as though a man's hand had twisted his face to the right, and, as he looked at the Lord's body in the priest's hands, in this position he fell off the bed onto the ground and kissed the priest's foot. He then accepted Christ's body, so that he might, at least under the guise of such false devotion, save the aforesaid *Ars*. What a marvelous temptation, or rather (so it seemed) divine dispensation! The patriarch Abraham had once placed "hope against hope" [Romans 4.18]; he always preferred his *Ars* or doctrine, through which many would come to know, love and worship God, to his own salvation. He was similar to the sun hidden by clouds, which, nevertheless, continues to burn. He despaired of God, in a miraculous way, under a certain darkness in his mind. Still, he proved that he loved God and others more than himself, which is clear from what has been said above.

While Ramon was weighed down in body and soul by a heavy tiredness, a report reached him that a certain ship was in port preparing to journey to Tunis. Hearing this, as if suddenly awakening from a deep sleep, he had himself taken to the ship with his books. His friends saw that he was on the brink of death and, taking pity on him, had him removed from the ship — a fact that saddened him very much. Again, Ramon thought about the matter and learned that a ship which the Genoese call in their dialect a *barca* was making ready to journey to the Saracen city, namely, Tunis. Despite the desires and counsel of his friends, he had himself taken to the barca with his books and other provisions. When the sailors had scarcely begun leaving port, Ramon suddenly regained the hope of his conscience, which he thought he had lost under the darkness which had covered him; joyful in the Lord, due to the merciful illumination of the Holy Spirit, he recovered not only the health of his weakened body, but also in a few days, much to everyone's amazement, he felt himself to possess a healthy mind and body such as he had previously possessed throughout his life.

After thanking God for such benefactions, they entered the port of Tunis, landed and entered the city. Every day he conversed with experts in Islamic law. Among other things he told them that he was well aware of the reasoning behind Christian law and all these matters, and that, after hearing the rational bases of Muslim law, he would be willing to hold conversations with them on these matters. Should their reasons be more convincing than those of the Christians, he would be willing to convert to their faith. As each day more and more experts in Islamic law met him, demonstrating the grounds of their law in order to convert him to their faith, he finally answered their arguments, saying, "The wise man ought to adhere to that faith which all the wise men of the world agree attributes to the Eternal God the greatest goodness, power, glory, perfection, and other qualities, and all of these qualities in the greatest equality and harmony. The most praiseworthy faith in God is the one which provides the greatest harmony and consistency between God, who is the highest and first Cause, and between His effects [*effectum*]. . . ."

When it appeared that Ramon had informed the minds of the infidels about these matters, it happened that a certain man who was famous among the Saracens, who understood Ramon's words and intentions, beseeched the king to have him beheaded as quickly as possible, for his attempts to subvert the Saracen people and his daring temerity would destroy the law of Mohammed. A council was called, and at this man's urging and that of other councilors the king tended to support Ramon's execution. But being prudent and learned, one of the council members suggested to the king that he should avoid such an evil deed; for although it would be very honorable to kill a man like Ramon, at the same time, while defending Christianity as best he could, he nevertheless appeared to be endowed with much goodness and prudence. He added that even a Saracen would be considered good if he dared to visit the Christians in order to convert their hearts to the Saracen faith. The king accepted these arguments and desisted from his decision to kill Ramon. Nevertheless, he ordered him expelled from Tunis. When Ramon was taken from prison, he was subjected to many insults, vituperation, and even physical attacks.

He was taken to the next ship bound for Genoa, while the king decreed that he should be stoned should he set foot in the country again. Ramon grieved very much for those persons of great reputation and others whom he could bring to baptism, and for those who before his departure he had influenced to reach the full light of the orthodox faith. While the man of God was afflicted with the sting of this kind of perplexity, the ship on which he was to be placed set sail. Ramon felt that he would face difficulties, whatever choice he might make. On the one hand, should he leave, those souls which were already favorably disposed toward Christianity would be again banished to the trap of eternal damnation. On the other hand, should he decide to remain, he knew that the Saracens in their anger had prepared his death. Utterly consumed with a love of God, he did not fear to undergo the dangers of death, if by his act he could bring these souls to salvation. And, getting off that ship, he entered another one bound for the same port, hoping that, if in some way he could reach land without encountering their beastly violence, he might accomplish the work which he had undertaken, as noted above.

At the same time, a certain Christian who was similar to Ramon in both gesture and clothes, came to town. The suspicious Saracens arrested him, believing him to be Ramon, and wanted to stone him. The man cried out, "I'm not Ramon!" When they looked into the matter, they discovered that Ramon was already aboard ship, and the man thus escaped their grasp. Ramon remained there on board for three weeks and saw that he could accomplish nothing there in Christ's service; he therefore went to Naples, where he lectured on his art and remained until the election of Pope Celestine V [1294].

Ramon then went to the Roman curia, hoping to achieve something in the service of the faith of God, as noted above, with the aid of the pope. There, he wrote books; and after Pope Boniface VIII succeeded Pope Celestine V [1296] everyone urged Ramon to beseech the pope's aid in order to forward the Christian faith. Although he suffered many difficulties as a result of his pursuing the pope, he didn't abandon his original intention, hoping to achieve his end, not seeking his own good or aggrandizement, but rather the good of the Christian faith.

When Ramon finally saw that he could get nothing from the pope, he went to Genoa, where he wrote many books. Next he visited the king of Majorca, and after they had a talk, he went to Paris [1297/99], where he lectured publicly on his art and wrote many books. He next spoke to the king [Philip IV (the Fair) of France] about certain matters of use to the holy church of God. But seeing that he could achieve little or nothing concerning these matters, he returned to Majorca, where he stayed in order to bring the many Saracens who lived there to salvation through disputation and preaching. He also wrote some books there.

While he was involved in this work, word reached him that Cassianus, the emperor of the Tartars [Ghazan, the khan of Persia (1295–1304)], had entered the kingdom of Syria in order to conquer this state. When Ramon heard this, he boarded a ship bound for Cyprus, where he discovered that the news was false. Ramon saw that he would be frustrated in his original aim, and began to conceive of a way whereby he could exploit the time allotted to him by God not in leisure, but in performing deeds acceptable and useful to God and of value to his fellow man. He weighed in his heart the apostolic advice which says, "Let us not be weary in well-doing, for in due season we shall reap, if we faint not" [Galatians 6.9]. And the words of the prophet, "He that goeth forth and weepeth, bearing precious seed, shall doubtless come again with rejoicing, bringing his sheaves with him" [Psalms 125.6].

Thus Ramon approached the king of Cyprus[7] and asked him whether he would encourage the infidels — namely Jacobites, Nestorians, and Monophysites — to attend his sermon and disputation.[8] After he had done this in order to edify his listeners, he asked the king of Cyprus to send him to the sultan, who is a Saracen, and to the king of Egypt and Syria, in order to inform them of the holy Catholic faith. The king did not, however, provide for any of these things. Placing his trust in him who "spreads the Gospel with much virtue" [Psalms 62.12], Ramon began with only God's help to act manfully among them by means of preaching and disputations. In the end, persisting in his preaching and doctrines, he suffered no small physical weakness. Two persons were serving him [at the time], a cleric and a manservant. Not "taking heed of God" [Psalms 53.5] and neglecting their own salvation, they thought of extorting money from this man of God through their evil hands. Thinking that he had been poisoned by them, Ramon dismissed them from his employ.

At Famagusta [1301/2], he was graciously received by the Master of the Templars,[9] staying in his house in the city of Limassol until he recovered

---

7. Henry II (1285–1324) of the Lusignan dynasty was also the last Latin king of Jerusalem (1286–91).

8. The Jacobites are a Christian sect founded by James Baradai, located largely in Syria. The Nestorians are an early Christian sect that stresses the two natures of Christ, one human and the other divine. This was the official teaching of the Persian church and was prevalent in central Asia. The Monophysites are an early Christian sect that stressed the single, divine nature of Christ. The term here employed is *Mominos*, which may refer to Muslims rather than Monophysites.

9. This refers to Jacques de Molay, the last grand master of the Templar order, who was burned at the stake following a series of trials that led to the disbanding of the order and the confiscation of its property.

his health. Ramon then returned to Genoa, where he edited many books, and then journeyed to Paris, where he taught his art very successfully and wrote many books. Leaving Paris at the time of Pope Clement V, he journeyed to Lyons, where the pope resided, and beseeched him to undertake a great project for the sake of the faith, namely, to establish monasteries populated by devoted and skillful persons who, having studied the languages of various peoples, would be able to evangelize the infidels in accordance with God's words, "Go forth to every part of the world, and proclaim the Good News to the whole of Creation" [Mark 15.16]. This request had little impact on either the pope or the cardinals.

Ramon then returned to Majorca, setting sail for a Saracen land known as Bugie [1305?]. In the town square Ramon stood calling out the following words: "The law of the Christians is true, holy and given by God. The law of the Saracens is false and erroneous, and I am prepared to prove this." When he said such things concerning the faith of Christ in the Saracen language to the large number of pagans who were present, many evil persons attacked him, wanting to stone him. Since such savagery was unleashed against him, the "high priest" or "bishop" of the city sent messengers ordering that he be brought before him, and he said to Ramon, "Why have you acted with such foolishness as to presume to impugn the true law of Mohammed? Don't you know that anyone who so presumes is to suffer capital punishment?" Ramon replied, "A true servant of Christ, who is knowledgeable in the Catholic faith, ought not to fear the dangers of physical death, when he can acquire the grace of spiritual life for the souls of the non-believers."

The "bishop" replied, "If you believe that the law of Christ is true, do you consider the law of Mohammed to be false? And can you provide the necessary proof of this contention?" This "bishop" was a well-known philosopher. Ramon replied, "Let's discuss a common issue and I will provide you with the necessary reasoning." When the "bishop" assented, Ramon asked him, "Is God not completely good?" The "bishop" answered in the affirmative. Ramon, wanting to prove the truth of the Trinity, began to argue. . . .

The "bishop" was dumbfounded by reasoning of this kind, and could not reply. He then ordered Ramon imprisoned in chains. Many Saracens waited outside, expecting to kill him. The "bishop" issued an edict that no one should conspire to kill him, since he intended exposing the man to a well-deserved death. As he was led to prison after leaving the "bishop"'s residence, Ramon was subjected to blows inflicted with sticks and hands, and his long beard was pulled. He was incarcerated in the latrine of the thieves' prison, where for some time he underwent a harsh experience; he was afterward removed to a cell in the same prison.

The next day the clergy of the Islamic law met in the presence of the "bishop" and asked for Ramon's death. After the council began, the majority conceived of a plan whereby they could kill him. Ramon was to be brought before them. If they found him to be a learned man, he would be killed. If it turned out that he was merely an ignorant fool, they would let him go. One of them, who had traveled with Ramon from Genoa to Tunis and had often heard his sermons and discussions, said, "Beware lest he be present at the tribunal. He may adduce arguments against our law that will be difficult or even impossible to contradict." It was agreed that he should not be brought to them, but a short time afterward he was transferred to a less stringent prison. Finally, the Catalans and Genoese who were present used their influence to have him placed in a more suitable place, which was done.

Ramon remained incarcerated for half a year, during which time the "bishop"'s clergy and messengers frequently visited in order to convert him to the Muslim law, promising him wives, honor, a home, and great wealth. But Ramon, like the man of God who dug deep and laid the foundations on firm rock [Luke 6.48], said, "If you want to believe in the Lord Jesus Christ, you should put aside that erroneous law, and I will offer you great wealth and promise you eternal life." After assaulting him often with such matters, they agreed to produce a book in which each side would confirm his law with the most efficient arguments. Whichever one could advance the stronger arguments, his law would be considered truer. After Ramon published his book, which was very effective, word arrived from the king of Bugie [Abû-l-Baqa Halid (1302–11)], who then resided in the city of Constantine, that Ramon was to be immediately expelled from Bugie.

When Ramon had boarded a ship that was in port, the ship's captain was told never to allow him to return to the country. On the voyage to Genoa, a violent storm arose when they were ten miles from the port of Pisa. The ship was subjected to severe hurricanes; some of the sailors drowned, while others escaped only with God's help. Among the latter were Ramon and his companion. All their books and goods were nevertheless lost, and they only managed to reach shore clinging half-naked to the barca. When he came to Pisa, some of the citizens greeted him with great honor. This man of God, although old and decrepit, there completed his *Ars generalis ultima* with Christ's aid. . . .

When the aforesaid *Ars* and many other books had been completed, he

wanted to encourage the people of Pisa to serve Christ and therefore suggested that a community of Christian knights be established in order to
undertake the conquest of the Holy Land from the perfidious Saracens.
They would send eloquent and convincing letters to the pope and cardinals
attempting to promote a plan of this kind. While such letters were being
procured in the city of Pisa, he went to Genoa and asked for similar letters.
There he was approached by many devoted noblewomen and widows who
promised twenty-five thousand Pisan florins for the succor of the Holy
Land. After he left Genoa, he traveled to Avignon, where the pope was then
residing. But seeing that he could not promote his plan there he went to
Paris, where he gave a public lecture on his art and on many other books
which he had written earlier. A large number of masters and students were
present at his lectures. He not only provided them with philosophical arguments to strengthen the faith, but also advanced the highest principles of
the Christian faith in a clever and convincing way.

Because of the words of the Commentator of Aristotle, that is, Averroës, it seemed that many had strayed from the path of the truth, and
especially of the Christian faith, saying that it is impossible for the Christian
faith to be understood intellectually in any way, although it might be understood through belief.[10] Because this was opposed by the community of
Christians, Ramon undertook to provide proof through scientific demonstration, so as to refute their views in various ways. If the Christian faith
cannot be understood intellectually, it is impossible for it to be true; concerning these matters he wrote several books.

After this, Ramon learned that the holy Pope Clement V was about to
hold a general council in the city of Vienne on the calends [first day] of
October 1311. He proposed to attend the council in order to advance his
three schemes for the advancement of the Christian faith: first, to establish a
suitable place to house religious and learned men, who would study various
languages in order to preach the Gospel to all creatures; second, to create
one order out of all the other military orders in order to wage a continuous
war abroad against the Saracens to recover the Holy Land; and third, in
opposition to the views of Averroës, who perverts the truth on so many
subjects, that the pope should quickly provide a way to oppose those views

10. Averroës — Abu-al-Walid Muhammad ibn-Ahmad ibn Rushd (1126–98) — born in
Cordoba, was an Arab Spanish diplomat, physician, and philosopher, whose summaries and
commentaries on the works of Aristotle were the chief means whereby the ancient philosopher's works reached Europe. His "double truth" doctrine was regarded as particularly dangerous to Christian belief.

which appear to obstruct the truth and the uncreated wisdom of the Son of God, thus preventing people from holding such opinions, so that learned Catholics should not seek their own glory, but rather the glory and honor of Christ. Ramon wrote a book concerning these matters, entitled the *Liber natalis*, promising to provide cogent philosophical and theological arguments against them. This he had done clearly in some of his other books. This servant of God and true spokesman of the highest and deepest truth of the Trinity, among his daily tasks, wrote over one hundred and thirty-three books.

Forty years have already passed since his heart, soul, strength, and mind were directed toward God. During this period he continually wrote books, as much as his time allowed, in order to fulfill the words of the prophet David, saying, "My heart is stirred by a noble theme, in a king's honor I utter the song I have made, and my tongue runs like the pen of an expert scribe" [Psalms 45.1–2], that is, the Holy Spirit, who grants the Word to those who spread the Gospel with much virtue, concerning which the apostolic Savior says, "For it is not you who will be speaking. It is the spirit of your Father speaking in you" [Matthew 10.20]. Since he wanted to assume the wide use of his books by all people, he published many in Arabic, since he knew that language. In fact, his books were published everywhere, but he had them especially collected in three places: at the Carthusian monastery in Paris, at the home of a certain noble of Genoa, and at the home of a certain noble of Palma de Majorca.

III

Sexual Nonconformists and the Fires of Lust

For medieval Christians, perhaps the most persistent trick employed by Satan was his exploitation of human sexuality as the means of tempting the believer. Since human procreation transmits original sin to future generations, it is fitting that Satan should exploit sexuality as the chief means of drawing souls to his side. Thus, despite the continuing effort of the Christian clergy to impose a uniform sexual ethic on their flocks, a wide gap remained between the ideological program of the faith and its fulfillment. This gap between ideology and behavior is reflected in the laity's frequent disregard of church doctrine concerning such subjects as incest, sacramental marriage, usury, bastardy, witchcraft, and trade with the Muslims. As David Greenberg and Warren Johansson have argued with reference to homosexuality, it cannot be assumed that the perennial distrust of pleasure, particularly of the sexual variety, voiced by philosophers, scholars, and churchmen was shared by others.[1] Medieval schoolmen argued that non-procreative sexuality — including adultery, bestiality, masturbation, and sodomy — are contrary to the laws of nature, the exercise of right reason, and the will of God. Nevertheless, the laity (and some of the clergy) acted otherwise, and contemporary sermons, conciliar and secular legislation, penitential manuals, and scholastic treatises indicate that those in authority paid considerable attention to the reform of sexual morals.

The medieval Aristotelian notion of natural law adapted by Thomas Aquinas and Albert the Great provided the intellectual background of the crusade against a variety of "sins against nature," including adultery, sodomy, and bestiality, to which were attached the label of infamy. Such sins were regarded as not only a danger to sinners themselves, but to society be-

---

1. David Greenberg, *The Construction of Homosexuality* (Chicago: University of Chicago Press, 1988).

cause they undermined the family. Infamy became the subject of many sermons, such as those delivered by Bernardino of Siena, who railled against the decaying morals of young people and the dangers this posed.

Youth in particular was often the focal point of the drama of salvation in which the soul is torn between the temptations of the Devil and the promise of God. The canonist Hostiensis spoke of the "via avis et sagitte" on which the youth was poised, like the Jewish people themselves, wavering between God and the Devil. The concupiscence and intemperance of young people were regarded as a consequence of their heated passions, whereby they are subject imprudently to instinct unmitigated by the restraints of reason. It was believed that the constant movement of the humors (blood, phlegm, black and yellow bile) and of the complexions (warmth, coldness, moistness, dryness) influence one's physical and mental constitution and create a changeability which may lead to error and reduce one's willpower. In his treatment of the moral dangers of adolescence, the encyclopedist Vincent of Beauvais (ca. 1250) cited Seneca the Elder's *Controversiae*, which warned of the sexual confusion of youth: "Look at our young men: they are lazy, their intellects asleep. . . . Libidinous delight in song and dance transfixes these effeminates, braiding the hair, refining the voice till it is as caressing as a woman's, competing in bodily softness with women, beautifying themselves with filthy fineries — this is the pattern our youths set themselves. . . . Born feeble and spineless, they stay like that throughout their lives, taking others' chastity by storm, careless of their own."[2]

The chief task of late adolescence was therefore to overcome the dangers of unbridled lust, by means of moral education, penance, marriage, sexual abstinence and the other tools whose acquisition was a major aim of religious propaganda. Patristic sources provided much of the evidence for the laziness, lust, confusion, and distress of youth. Augustine himself in his *Confessions* served as a model for those torn between lustful urges and the desire for chastity. Isidore of Seville had derived *adolescent* from *adolere*, which implies burning, since the youth is threatened by the consuming fires of lust due to his natural viscosity, humidity, instability, vanity, recklessness, tendency to violence, and malleability. Thomas of Cantimpré noted that at the very moment when the adolescent is capable of generation, and has reached his greatest strength, he is filled with passion and his natural virtues are weakened. Both Thomas Aquinas and Giles of Rome argued that the

---

2. Annaeus Seneca, *Declamationes*, ed. and trans. M. Winterbottom, 2 vols. (Cambridge, Mass.: Harvard University Press, 1974), 1: preface, 8–9.

flux of the libido begins only to weaken after the age of twenty, and may at least be controlled and channeled through marriage.

Women, who were viewed by the scholastics as incomplete men, were regarded as untamed and lacking reason, intemperate, garrulous, quarrelsome, lazy, and frivolous. Their moral education stressed pious love of God, frequent confession, charity, humility, modesty, and obedience. Gilbert of Limerick (d. 1140), for example, described the ideal woman as "a servant, mild, obedient, humble, patient, sweet, charming, innocent, devoted, faithful in deed, consoling to those who complain, chaste, amicable to those giving birth, pious to the suffering . . . gracious to all and sundry on every occasion."[3] Humbert of Romans (d. 1272) suggested saints Agnes, Catherine, Caecilia, Lucia, and Esther as suitable examples of the humility, chastity, piety, charitability, and taciturnity required of women.

The resolution of the sexual conflicts of adolescence, when "the temptations of the flesh are violent," had long been a focus of preaching, hagiography, and didactic literature.[4] Many of the moral examples presented to youth stressed the need to overcome "unnatural" sexual urges. Jerome's life of Paul the Hermit, for example, reported the first bloom of youth and the saint's victory over the temptations of a lustful harlot. His crisis reached a decisive point when he feared the betrayal of his new faith by his brother-in-law, leading him to flee the world for life as a hermit. The life of Anthony by Athanasius also dwelt on the Devil's lascivious tricks during adolescence; and Benedict nearly abandoned his hermitage due to the temptations of lustful women, until he "conquered pleasure through suffering" by throwing himself naked on a bed of brambles and nettles.[5]

During the Gregorian reform period of the eleventh century, the sexual crisis of adolescence assumed greater importance as the focal struggle of those who wished to abandon the world, family, and friends in pursuit of the faith. Perhaps the most eloquent (and extreme) example of the distress caused by the conflict between the demand for celibacy and the pangs of the flesh was Peter Damian (ca. 1007–72). He described sexuality in the most pejorative terms, born of lust rather than love. He regarded the pangs of birth as the just punishment for the pleasures of sexual congress and he saw the urge to bear children as the proud result of an unwillingness to abandon

3. Gilbert of Limerick, *Liber de statu ecclesiae*, in Jacques-Paul Migne, ed., *Patrologia Latina. Cursus completus*, 221 vols. (Paris: J. P. Migne, 1844–55), 159: 997.

4. Gregory the Great, *Dialogi*, ed. Adalbert de Vogüé and Paul Antin, 2 vols. (Begrolles en Mauges: Abbaye de Bellefontaine: 1978–80), 1: 3.

5. Ibid., *Dialogi*, II.1.1.

the sensuality of the world, even when approaching death. Damian argued that we are all born in "hideous putrefaction and filth."[6] While brute beasts may be satisfied with procreation alone, human beings seek the satisfaction of lust. He described the human body as dirt, filth, or ordure, consumed by the fires of lust, particularly in adolescence. His call to the Virgin Mary echoes the despair of one caught in a prison of sensual degradation: "O my glorious mother, mirror of virginal purity and standard of virtue. How have I, a wretched and unhappy creature, offended you by the filthy putridness of my flesh and have violated the chastity of my body, of which you are mother and author." When threatened by a nocturnal emission in the middle of the night, Peter customarily jumped out of bed and threw himself into ice cold water in order to stanch the burning flames of lust. After the diabolical urges had ceased, he recited several Psalms and went back to sleep. Jacobus of Voragine's widely distributed life of Bernard of Clairvaux also reported how the saint had stanched the fires of lust by jumping into cold water until he was nearly bloodless.

In the thirteenth century, the eremitical tradition of battle with the pangs of sexuality is represented by William of Oliva (1174–1240), for example, who had at first tried to undo his fellows in debauchery. Torn by lust, he abandoned his home and wandered at sea, until several visions induced him to become a hermit. Even then, he was often visited by "demons in the form of beautiful women," who danced about and sang lascivious songs. He likewise prostrated himself in prayer, thrust himself into cold running water, ran about in the snow, and flagellated himself.[7] Pope Celestine V's sense of guilt over the pollution of a nocturnal emission prior to saying mass was relieved only after a vision reaffirming his sense of mission (see his autobiograpical account in Chapter 4 on the possessed). A similar danger of adolescent sexuality hampered women. Benvenuta Bojani (d. 1295) of Forlì was visited by an evil spirit who inquired, "Why do you behave this way? You can do it at another time. For I have come and let us experience the pleasures of the world."[8]

At the same time, the new heretical sects suggested a sexual ethic which radically differed from the Catholic program. Their allegedly polluting sexual profligacy was often employed by the church as a polemical tool in order

6. John of Lodi, *Vita Petri Damiani*, in *Acta Sanctorum*, ed. Socii Bollandiani, 69 vols. (Paris: V. Palme, 1863–1940), 23 February III: 424.

7. Anonymous, *Vita Gullelmi*, in *Acta Sanctorum*, 11 February I: 496ff.

8. Conrad of Castellario, *Vita Benvenutae de Foro-Julii*, in *Acta Sanctorum*, 29 October XIII: 154.

to exclude them from the body politic. The Brethren of the Free Spirit, for
example, were accused of sexual libertinism, including polygamy and sexual
orgies in which acts against nature were performed. Cathar theology, in
contrast, extended the prohibition on sexual congress leading to generation
to all, not simply the clergy and the unmarried, thus challenging the traditional Catholic distinction between the celibacy of the priesthood and the
monogamous marriage of the laity. In 1178, for example, it was reported
that the Cathars had preached "that a man and wife could not be saved if
each rendered the other their marital debt."[9] These Cathars denied the
possibility of reconciling salvation and sexual generation in marriage, nor
was marriage regarded as a sacrament. It is therefore fitting that the arch-
heretic is portrayed as the antithesis of the saint, and his or her sexual
behavior as a confirmation of the Devil's machinations.

The Inquisitorial trials thus stress in particular the sexual misdemeanors of the heretics. For example, the best-documented case of someone we
would consider a gay person hailed before the Inquisition, accused of both
sodomy and heresy, concerned Arnaud of Verniolle, whose testimony appears below. His frequent sexual contacts with fellow-students at Pamiers
are reported in testimony from both the accused and his bed-partners. The
inquisitors were, however, no less concerned with Arnaud's illicit hearing of
confessions while posing as a priest and the ideological justification he gave
for his sex acts. His argument — that nature demands the fulfillment of one's
sexual appetite and that sodomy is no less sinful than adultery — smacks of
the kind of radical Aristotelian philosophy of nature which the church had
roundly condemned since the mid-thirteenth century. Although his trial
and punishment, like the adulterers and others who appeared before the
same court, stemmed more from his heresy than his sexual adventures, they
provide a good example of the link made between sexual nonconformity
and theological heterodoxy in the eyes of the Church. This same investigation of alleged heresy in the Ariège, centered at Montaillou, incidentally
also tarred many of the victims as adulterers and practitioners of incest and a
variety of other sexual misdemeanors.

The Church attempted to provide only two acceptable standards of
sexual behavior, the celibacy of the cloistered man and woman and monogamous marriage. The new ideal of sacramental marriage as an antidote to
sexual profligacy among the laity was exemplified by such figures as Dau-

---

9. Cited in Walter L. Wakefield and Austin P. Evans, eds., *Heresies of the High Middle Ages*
(New York: Columbia University Press, 1969), 198.

phine of Languedoc (d. 1360), who combined chastity with child-bearing. Dauphine was known for her "exemplary life and perfect chastity, the rejection of fleshly desire and the relegation of earthly longings."[10] Despite her marriage to Elzéar of Sabran, she sought to induce him to follow the example of such married saints as Caecilia, Alexis, and Valerian, who had taken vows of celibacy with their spouses, even after having born children. Following the celebration of their marriage, she had allegedly said, "I was forced into the married state by my parents; I came unwillingly." Her bridal night was spent in tearful sleeplessness. A feigned illness eventually turned into a real one, as physicians feared for her life. She reportedly said, "You know, Elzéar, that unless you consent not to bother me any further about carnal intercourse, I will never get out of this bed alive, since you know I'd rather die than consent to carnal relations."

Cunegunda of Cracow (d. 1292), in another example, gave into her husband's sexual demands with reluctance, eventually becoming a nun after his death. The new model demanded that marriage fulfill God's commandment to increase and multiply, rather than the satisfaction of bodily lusts. Hedwig of Silesia (d. 1243), "Like another Sarah, in fear of the Lord, rather than because of her lust . . . consented to marry a nobleman."[11] Her marriage-bed nevertheless remained "unstained," and she avoided her husband during each pregnancy in order to avoid the sin of barren sexuality.

Many of the thirteenth-century evangelical movements were led by moral busybodies — often a bit self-righteous — bent on reforming the sexual mores of others, such as prostitutes. They took part in the 1233 Alleluia evangelical campaign in Italy in order to pass legislation against adulterers, sodomites, and other sexual offenders, first punishing them, and then excluding them from civil society. The efforts of Franciscans and Dominicans like Peter of Verona, Ranier Fasani, and John of Vicenza to reform municipal statutes had led to the passage of legislation which required heavy fines, banishment, and even capital punishment of convicted sodomites, for example. Much of this legislation was prefaced by a citation from the Epistle to the Ephesians 5.6: "because of this the wrath of God came down on the sons of disobedience." In medieval exegesis, the phrase "wrath of God" referred back to God's reaction to the behavior of the Sodomites, which had led to their destruction. Contemporary Biblical commentaries identi-

10. Jacques Cambell, ed., *Enquête pour la procès de canonisation de Dauphine de Puimichel comtesse d'Ariano* (Turin: Bottega d'Erasmo, 1978), 9, 17–18, 36–37.

11. Simon of Trebnitz, *Vita maior S. Hedwigis*, ed. A. Semkowicz, in *Monumenta poloniae historica*, 6 vols. (Lvov: W. Komisie Ksiegarni Gubrynowicza i Schmidta, 1896), 4: 514.

fied the sin of the Sodomites not merely as inhospitality, as some would
have it, but what would now be termed homoeroticism.

Although thus far not clearly documented, this heightened reform
activity against sexual "deviants" may have occurred in a background of the
relaxed sexual behavior prevalent in the early Renaissance city-states. One
of the consequences was the establishment of confraternities of Flagellants,
whose members flagellated themselves as a form of penance. The preface to
the statutes of the first such group, founded at Perugia about 1260 by
Ranier Fasani, specifically cites Ephesians and the coming doom which
awaits any society which permitted sexual disorder. The program of the
great thirteenth-century reformers thus had a strong sexual dimension. All
of the surviving "orthodox" autobiographical sources—Ramon Llull, Celestine V, Angela of Foligno, Hermann of Scheda, Salimbene de Adam—
stress the author's revulsion of sexuality as a central trigger and foil to
religious "conversion"; Ramon Llull left wife and family, repelled by his
former flirtations and sexual adventures; Hermann of Scheda was frightened by the anticipation of the sexual demands of Jewish marriage and
avoided congress with his wife; Pope Celestine V undertook gargantuan
efforts in order to flee the sight of women.

Those who gave their sexual appetites free rein, in contrast, were threatened with eternal damnation in the next world, and could be expelled from
civil society in this world. Among them were the lepers. Many characteristics
of marginality are to be found highlighted among the lepers, whose condition was regarded as the product of sexual aberration. The attitude of society
was often one of disgust, disdain, self-righteousness, and pity. Like those
possessed by the Devil, lepers could be freed of their disorder through penitential faith and miracle. A vision of Purgatory from Eynsham, for example,
dated about 1196, describes the sufferings of a leper who is freed through
penance. One of Francis of Assisi's first penitential acts was ministry to the
leprous. Humbert of Romans' model sermon to the lepers highlights the bitterness and grief of the afflicted, which at the same time opens up the possibility of salvation. Medieval moral theologians regarded physical diseases as
a consequence of sexual immorality, and in the case of the leper, such spiritual ill-health acquired an outward expression in the victim's physical appearance. It was argued that the body could be disposed to contagion as a result of sexual transmission. Regarded by physicians as venereal, contagious,
and congenital, leprosy could allegedly be caused by corruption during
conception, and after birth, by bad air, the use of "melancholic foods" such
as legumes, and excessive contact with leprous women. If one had lain with a
woman who had lain with a leprous man whose seed remained within her, a

leprous child could result. In medieval tradition, there appears to have been some confusion between the Biblical Lazarus the beggar and Lazarus of Bethany, whom Jesus allegedly raised from the dead. The disease described in Leviticus 13.43–46 ("The priest shall examine him, and if the discolored sore on the bald patch behind or on the forehead is reddish-white, similar in appearance to a malignant skin-disease on the body, the man is suffering from such a disease; he is ritually unclean and the priest must not fail to pronounce him so") was taken to refer to the leper, regarded as ritually unclean, to be separated from the community as long as his condition persisted.

The disease known as leprosy (*lepra*) probably appeared after the fourth century, reached its peak ca. 1100–1300, and began to disappear in the fourteenth century. Some physicians failed to distinguish among a number of skin disorders such as psoriasis, eczema, and scrofula, although by the fourteenth century various strains were identified. While the nobility were first reported as its victims, the disease later encompassed all social classes, and Andreas Capellanus compared the sexual mores of the leper to those of the poor and rural folk. Beginning in the twelfth century, the leper was separated from other persons by means of a ceremony, which placed him in a marginal position. In 1112 the order of St. Lazarus was established, perhaps as a military order (later renamed the knights of St. Lazarus and St. Mary), to care for lepers, and leprosaria sprang up all over Europe (see the legislation of the Third Lateran Council held in 1179). Municipal authorities, fearing infection, excluded lepers from the city limits and required that they be shod, wear special dress, and carry a bell to warn of their approach. The leprous were often treated as monsters who could destroy society, but at the same time as instruments of God's will. In 1174, the thirteen-year-old leper Baldwin IV became king of the Latin kingdom of Jerusalem. Shortly thereafter, the fortunes of the Crusaders in the Holy Land began to turn, and Pope Alexander III implied that this was perhaps caused by Baldwin's leprosy. Again, in 1321, a cabal of lepers, Jews, and Muslims in France were accused of poisoning the wells of Christendom, and numerous lepers (along with their Jewish "co-conspirators") were put to death by angry mobs. It was in this context that the Jew Baruch of Languedoc was forced to renounce his faith; and Arnaud of Verniolle's contact with a prostitute, followed by leprous sores, led him to homosexual contacts, for fear of being branded a leper.

Those who had succumbed to Satan's use of the sexual drive as a means of tempting the wayward to his side, therefore were the subject of canonical and secular legislation, marked with the brand of shame, the continuing objects of condemnation and abuse. Sexual nonconformists were driven to the peripheries of society and often became outlaws. Married clergy were to be deprived of their office and their children declared illegitimate. Although tolerated, prostitutes were restricted in their movements and subject to a variety of liabilities. Sodomites were to be ultimately executed as sinners not only against the laws of man but of God.

Robert of Flamborough, *Liber poenitentialis* (1210/13)

The chief means of controlling sexual behavior was the sacrament of confession. The Fourth Lateran Council (1215) required all believers to confess at least once a year, and those who failed to appear might be suspected of heresy or some other grave sin. During the thirteenth century, numerous treatises aimed at providing confessors with systematic, clear guidelines based on canon law and removing many of the conflicting penitential tariffs which had formerly been imposed on the faithful. The *Summa confessorum* (1208–15) by Robert of Flamborough contains a rather unique mock interview held between a confessor and his congregant, which summarizes the sexual sins prohibited in church law. It was probably produced in university circles at Paris, and therefore incorporated the most up-to-date scholarly approach. Many other such manuals of pastoral instruction followed, often produced by members of the new mendicant orders like the Franciscans and Dominicans, which stressed the importance of confession and penance for Christian salvation.

Source: Robert of Flamborough, *Liber poenitentialis*, ed. J. J. Firth (Toronto: University of Toronto Press, 1971), 195–99.

Bibliography: Aron Iakovlevich Gurevich, *Medieval Popular Culture: Problems of Belief and Perception*, trans. János M. Bak and Paul A. Hollingsworth (Cambridge: Cambridge University Press, 1988), 78–103.

*   *   *

Chapter. viii. On Lust [Luxuria]

222. Have you been lustful? The following things pertain to lust: extravagance, shamelessness, licentiousness, impudence, hesitation, flattery, allurements, voluptuousness, dissoluteness, feebleness, scurrility, and coitus. Extravagance is clear; likewise shamelessness. Hesitation is when a man acts without confidence. Flattery is when a man flatters others and accepts flat-

tery from others. Allurements are clear. Voluptuousness is when a man follows his longings, his desires. Dissoluteness may be found in gestures, words, deeds and attire. Feebleness is clear. Scurrility is when a man acts like a clown. Concerning all these things, do you ask pardon, etc.?
Priest: Those things which you otherwise do, do with confidence . . . and patiently . . . and firmly . . . and with perseverance . . . and with a relaxed mind. . . .

223. There remains coitus, which is lust in the strict sense of the word. Have you ever been polluted with lust?
Penitent: Many times.
Priest: Ever against nature?
Penitent: Many times.
Priest: Ever with a man?
Penitent: Many times.
Priest: With clerics or laymen?
Penitent: With both clerics and laymen.
Priest: Married or single laymen?
Penitent: Both.
Priest: With how many married persons?
Penitent: I don't know.
Priest: You therefore don't know how often?
Penitent: Correct.
Priest: Let's try to find out what we can. How long were you with those persons?
Penitent: For seven years.
Priest: In what [priestly] order?
Penitent: In the priesthood for two years, in the diaconate for two years, in the sub-diaconate for two years, and as an acolyte for a year. I sinned with single persons, but I don't know how many or how often.
Priest: Did you sin with clerics?
Penitent: I sinned with both secular clergy and religious [monastic clergy].
Priest: Tell me with how many secular and how many religious clergy, in which order you and they were in when you sinned together, and whether they possessed the office of archdeacon, dean, abbot, or bishop. Did you ever introduce some innocent person to that sin? Tell me how many and what order you were then in.

224. He may afterward be asked whether he ever sinned any more against nature, if he had anyone "in an extraordinary way." If he should ask in what

"extraordinary way," I won't answer him; he'll see for himself. I never mention anything to him from which he might derive some reason to sin, but only speak in a general way about things which everyone knows are sins. I painfully wrench a confession of masturbation out of him and likewise from a woman, but the method of getting this out should not be written down. Just as I asked a man whether he has done anything against nature, so I ask a woman, and in fact about every kind of fornication. Second, I inquire about adultery, then about every kind of fornication; afterward I ask about incest in this way:

225. Did you approach your female cousins? Say how often and how they were related to you. Afterward I inquire as above. Did you approach two females related to you by blood? Say how many times and how they are related, and afterward as above. You had how many [such female relatives] after your male relatives [had them]? Say how they [the males] are related to you, and afterward as above.

Did you approach a nun or another *conversa*?[1] Say to which order they belonged, and afterward as above.

Did you deflower a virgin? Did you approach your godmother (*commater*)? Your aunt? Your daughter? Your father's daughter? Your godfather's daughter? A woman during menstruation? An infidel, Jew, Gentile, heretic? Say how many times and how much. A woman in childbirth? A woman who has not been purified?[2] You should inquire about all of this as above.

226. Did you approach a pregnant woman? I ask this because many little children are weakened in this way, crippled and oppressed. If someone is oppressed by your having sexual relations you should in my opinion never serve as a minister in any order or be promoted without papal dispensation. During menstruation or childbirth many lepers, epileptics, and children with evil characteristics are conceived.

227. Have you committed fornication in a holy place or on a holy day? Ask where and how often this has happened, in what order, with whom and what kind of fornication it was. If you have fornicated in a holy place like a church which has been consecrated or a cemetery, the place itself is reconciled by a simple priest in a private capacity, or solemnly by a bishop. It is reconciled by a simple priest in a private capacity if the crime is hidden, and solemnly by a bishop if the crime becomes known. For this purpose a

1. A woman who has taken a vow.
2. Forty days after childbirth.

special office and special masses are held. The simple priest ought to walk around the place and sprinkle water which has been blessed in a dedicated church, singing seven Psalms and a litany. It is reconciled as for homicide, for whatever kind of fornication, if blood was shed there during a quarrel, [but] as if for theft according to some.

228. Did you approach prostitutes? You should be afraid lest she be your cousin or related by marriage, or vowed to enter religion, or because one of your relatives had had her, or for some other reason.

Did you procure her not for yourself? Say how often. . . . From the aforesaid inquiries you should know well enough what is to be investigated. Have you ever solicited another person through someone else? Inquire as above.

Were you ever "infamous" due to fornication? Something was said above concerning infamy. Did you ever fail to confess and approach the altar without contrition after fornication or in hatred or with a desire to sin? . . .

Municipal Legislation of Pisa (1286) and Bologna (1288)

Much of the direct responsibility for the punishment of sexual offenders fell on local authorities. Communal legislation beginning in the thirteenth century contained detailed regulations concerning the punishment of adulterers, prostitutes, procurers, bordello owners, sodomites, and other offenders. The newly established Franciscan and Dominican orders were especially active in arousing public indignation against such persons and establishing religious confraternities dedicated to their reformation. In addition to severe fines imposed on both offenders and those aiding and abetting their activities, their dwellings could be destroyed, and they could be paraded through the streets, imprisoned, subjected to public ridicule, pelted with refuse or worse, and expelled. Those public officials who failed to act could have their salaries reduced and they could be dismissed. The following legislation comes from the cities of Pisa and Bologna, both flourishing Italian communes involved in trade and banking. Their economic prosperity presumably attracted an "undesirable" element to the city, and residents of the more prosperous neighborhoods were particularly appalled. The Pisan legislation therefore contains considerable detail concerning those parts of the city from which prostitutes were expelled, although their activities were allowed within restricted areas — an early example of a red-light district. The legislation also takes note of the possible connection between heresy and homosexual behavior, at least in the eyes of the city fathers.

Sources: Francesco Bonaini, ed., *Statuti inediti della città di Pisa dal xii al xiv secolo*, 3 vols. (Florence: Presso G. P. Vieusseux, 1854–57), 3: 364, 395–97, and *Statuti di Bologna dell'anno 1288*, ed. Gina Fasoli and Pietro Sella (Vatican City: Biblioteca Apostolica Vaticana, 1937–39), 195.

Bibliography: James Brundage, *Law, Sex and Christian Society in Medieval Europe* (Chicago: University of Chicago Press, 1987), 420–79.

Pisan Legislation (1286)

III. Concerning apostolic regulations against heretics and sodomites

We will take heed of apostolic regulations which have been laid down against heretics, will observe them to the letter, and will have others do likewise during the entire period of our governance. We and others will harass and threaten sodomites, buggers, and other persons found guilty of the depravity of heresy, proceeding against them in accordance with the form of the law. And any outsider coming from outside the district into the city of Pisa who is found to be a heretic and is convicted by the inquisitor, or in our presence, and is condemned by him, in addition to the punishment and sentence determined against such a heretic, will be expelled from the city and district of Pisa by the *podestàs*[1] of Pisa and the captains of the people. By this law those podestàs and captains who act otherwise will be punished. And we will have this proclaimed publicly throughout the city.

IV. Concerning prostitutes and men of ill-fame

We will not allow any public prostitute or female go-between, or one who receives prostitutes, or pimps, male or female to remain within the walls of the city of Pisa, in "good" public places, from which we will have them expelled in accordance with the desires of the local residents, or at least three of them, who are of good reputation, neither near, inside or outside the walls of the city of Pisa[2] . . . and they are not to stay or dwell in any street or public square. The podestàs and captains are to do and observe this. If

---

1. The *podestà* was a local official responsible for the prosecution of criminals.
2. This is followed by a very detailed list of the boundaries of those parts of the city from which they are excluded.

they don't they are to forfeit one hundred *denarii*. . . . Nor may anyone sell any cooked food [in those places] to the aforesaid prostitutes and pimps, or dare to provide them with any kind of hospitality, to receive them in their homes, to rent to them or maintain them during the day or the night. Each time this occurs we impose a find of one hundred pounds on anyone who acts otherwise, while the prostitute will be beaten or dunked in the Arno River. Such men and women are to be expelled by the city police. This is to be written down in their rules and to be sworn by them: if they don't do so, they may be deprived of their office.

Persons may expel such prostitutes by force if necessary from the aforementioned places without incurring any punishment. No prostitute may presume to enter a bathhouse, except on Wednesday, under penalty of a fine of fifty *solidi*, to be paid every time they break the law. The bathhouse attendants (or owners) are to pay the same fine, and this is to be announced throughout the city. No public prostitute may wear a cloak, under penalty of the same fine; this is to be overseen by the police. Any Pisan who allows his home to serve as a dwelling for a prostitute or for any of the aforementioned persons, male or female, that is, persons of ill fame, reputation, class or conduct; who received thieves, buggers, sodomites, gamblers, dice throwers or other persons of ill fame, should be condemned to pay one hundred *denarii*. . . .

Bolognese Legislation (1288)

xix. Punishment for adultery, rape, and incest committed by men and women

We order that if anyone commits adultery, if he is a knight or son of a knight or *potens*, he should be condemned to pay fifty pounds of Bolognese currency; and if he is a footsoldier he is condemned to pay thirty pounds. An adulteress is condemned to pay one hundred pounds and in order to pay such a large amount it may be deducted from her dowry and the addition to the dowry.

Arnaud of Verniolle (1323/4)

In medieval theology, it was argued alternately that sodomites (for example) are enslaved to demonic powers and should be punished with the utmost severity; that sodomy causes eternal damnation, is contagious, loath-some to everyone, undermines moral character, causes natural catastrophes, and would lead to collective suicide. Most important for historians, ter-ming it the "unmentionable vice," the heinous sin was even to be blotted out from consciousness, memory, and written record, thereby limiting our knowledge of its practice in the Middle Ages. The great judicial scholar Luca da Penna had even argued in his commentary on the code of Roman law that sodomy is worse than murder, and that if by chance an executed sodomite has been revived several times during hanging (which would otherwise justify setting a convicted murderer free), he should be punished each time more severely.

The records of the inquisitorial trials held by Jacques Fournier, bishop of Pamiers (see also the cases of Baruch the German of Languedoc and Beatrice of Planisolles in this volume), contain a rare report of the activities of the renegade subdeacon Arnaud of Verniolle, accused of sodomy, falsely posing as a priest, and hearing confessions. The many witnesses called to corroborate these accusations reported that Arnaud had justified his "act against nature" on the grounds that such a sin is no graver than fornication, is less serious than incest, adultery, rape, and so on, and that one's nature must be satisfied. Such an argument implies his adherence to some unspec-ified heretical sect, although his hearing confessions without being a priest, and the fact that the court asked if he knew any Waldensians, suggests he might have been connected to this sect. The church regarded sodomy as a particularly heinous crime, which could bring down the wrath of God against all of Christian society, as had occurred at Sodom and Gomorrah.

Although also involved illicitly with women, Arnaud allegedly became more attached to men after having dallied with a prostitute in about 1320; his face swelled up, and he feared being persecuted along with the lepers. The following selections suggest the existence of a subculture of students at Pamiers who led varied sex lives, despite the severe civil and ecclesiastical punishment demanded for both sodomy and fornication. Arnaud found companions, mostly in their teens, among the student and clerical popula-tion of Pamiers, which at the time boasted a university (later disbanded); he claimed that his first encounters took place when he was still a child and shared a bed with some other students, although he did not yet feel the pangs of lust. Those who testified against him claimed that Arnaud often forced himself upon them, although this may have been intended to miti-gate their own guilt before the court. The large number of persons involved in illicit sex raises doubts about the effectiveness of the church's sexual program; such unorthodox behavior, including fornication, adultery, and clerical "marriage" is also attested among the residents of the village of Montaillou, who were investigated at the same series of trials. Nevertheless, the Inquisition's attention appears to be directed more toward the defendant's posing as a priest and granting absolution and the false theology he allegedly propagated among those who confessed to him than toward his alleged sexual transgressions.

Source: Adapted from Michael Goodich, *The Unmentionable Vice: Homosexuality in the Later Medieval Period* (Santa Barbara, Calif.: ABC-Clio, 1979), 93–123. Text translated from Pierre Duvernoy, ed., *Le registre de Pierre Fournier*, 3 vols. (Toulouse: Édouard Privat, 1966–68), 3: 14–50.

Bibliography: James Brundage, *Law, Sex and Christian Society in Medieval Europe* (Chicago: University of Chicago Press, 1987), 212–14, 398–400, 472–74, 533–36.

*   *   *

Against Arnaud of Verniolle, Son of William of Verniolle of Le Mercadal Parish of Pamiers, Concerning the Crime of Heresy and Sodomy

On June 9, 1323, Jean Ferrié, son of Raymond Ferrié of Bouriege in the diocese of Alet, a student of liberal arts at Pamiers, came to our reverend father in Christ, Jacques, by the grace of God bishop of Pamiers, to reveal the following facts concerning the crime of heresy, recorded in his presence in the portico of the episcopal see of Pamiers. He swore on the Gospels to speak the whole truth and nothing but the truth concerning the crime of heresy, about himself and about all persons living and dead. After he took the oath, he spoke, confessed, and testified as follows:

He said that when he, in that same year on a day in March during Holy Week, as he recalls, went to the Dominican monastery in Pamiers in order to confess to friar Bernard Scandala, he encountered Arnaud of Verniolle of the Le Mercadal parish of Pamiers on the street near the convent. Arnaud told him to accompany him, to bring a book to the market [or the Le Mercadal parish] of Pamiers, and he would free him from his task.

He replied that he had to go to the Dominican house to confess his sins. Nevertheless, he went with Arnaud, but he did not bring along a book. Along the way Arnaud asked if he wanted to confess, and the speaker said he had already confessed to a certain Dominican, and wanted to confess only to him, because he had heard that one should confess all one's sins to only one priest and that if the penitent remembered something afterward, he should confess to the same priest. Arnaud said that it was just as valid to confess to him as to anyone else, "because I will be as much your confessor as the other one was, since it is just as valid to confess to one man as to another."

When they approached the church of Le Mercadal, the speaker suggested they go in, and Arnaud could hear his confession there. Arnaud replied that he would not hear his confession in that church because if he entered the church and sit down there in order to hear confession, because of the many people who would come to him to confess, he would have to linger there a long time. For this reason he would hear Jean's confession in his own home, because it is just as pleasing to God in a house as in a church.

The two of them then went to a house situated near the church of Le Mercadal, Arnaud sat down with the speaker beside him at the head of the table in the hall, and Arnaud heard his confession. Among other things, he confessed that he had once sworn falsely on a calendar which contained the Gospels, and certain other mortal sins. Afterward Arnaud absolved him and enjoined him to say, on bent and naked knees from then until the feast of All Saints, "Miserere mei Deus" once, the Lord's Prayer seven times, Hail Mary seven times, and "Laudatum". He made the sign of the cross on the ground, kissed him, and said "In rememorationem. . . ."

After confession, the speaker asked Arnaud to give him proof to show the parish priest that he had already confessed. Arnaud replied that he would not give him such proof because it was enough for him to say that he had confessed to a chaplain and a Dominican. The speaker asked Arnaud what his name was so that if he should remember any sin he could come back to confess to him. Arnaud replied that his name was Arnaud of Catalonia.

Afterward, the speaker confirmed that this same Arnaud was named Arnaud of Verniolle and that he was not a priest, because he had asked many people; and later, at Le Pomarol, Arnaud told him that twelve students had already come to him to lighten their penance. . . .

Arnaud told him he had celebrated mass at the Dominican convent in Toulouse assisted by a certain student who at the time tutored Baudouin of Pamier's sons. . . .

On June 13, 1323, Guillaume Roux, son of Pierre Roux of Ribouisse in the diocese of Mirepoix, a student in the liberal arts at Pamiers, slightly over sixteen years of age . . . testified as follows:

He said that in that year, around the first day of Lent [Feburary 13,

1323], on a Sunday between noon and three P.M. on a day and time not
otherwise recalled, when the speaker was in the convent church of the
Augustinians at Pamiers, he met Arnaud of Verniolle, who took him out of
the church into the garden. Arnaud told him that if he wanted to stay with a
certain canon of St. Saturninus of Toulouse who had forty pounds in rents
and was prior of Lavelanet and [if he] would assist the canon by carrying
his books to school, Arnaud could secure the position for him and the
canon would provide his needs, food, and clothing.

The speaker replied that he would willingly stay with the canon if he
could study with him; the two of them then went to the Augustinian
sacristy. Arnaud made Guillaume swear on a missal that he would reveal to
no one the canon's secrets and manner of living. Arnaud then said that the
canon frequently got drunk and in his drunkenness easily assaulted others.
If the speaker should see the canon drunk, it was advisable to put him to
bed. He said the canon wanted women very much and usually either the
speaker or any other servant who stayed with him would have to bring him
women. If he wanted to stay, Guillaume should not reveal his knowledge of
this to the canon.

The speaker promised Arnaud to do this since Arnaud told him that it
could be accomplished easily. He even told him that during the winter
Guillaume would have to sleep in bed with the canon and that he ought to
do whatever the canon wanted done; in the summer while asleep at midday,
he would likely have to rub the speaker's feet; but Arnaud said he should tell
no one about this.

When Guillaume said that it was sinful to bring such women to the
canon, Arnaud told him that it was not such a grave sin and that he would
introduce him to some friars who would absolve him of any sin and impose
a light penance. If he did the canon's bidding, he would make money and
could give charity [as penance] from the canon's goods.

Arnaud then suggested that Guillaume come to his house where he
would show him books and he could stay. The two then went to Arnaud's
house and entered an upper room. When they were alone, Arnaud showed
him a book, saying it contained decretals,[1] and after reading a bit told the
speaker, "See what these decretals say here!" When the speaker said that he
didn't understand the words of the decretals, Arnaud told him in the vernacular [Provençal] that it was written that if a man lies with another, and
because of the warmth of their bodies semen flows, it is not as grave a sin as

---

1. Decretals are decrees that have the force of canon law.

if a man carnally knows a woman; because, so he said, nature demands this and a man is made healthier as a result. And, so he said, he himself could not stay with either a man or a woman, without semen flowing out.

When Guillaume said he didn't believe that it was a lesser sin to so behave with a man than to know a woman carnally, Arnaud told him that it is a lesser sin and that the decretals said so. Arnaud then threw the speaker down on the ground, placed his hands on his back, and lay on Guillaume. He then removed the speaker's clothes and told him to spread his thighs or some evil would befall him. The speaker then spread his thighs, and Arnaud got completely undressed, embraced the naked youth, kissed him, placed his penis between Guillaume's buttocks, and, moving himself as with a woman, his semen flowed between the speaker's legs. When this was accomplished, Arnaud told Guillaume to do likewise to him and that he could not leave the room until he had done so. Guillaume then likewise let his semen flow out between Arnaud's buttocks, and Arnaud then made a similar movement.

When this was over, Arnaud said that they must mutually swear never to do this again, either with each other or with anyone else. They then swore on the speaker's calendar in which the four Gospels are written.

When Guillaume said that they had committed a grave sin and heresy, Arnaud said he would bring him to a Franciscan who would absolve him of this sin and impose a light penance on him. Arnaud also gave him a book containing ten parchment folios which he kept in his home. Arnaud said that if he wanted to stay in his house until the feast of the Nativity of John the Baptist and on some night lie with him, he would pay him. The speaker said he wouldn't do this and left Arnaud's house while Arnaud remained.

Afterward, Arnaud frequently met him in town, and when he encountered him he called Guillaume a heretic. Nevertheless, he did not bring him to that Franciscan to hear his confession concerning said sin, although Guillaume frequently asked him to do so.

Finally, about eight days later [i.e., after the beginning of Lent], Guillaume was with Arnaud's illegitimate son in the furrier Tignol's workshop in the Villeneuve quarter of Pamiers. Arnaud, who was also there, told the speaker to accompany him to a parcel of land which he owned in Le Pomarol where, so he said, there were some men. The speaker consented to join him and the two of them went to the field, but there was no one there. When they arrived, Arnaud told him to undress and nap a bit because it was getting warm, and they could then carry on as they had done earlier in Arnaud's house.

The speaker at first refused and fled; but Arnaud pursued him and threw one of Guillaume's textbooks at him three times; as a result its binding broke. Arnaud then unsheathed a knife, pursued and assaulted him and brought him back to the field; with one hand he twisted the speaker's arm and in the other he held the unsheathed knife.

He then threw Guillaume on the ground and coiled his arms around his chest. He tried to lift him up and carry him to the spot where they had been, but when he couldn't, grabbing and pulling his hair, he dragged him there. While they were still dressed, Arnaud threw him on the ground, and in the manner described earlier, thrust his penis between the speaker's thighs and, embracing and kissing him, released his semen. Both before and after perpetrating this sin, Arnaud told him that this sin was less sinful than to know a woman carnally; and because Guillaume refused to commit this act with Arnaud due to the oath he had sworn, and from which no one could absolve, Arnaud said he would absolve him. After it was over, Guillaume took his robe and left while Arnaud remained in the field.

About eight days later, they met near the Carmelite house in Pamiers and Arnaud asked Guillaume to join him visiting his son's fiancée and to give her a ring; after many stops, they came to Arnaud's house and went to the aforementioned room. Arnaud then closed the door and swore on the decretals and on his holy tonsure that they would not leave the room until they had again done what they had done before. Guillaume wanted to leave, but when he stepped on the doormat Arnaud pulled it toward him and the speaker fell down. Arnaud held his shinbone, dragged him to the bed, put him on it, and sodomized him in the manner noted above. When the deed was done, the speaker left the room and went away. Arnaud also told him twice that if he wanted to carnally know his maidservant, he would make sure he could have her.

Asked if Arnaud had told him to confess to him and that he could as easily be absolved by him as by anyone else, he replied that he had not. But now Guillaume very much regretted what he had done, and he had never believed that it was less sinful to commit sodomy than to know a woman carnally. He offered to undergo the complete penance that the lord bishop wanted to impose on him for the aforementioned acts. He said that he had heard in school, although he didn't remember by whom or about whom it was said, that some of the students had confessed to Arnaud.

He said that after perpetrating the last sin, he told Arnaud that the lord bishop would find out about it. Arnaud responded by lifting something from the ground and saying that this object was as little value to him as if this deed would become known to the bishop [i.e., he didn't care]. He said nothing else pertinent. . . .

He further remembered that in addition to the instances already noted, in the same house, room, and bed, Arnaud had twice committed sodomy with him; that on other days and times, at Arnaud's instigation, in the same way Arnaud committed sodomy with him and vice versa. He said he never did so with anyone else nor did anyone else solicit him to commit said crime. He added that Arnaud promised to lend him his books and give him a knife if he would consent to commit this crime.

Arnaud suggested to him that he could carnally know Jacoba, the wife of Raymond Faur of the Loumet quarter of Pamiers, in whose house he dwelt and whose son he tutored. And although Arnaud suggested that he have either Jacoba or her daughter, Bosaurs, the speaker himself never solicited either one. . . .

On another occasion, in the portico connecting the dormitory and latrines of the Franciscan convent of Pamiers, to which he had come to confess about his aforementioned sins, Arnaud solicited him to commit sodomy, telling him that he would introduce him to a friar of the same house who would lighten his penance and would absolve him of the oath they had sworn about not committing that crime. Arnaud said that if they committed this act then Arnaud would bring him the means of loosening his penance. Because Guillaume refused, Arnaud would not introduce him to that friar. . . .

The same year noted above, on June 23 [1323], Guillaume Roux . . . confessed and testified the following:

That same year, around the Feast of the Ascension [May 5, 1323] on a rainy day between noon and three p.m., and on another day and time which he didn't recollect, when the speaker was at the school situated near the Carmelite house in Pamiers, Arnaud of Verniolle came to him. He said that if Guillaume would come along with him, he would give him a writing tablet. The two of them came to a house situated near the home of the Minorissi family of Pamiers, although he didn't know whose house it was. While they were there Arnaud found four small tablets in a box that he wanted to give to Guillaume and that Guillaume refused to take, saying that they weren't particularly valuable. Next, Arnaud shut the door, and on the ground floor room in which a bed was situated, Arnaud lay down with his clothes on and asked Guillaume to lie down beside him on the bed. He did so and, in the manner described in the previous confession, Arnaud committed sodomy on the speaker as they lay side by side. Arnaud then told Guillaume to do the same to him, which he did. When that was done, they separated and Guillaume returned to school.

In Arnaud's house, Arnaud told him that he had committed the crime with only one other man. Asked if he told Arnaud that he had committed a similar crime with a certain squire of his country or with any other man, he replied that he didn't remember. . . .

On June 13, 1323, Guillaume Bernard, son of Jean Jeu of Gaudiès in the diocese of Mirepoix, student of the liberal arts at Pamiers, aged about fifteen and a half . . . made the following deposition:

In that same year, around the Feast of All Saints just past, one Sunday when Guillaume was at the Augustinian house of Pamiers, during mass after the elevation of the host, Arnaud met him and inquired where he had come from. Guillaume replied that he was from Gaudiès. Arnaud said that he was acquainted with some people from Gaudiès who were staying in Toulouse, and among them was Bernard Faur, a student at Toulouse. The speaker said that this same Bernard was his second cousin. No other words were exchanged between them.

After lunch, Guillaume returned to the Augustinian house to hear the sermon; when Arnaud saw him in the church, he led him to the friars' refectory. There, he told Guillaume that if he wanted to lodge with a certain canon in Toulouse and bring his books back and forth from school for him, the canon would give him food and clothing; also, by staying with him, he could study with him. Guillaume replied that he would be willing to stay with the canon.

Arnaud told him to swear never to reveal the canon's manner of living to anyone. . . . He said he would willingly so swear, and made this oath on a Bible in the refectory in which the friars gathered to eat. After this oath, Arnaud invited him to his home. There, in the south portico, Arnaud asked if he would like to hear about the canon's mores and manner of living, and he said that he would. Arnaud then took him to an upper chamber, and in the hall he saw Arnaud's mother and nurse, although he did not know their names. When they were alone in the room, Arnaud closed the door and again asked if he wanted to hear about the canon's way of life. When he again replied yes, Arnaud asked him to remove his overcoat and lie down on the bed, which he did. Arnaud then lay down beside him, undressed both himself and Guillaume and spread his thighs. . . .

On June 13, 1323, Guillaume Boyer, son of Bernard Boyer of Plavilla in the diocese of Mirepoix, as student of the arts at Pamiers, aged about eighteen . . . made the following deposition:

That same year, on the second day of Rogations, Guillaume and Arnaud went to the church of St. John the Martyr, to which Guillaume de Voisin's wife had come with some of her friends to hear mass. After they had witnessed communion, Guillaume and Arnaud went out into the church cemetery and there Arnaud asked him which woman he would prefer to have sex with. Guillaume replied that he preferred a girl who had come along with Voisin's wife. But he also told Arnaud that it wasn't right to speak of such matters in a graveyard.

They then went to Arnaud's house; on the way, Arnaud asked, among other things, if he knew which sin was greater, a man lying carnally with a man or polluting himself with his hand on his virile member. He replied that he didn't know. Arnaud then told him that these two sins were widespread among the religious [i.e., monks and friars]. Guillaume, surprised to hear this, said, "Is that so?" And Arnaud said that it was so. Afterward, because they were near Arnaud's house, they went in and went up to the upper chamber. In the hall they encountered the maid and another woman who were cooking.

When they were in that room, Arnaud took off his overcoat, sat down on a chair, and showed Guillaume his books; among other things he asked Guillaume if he wanted him to write down a certain obsequy for the dead.

Afterward they returned toward the castle of Pamiers, and when they were near the castle, Arnaud said it would be fun to have sex with Gaillarda, Bartholomew of Rieu's maid, and Fina, Germani of Rieu's wife, in whose house Guillaume was then staying; that Guillaume ought to make an effort to know Gaillarda carnally; and that she was an animal who didn't know how to do anything. It would also be good to have sex or stay with Fina, the speaker's mistress, who was Bartholomew of Rieu's widow. Guillaume said he didn't care about such things. They then had lunch at his house.

After lunch, although it was late, Arnaud went to Fina's house, where Guillaume was staying. He asked the speaker to take a short walk with him. They then went to Arnaud's field at Le Pomarol and sat down there. Arnaud said, "If we were to get a hold of a woman here, what would you do with her?" Bernard said [he would do] nothing, and Arnaud embraced him and kissed his cheeks; the speaker told him to leave him alone. Afterward they got up and Arnaud embraced him again, but they didn't touch each other in any other way.

When they walked through that field, Arnaud asked Guillaume whom he had confessed to this year, and he said he had confessed to the Franciscan friar Arnaud Marti, who had refused to absolve him on the first day of his confession. Arnaud asked him which sins the friar had refused to absolve;

but the speaker said he wouldn't do this since it is forbidden to reveal such things. Arnaud then said: "Do you want to confess to me?" But Bernard replied that he didn't because he had already confessed this year and because Arnaud wasn't even a priest. Arnaud then said that there was a certain Dominican friar who had heard confession this year and had asked Arnaud what penance was suitable to impose for certain sins. There were no other words between Guillaume and Arnaud concerning this matter. . . .

In the same year, on June 2, friar Pierre Recort of the Carmelite order,[2] who had stayed in Arnaud's cell for several days and heard him speak about the crimes of heresy and sodomy . . . made the following deposition:

During the feast of St. Barnabas the Apostle just past, Arnaud of Verniolle was incarcerated along with the speaker and Raymund Bar of Montaillou. Arnaud pulled the speaker to one side and asked why he had been imprisoned. Pierre likewise asked why Arnaud had been imprisoned. He replied that he had been accused of committing the crime of sodomy with three youths, one from Gaudiès and the other two from Ribouisse. He was also accused of posing as a priest, of hearing confessions, and of absolving penitents of their sins.

Pierre asked: "Did you indeed commit these crimes?" Arnaud replied that he had. Arnaud said that because they wanted him to write parables or verses for them, Arnaud used to go with one or another of the aforementioned youths, bringing along some wine, silver cups, and food to a field that is situated opposite the leprosary of Pamiers. When they were there, they sometimes used to spread out a robe, dance, and wrestle, and afterward commit sodomy with each other. The boys would even come to his home and there, in an upper chamber, which was his study, they committed sodomy with him and he with them. And in that way one day the three youths fooled around with Arnaud, lying down together on the bed, one of them committing sodomy with the other as the third one watched. Because one of them already knew about it, they were all fired up about this sin. Arnaud started to do this on the feast of All Saints [November 1, 1322] last year and frequently committed that crime with the youths.

He told Pierre that he believed that sodomy was a mortal sin, although it is equal to simple fornication with prostitutes. Although he had heard that sodomy is was graver sin than simple fornication, he didn't believe it

2. This friar was himself sentenced on January 17, 1329 to ten years' imprisonment in irons at the Carmelite house in Toulouse, to be fed bread and water, for having seduced two women and having practiced sorcery.

was, unless a man lay on top of another man like a woman or committed the
sin through the rear. When Pierre asked why he carried on in this way with
youths when he could have had enough women, Arnaud told him that
during the period that they were burning lepers, he was in Toulouse and
had sex with a prostitute. After perpetrating that sin, his face swelled up and
as a result he was afraid of becoming a leper. He therefore swore from then
on not to know women carnally; and, in order to keep that oath, he carried
on in the above manner with those young men.

Arnaud told him that when he was caught, he came back from Toulouse with a certain youth of Moissac, of good family; during the journey
Arnaud committed sodomy with him. The youth promised never to reveal
anything about the crime, even if he knew that because of it he would be
flayed. Arnaud was very much afraid that the youth would be captured by
the lord bishop along with Arnaud's nephew, his illegitimate sister's son,
named Estaunie. He said that he had, however, not committed sodomy
with his nephew. Arnaud said that the fellow knew his secrets well and he
feared that if they were captured he would reveal all.

Arnaud told him that even before he had become a Franciscan, Arnaud
had committed that sin. Because of that same sin, a certain Franciscan friar
of Toulouse, either the son or nephew of Raymund of Gaudiès, had left
the order. He was his friend in the order and maligned the friars because
of this sin.

When he was a student at Toulouse, Arnaud lodged in rue Argulhieras,
near a canonry. At that time, a certain woman sent her son Arnaud Refec-
torarii, who could already recite seven psalms, to receive instruction from
Arnaud. Arnaud carried on with the boy, committing sodomy with him.
Arnaud did not tell Pierre about committing sodomy with the boy at any
other time.

Arnaud had said that the bishop would have enough on his hands if he
were to apprehend everyone in Pamiers who had been infected with that
crime because there were more than three thousand persons. But he did not
name anyone whom Pierre could recall.

Arnaud told him in the cell that while he was a student at the Franciscan convent of Bordeaux, friar Bernard Raynier had been accused of seduc-
ing the niece of the former bishop of Toulouse, Gaillard de Preyssac, and
was incarcerated at the Franciscan convent of Mirepoix. Arnaud was placed
in the same prison and the two of them used to discuss their incarceration
and what they would do, that is, how they would live, outside the prison.
Among other things, Bernard told Arnaud how they would hear confes-

sions when they got out, while Arnaud told him how he would absolve penitents: "May the Lord take pity on you and relieve you of your sins, and may he lead you to eternal life;" and he would add, "May God absolve you of your sins." But he did not say "I absolve you."

Arnaud said that when more intelligent folk came to him to confess, he would not apply that kind of absolution but would send them to Bernard to receive absolution. Arnaud told Pierre that Bernard had instructed him that if he had absolved penitents in the aforesaid manner, they were absolved. When Arnaud and Bernard left prison, they went to different places and churches, and Arnaud heard the confessions of many and diverse persons and absolved them in this way. Arnaud did not, however, reveal to Pierre either the persons or the places.

Finally, Arnaud separated from Bernard and went to Rome alone, and somehow he earned his needs along the way. But he never told Pierre that he heard confessions along the way, nor did he say that he believed that penitents were absolved in this way, that although he was a subdeacon they were absolved.

Arnaud said that some of the aforementioned youths confessed to him that year, and he absolved them in the same way and told many that he was a priest, although this was not true.

Arnaud told him that he went to the baths of Ax-les-Thermes with a certain Raymund, whose name he didn't recall, although Arnaud said his name was Raymund. At Tarascon, they went to the church of the Blessed Virgin of Sabartès, where they met two cleaning women commonly called nuns; Arnaud told them that out of devotion to that church, he wanted to celebrate his first mass secretly, so that none of his friends would know and so that he could celebrate it that much more devoutly. When he entered the church, Arnaud donned priestly garments and celebrated the mass. Afterward, the two nuns who took part in the mass along with Raymund told Arnaud that if he wanted to eat with them, they should bring food from Sabartès and they would be happy to join them. But Arnaud did not tell Pierre whether he ate with the nuns.

After brother Gaillard de Pomiès had told Arnaud that among other things he had gravely erred by celebrating mass and hearing confessions, Arnaud wanted to cancel what he had said about the mass; that because there were no wafers in the church, he had not celebrated the mass. He sometimes even told the speaker that what he had said about celebrating the mass was out of stupidity and foolishness.

Arnaud told him that he frequently spoke with the Waldensian Raymund de Costa, who was staying in Pamiers, whom Arnaud commended for his learning and wisdom; Pierre did not recall what else touching heresy had been said by Arnaud.

Pierre said that about a year ago Arnaud Maury of Montaillou stayed with brother Pierre Genies, a monk of Fontfroide, a penitent of the bishop, in a room situated beside the tower where the speaker was staying. Among other things, Arnaud told him one day that he had a brother who had fled from the kingdom of France because of heresy. And the brother, who was his fourth, came to the hospice of St. Susanna;[3] but because he dared not proceed further, he sent for Arnaud to bring him an alb, finding him beside the hospice. Afterward the fugitive, after taking counsel with them, left with the aforementioned three men in the direction of Catalonia. Arnaud did not tell him the names of the brother's three friends.

On another day, when the speaker had cried about the length of his incarceration and because he could not go to church, as consolation Arnaud told him what is written in Scripture: "I send you forth as lambs among wolves" [Luke 10.3]. And he added that Pierre said that he would not be able to go to church because he was of low moral standing, that that church is good in which the souls of good people are found.

Arnaud spoke to him of the human soul, but Pierre didn't remember what he said; but it seems that he held erroneous views in this area. He said nothing more pertinent regarding Arnaud.

Confession of Arnaud of Verniolle, Son of the Subdeacon Guillaume of Verniolle of Le Mercadal Quarter of Pamiers, Concerning the Crimes of Heresy and Sodomy

On June 23, 1323, Arnaud of Verniolle, son on the subdeacon Guillaume of Verniolle of the Le Mercadal quarter of Pamiers, an apostate from the Franciscan order, strongly suspected and accused of the crimes of heresy and sodomy, was arrested and, at the order of the reverend father in Christ, the lord Jacques, by the grace of God bishop of Pamiers, was bound over in prison at the order of the aforesaid lord bishop and was led into the bishop's presence to the upper gallery of the episcopal see at Pamiers, to a court set up in his presence. He swore on the Gospels that he would speak the whole truth and nothing but the truth concerning said crimes and others touching on the Catholic faith and the office of the Inquisition touching depraved

3. Situated at Hospitallet.

heresy, both about himself and about all others living and dead; after taking his oath, he said, confessed, and made a deposition as follows:

That same year, during Lent, although he doesn't remember whether it was the seventh day or some other, he was at the Augustinian church in Pamiers. While he was there a large number of people wanted to confess, including a student aged between sixteen and eighteen, whose name he didn't know, dressed in blue and not from Pamiers. The youth came to him and asked if he were a priest, because he wanted to confess. Arnaud said that he was a priest and was willing to hear his confession. They then prostrated themselves in the church and prayed and he heard the student's confession.

Among other things, the student confessed about the sin of fornication with public prostitutes, the theft of fruit, grain, and herbs from the fields, and similar deeds. Arnaud did not recall what other kinds of mortal sins the student confessed to.

After the confession Arnaud told him to say the "Confiteor." The student did so and Arnaud said: "May the Omnipotent Lord take pity on you and wash away your sins; may he grant you eternal life." Then he added, "May the Omnipotent God grant you absolution and remission of all your sins." He then placed his hands on the penitent's head and recalls saying: "By the authority of God I absolve you of your sins." But he does not recall completely if he said this or not. Finally, he imposed the following penance upon him: every day until the feast of the Nativity of John the Baptist he must say the Lord's Prayer five times, Hail Mary seven times, and "Miserere mei Deus". He then prayed on bared knees. But he did not impose any penitence upon him nor grant him satisfaction. He told him that before he went to communion, should he remember any sin, he should come back to confess that sin. He told him that his name was Arnaud of Catalonia. But the student did not come back to confess his sins, since Arnaud saw him going into town. He said nothing to him about these matters.

Finally, after several days, although he doesn't remember when exactly, at about three o'clock, the speaker and a student, not from Pamiers (he doesn't know his name or place of origin), aged between sixteen and eighteen and a half, went to the street where the Dominicans are situated, opposite the former home of Raymund de Surp. The student asked Arnaud if he were a priest, because he wanted to confess. He said that he was and would hear his confession if the youth so desired. They went to Raymund de Surp's house; in the hallway the speaker sat down on the bench beside the head of the dining table and the student either sat down or bent down on the ground beside Arnaud (he does not recall if he bent his knees or sat down). Arnaud, holding a cowl over his head, heard the student's confession; among other things, he confessed that he had stolen fruit from someone and had sworn falsely. About the other kinds of sins confessed, Arnaud did not recall.

When the confession was completed, Arnaud told the student to say his "Confiteor," absolving him in the manner described above, and imposed a similar penance. He didn't recall if he told the youth that he was named Arnaud of Catalonia or that should he remember any other sins he should return.

Asked if he had heard anyone else's confession or had absolved anyone else in a similar way, he said that he had not.

Asked if he had spoken to someone else or suggested to anyone else that they ought to confess to him, he replied that this year during Easter, while he and a certain student who was lodging with either Pierre or Jean Rieux of Le Mercadal, whose name he didn't recall, were going to or leaving Arnaud's field at Le Pomarol, the student told Arnaud that he had confessed to friar Arnaud Martini, a Franciscan of Pamiers; the youth had noted that after confession he remembered another sin and wanted to go back to the friar to confess it. Arnaud thereupon told the youth to confess the sin to him and he would absolve him, because he was a priest. But the student replied that he could not give him solace[4] and hear his confession, since he knew well that he wasn't a priest. He did not recall whether he said similar things to anyone else.

Asked if he had celebrated mass or masses or had worn holy garments as a subdeacon in the church of the Evangelists, he replied that he had not. Asked if he had told anyone that he was a priest, he said he had so told the three aforementioned students. He told a certain student who stayed with Jacques of Paris, a dyer of Le Camp in Pamiers, that he was a priest and had celebrated mass. But he didn't tell him where he had celebrated mass.

He recalled further that after he had heard the second student's confession for the first time, at the home of Raymund de Surp, the next day the two of them crossed the city and passed the church of Le Mercadal in Pamiers. The student said that he had just then recalled some sins which he wanted to confess and they entered the church. The two of them prostrated themselves on the steps before the altar of St. Bartholomew and the student

---

4. This term is often used by the Cathars, which suggests possible connections with this sect.

confessed again. Arnaud absolved him of these sins in the aforementioned way and imposed a penance similar to the first.

Asked if he had later told those students whose confessions he had heard in his guise as a priest that he was not a priest, he said that he had not, although he frequently saw and greeted them. Asked if at that time when he had heard these students' confessions as a priest and absolved them as a priest he believed before or after or now believed that he could hear anyone's sacramental confession or absolve anyone of sin, especially mortal sins, so that they were truly absolved of sin, he replied that he had not; nevertheless, he had heard their confessions, wanting to know their consciences, and what sins they had committed. Afterward, he didn't tell them that he wasn't a priest, having told them earlier that he was.

He was asked why, when he heard the confessions of these students in order to know their consciences and what sins they had committed, he had nevertheless absolved them of their sins, even though he didn't believe he had the power to do so. He replied that he had at first said that he was a priest and had heard confessions as a priest but was afterward embarrassed to say he wasn't a priest and couldn't absolve them. Because of this embarrassment, he absolved these students, although he didn't believe this absolution was valid.

Asked if anyone had taught him that he could pose as a priest and hear anyone's confession and absolve them, he replied in the negative; nor did he know anyone else who, although not a priest, had dared to hear confessions as he did.

He further recalled that during the same year at Easter, although he didn't recall the time or day nor whether it was before or after the preceding events occurred, he was in the Dominican chapel where at about three he was accustomed to read theology. A student, not from Pamiers, dressed in a brown mantle, about twenty years old, came in and said he was looking for a Dominican to confess to. The two of them sat down at the foot of the pulpit and as they spoke the student said, among other things, "Are you a priest?" Arnaud said that he was. The student said he would prefer to confess to Arnaud more than to anyone else, while Arnaud said he would be pleased to hear his confession. The two of them prostrated themselves on the stairs where they were and the student confessed his sins. Among other things, he confessed that he had committed fornication with prostitutes and solicited both married and unmarried women to commit that vice; that he was sometimes drunk and frequently considered how he could commit that sin; he had also stolen some fruit and other things. He likewise spoke about other kinds of sins, which Arnaud didn't remember.

After the student had confessed his sins, Arnaud absolved him and imposed a certain penitence as satisfaction. But he did not recall which penitence he had imposed. Afterward he never saw the student again.

Arnaud said and confessed the following regarding the sin of sodomy:

About twenty years ago, although he doesn't remember when, when he was about ten or twelve, his father sent him to study grammar in Pamiers, at Master Pons de Massabucci's place in the Borayria. Pons later became a Dominican. At this school he boarded with Master Pons; Pierre Illat of Montsegut; Bernard Balessa of Le Mercadal; Arnaud Auriol, son of Pierre, a knight near Bastide de Serou, who already shaved his beard and is now a priest; Bernard of Verniolle, the speaker's brother; and other students whose names he did not remember.

While Arnaud lodged in that room with these students; for about six weeks he shared a bed with Arnaud Auriol. After they had been together for about two or three nights and Arnaud Auriol thought that Arnaud was asleep, he started to kiss the speaker and placed himself over Arnaud's thighs. He then placed his penis between Arnaud's thighs and moving himself about as with a woman, he ejaculated between Arnaud's thighs. He continued this sin all night, as long as the speaker slept with Arnaud Auriol. Because Arnaud of Verniolle was still a boy, this act was displeasing to him; but because of shame, he didn't dare reveal it to anyone. At that time, he didn't even have the will or desire to commit that sin, for, so he said, he did not yet have such desires. After six weeks, the speaker, along with Master Pons, Arnaud Auriol, the speaker's brother Bernard of Verniolle, and a certain Theobald of Cintegabelle, who had already shaved his beard, moved to another house near Pont de Lasclades. This house now belongs to someone named Salvetati. Arnaud slept there in one bed with his brother and Master Pons, who solicited Arnaud to commit that vice. At that time Arnaud Auriol slept with Theobald, but Arnaud Auriol did not commit that sin with him nor discuss it with him.

He said that about a month ago a certain youth, aged about eighteen, whose name he didn't know, came to Pamiers to stay with Bartholomew of Auterive, a shoemaker of Le Mercadal, from whom Arnaud customarily purchased his shoes. Since Arnaud knew him from Toulouse, the youth came and told him that he no longer had a place to stay; Arnaud therefore asked if he would like to lodge with him. The youth came to Arnaud's house and in a room adjacent to the hall spent one night naked in bed with Arnaud. When the two of them were in bed together naked, Arnaud embraced and kissed the youth and asked if he would like Arnaud to put his penis between the boy's thighs. The youth replied that he could do as he wanted. Arnaud, putting his penis between the boy's thighs as they stood side by side, ejaculated semen and committed sodomy with the youth twice that night, behaving as described above. The youth, however, did not sodomize Arnaud, nor did Arnaud ask him to do so. The next morning when they got up, Arnaud told the youth not to tell anyone what had happened that night, for, he said, "If anyone should find out, I'll get in trouble." Nevertheless, he didn't ask the boy to swear not to reveal these events to anyone. Nor did Arnaud give him anything except food; nor did he commit that sin with him afterward, although he spoke with him frequently.

He said that the same year around last Christmas on a day which he didn't remember Guillaume Roux of Ribouisse in the diocese of Mirepoix, a student at Pamiers and tutor to the sons of Raymund Faur (also called "Recurul") of the Loumet quarter of Pamiers, came to Arnaud's house and asked if he knew a cleric, whom he could serve and who would be willing to hear his lessons, because his brother didn't want to provide for his studies. Arnaud replied that master Maurand, prior of Lavelanet and canon of St. Saturnin of Toulouse, was looking for a cleric like him to bring his books back and forth for him to school. Arnaud made this Guillaume swear on a martyrology or liturgical book not to reveal, even to the canon, the things that Arnaud would tell him about this canon.

After Guillaume had so sworn, Arnaud told him that he had heard that the canon sometimes kissed and embraced youths and afterward he would put his penis between their thighs and perpetrate that sin, "and if by chance, you lodge with him, you'll have to allow him to do likewise with you if he so desires."

Guillaume answered that he was willing; Arnaud then asked if he had already committed this sin with someone else. Guillaume replied that he had done so with a certain squire of his country, who had shared his bed; he added that he knew well how to commit that crime, and even told Arnaud the squire's name, although Arnaud didn't remember it. This conversation took place in the upper chamber of Arnaud's house, in which there was a bed. Arnaud thereupon said to Guillaume, "Do you want me to demonstrate that act to you, and will you show me how the squire acted with you?" Guillaume replied that he was willing. They then undressed, lay down nude on the bed and, in the aforementioned way, first one and then the other committed sodomy; they then swore on the Gospels never to reveal anything about this sin to anyone. Arnaud then borrowed from Guillaume a book by Ovid,[5] whose title he didn't know. Guillaume then

---

5. Ovid's work on love was widely read and copied during the Middle Ages.

asked Arnaud to give him a knife which he carried with his knives, but Arnaud refused and said he would give him a different one.

Asked who told him that master Maurand committed such acts, he said that around the feast of the Nativity of John the Baptist last year, when he was studying in Toulouse, a book porter who lodged with Maurand told Arnaud on rue Agulhieras that he would willingly leave his master. This is because he didn't like Maurand's habits, that when he was in bed he made him rub his feet; when he was warm he embraced and kissed him and put him to bed. Arnaud surmised from this statement that the canon carried on that vice and the porter explicitly admitted it when asked. It seems to the speaker that the porter's name was Gerald and he was from either Limoges or Cahors; and he told Arnaud that he had lived with the canon for a year.

Arnaud said that afterward he and Guillaume Roux committed sodomy with each other in the same room and bed, on different occasions, two or three times. The speaker likewise committed that sin with Guillaume Roux in the same way, except that they only lay down on the bed naked the first time. Guillaume often even committed the crime with the speaker, and it seems that he enjoyed it as much as Arnaud did, to tell from his words and deeds. On the last occasion that they did this, they swore on the Gospels not to do so with anyone else. Guillaume excepted the canon, since he was going to lodge with him. They swore otherwise not to commit the sin again with each other.

After this oath, about eight days later, Arnaud and Guillaume Roux went to Arnaud's brother Guillaume's field at Le Pomarol. When they got there, Arnaud told Guillaume Roux that they should remove their mantles and commit sodomy as they had done before. Guillaume said that he wouldn't do so. Arnaud said that if they committed sodomy after having sworn not to do so again, the Franciscan lector of Pamiers, who had power over such things, would absolve them. Guillaume refused to consent to this; but because Arnaud still wanted to commit sodomy with him, he made certain signs, embraced him, wrestled him down to the ground, and turned Guillaume over, as if to commit sodomy. But this didn't happen; he had only acted to test and tempt Guillaume to see if he wanted to commit that sin or not; but at that time the speaker did not commit sodomy with Guillaume, nor Guillaume with him.

Asked if he had solicited Guillaume to commit sodomy in the Franciscan house at Pamiers, he replied that he was not sure if he had spoken to them or not. He said that in various places he and Guillaume had discussed committing that sin.

Asked if he had sometimes told Guillaume or anyone else that sodomy was a lesser sin than carnal knowledge of women, he replied that he had so told Guillaume Roux but did not recall where or when. He had said that he believed that simple fornication and sodomy were equal sins and that rape, deflowering of a virgin, adultery, and incest were greater and graver sins than sodomy. He said that he maintained this belief from the feast of All Saints until very recently. But he always believed that sodomy and simple fornication were mortal sins.

The speaker even told Guillaume Bernardi, son of Jean Jeu du Gaudiès, that sodomy and simple fornication were equal sins. He had said this to both Guillaume Roux and Guillaume Bernardi because they had asked him if the sin of sodomy, which he had committed with them, was a sin of heresy. He answered them that it was not a sin of heresy but was rather equal to carnal knowledge of women or prostitutes.

Asked if he had told these people that sodomy and fornication were equal in order to induce them to commit sodomy, he replied that he had not, since they had both voluntarily committed the act with him, and the speaker with them, as it appeared to him from their words and deeds. For Guillaume Roux had told Arnaud in his house when they discussed the matter, "Do you want me to show you what a man can do when he wants to have sex with another man but doesn't have the chance, so that he can satisfy his lust?" Guillaume then added that he frequently took his penis in his own hand and rubbed it in order to satisfy his lust; he also told Arnaud that he would show him how to do it if he ever wanted him to, but Arnaud had said he wasn't interested because he would never do it.

Asked if anyone had told him that sodomy and simple fornication were equally blameworthy, or if he had heard the contrary preached in church or had read it somewhere, or if anyone had told him that sodomy is graver than any other type of lust, with the exception of bestiality, he replied in the negative; except that he well knew that the rectors of churches and chaplains could not commonly absolve penitents of sodomy, but only bishops or those so licensed by bishops could absolve sodomites.[6] On the other hand, simple rectors and chaplains could absolve penitents guilty of simple fornication and adultery without special permission from the bishop.

Asked if he had told any of the above persons, showing or pointing out in a book of decretals that it was so written, that sodomy was a lesser sin or

6. In other words, sodomy is classified as a reserved sin which could only be absolved by a bishop or higher ecclesiastic, and not by a parish priest.

equal to simple fornication, he replied that he had not shown this in decretals nor had said that it is written in the decretals that said sin of sodomy is lesser or equal to the sin of simple fornication. But he had told Guillaume Roux that in some men nature demands that they perform that act or know women carnally; and, he said that he very much felt in himself that his body would suffer if he should abstain for more than eight or fifteen days if he did not have sex with a woman or didn't commit that crime with a man. Nor, he said, did he believe that he committed a greater sin by committing sodomy with a man than by knowing a woman carnally.

Last year, around the feast of All Saints just past, at the Augustinian house in Pamiers, Arnaud encountered Guillaume Bernardi, a student from Gaudiès. He said that if he wanted to lodge with a certain canon of St. Saturninus of Toulouse who was also a prior of Lavelanet, in return for which he would carry the prior's books back and forth from school for him, Arnaud would get him the position. Guillaume asked about the canon's manner of living and habits; Arnaud made Guillaume swear on a book never to disclose or reveal to anyone what he would tell him about the canon's manner of living. Arnaud did not remember where that oath was made, but it was either in the Augustinian house or in Arnaud's house. After the oath was made, Arnaud told Guillaume that the canon occasionally drank wine and afterward had his servant rub his feet and then kissed and embraced the servant, so he had heard. But he didn't know if he did something afterward with the servant. But when Guillaume Bernardi asked Arnaud what the canon had done, Arnaud told him that the canon put his penis between the servant's thighs and satisfied his lust; and the speaker believes that he also added, "Have you occasionally done this?" Guillaume Bernardi replied embarrassedly that he did not know what it was and said, "Do you want to show me?" Arnaud replied that he would. These last words were exchanged in the upper chamber the home of Arnaud and his brother Guillaume of Verniolle. Arnaud then said to Guillaume Bernardi, "Should we do it naked or dressed?" Guillaume replied that they should do it in whatever fashion Arnaud preferred; the speaker replied that they should undress and lie down naked on the bed, which they did. There, in the same manner in which he committed sodomy with Guillaume Roux, Arnaud committed sodomy with Guillaume Bernardi, and Guillaume with him. After this, Arnaud committed sodomy with Guillaume three or four times thereafter, at different times, during different holidays, but in the same room and bed. But they only lay down nude the first time.

Asked if he had committed sodomy anywhere else with Guillaume

Bernardi, he replied in the negative. Asked if he had instigated Guillaume to commit sodomy with the speaker, he said that he had and that Guillaume had committed sodomy in the same way with the speaker three or four times. Asked about how old Guillaume was, Arnaud replied that he didn't know for sure, but he seemed to be between sixteen and eighteen years old. Asked if he had made Guillaume swear never to commit sodomy with anyone else or even with Arnaud, or if he himself had so sworn, he replied in the negative. Asked if he told Guillaume or made him swear never to reveal that vice which he had committed nor even to confess about that sin, he replied that he had not, except as stated above.

He said that on the feast of Pentecost just past, but at a time he didn't recall, on a certain holiday after vespers, Arnaud went to a garden belonging to Germain Fromagerii, situated at the far end of Las Gransas; he was followed by an eighteen-year-old youth at Mirepoix, whose name he didn't remember, an apprentice to the shoemaker Bernard of Toulouse of Le Mercadal in Pamiers. They went together to the garden; along the way the youth told Arnaud that he couldn't earn enough as a shoemaker and would willingly serve another master, asking if he could find him one. Arnaud replied that he believed that Master Bernard Saisset, canon of Pamiers, needed such a servant and that Arnaud was willing to ask if he was interested in the youth's services. The youth replied that if Arnaud should secure the position for him, he would get Arnaud some good-looking women he knew. Arnaud replied, "If you could procure such women for me, I would be very pleased, and you would have done well." As they spoke of such matters, they entered the garden and lay down on a mound of dirt. Arnaud removed his mantle because he was warm. When they sat down on the ground, the youth told Arnaud that he would tell him how he satisfied his lust when he had no women. Arnaud asked him about this method; the youth then embraced him and put Arnaud under himself, saying that he would demonstrate the aforementioned technique. Arnaud told him that he knew well how to do it and put the youth under himself. But neither he nor the youth did anything.

Finally, the youth told Arnaud that he would teach him another method, that is, while they were standing side by side he would place his penis between Arnaud's legs in order to commit sodomy and that they should get ready to do it that way. But Arnaud didn't want to do this and said that he knew that method well. The youth told him that many good men did this, and Arnaud replied that it was so, as he heard said, even the religious [priests and monks]. The youth asked if the canon did such things and Arnaud replied that he didn't believe so, since he was an upright man.

Asked if he had committed sodomy with anyone else, or anyone had solicited him to commit that crime, he replied in the negative.

Asked if he had confessed to any priest or religious about that crime which he had committed, he replied that he had not; and he had also not confessed during Lent that year, or since the feast of St. Luke; but when he was sick he had confessed to a certain Carmelite lector. Asked if he had taken communion during Easter, he replied that he had not, nor for the past twelve years since he left the Franciscan order. He had refused to take communion for the past twelve years or to confess his sins during last Lent because every day he resolved to enter a new religious order. Then he would confess his sins and he would begin to do what he ought to do in order to be a good man and he would cease his sins.

Asked if he had absolved anyone who had confessed to him of sodomy, he replied that he hadn't. Asked if he had told anyone with whom he had committed sodomy or whom he had solicited to commit that crime that he would take them to a religious who would absolve them of that sin and would impose a light penance, he said that he had not.

Asked if he had heard the confessions of many others aside from those mentioned above, or had solicited others to confess to him, he replied that he had not. Asked if when he had absolved penitents in the above manner he believed that he could in fact absolve and that they were completely absolved of their sins, he replied in the negative. Nevertheless, he had not told those who confessed to him and were absolved in the above manner, and to whom he said he was a priest, that they ought to confess to another priest since they were not absolved because he wasn't a priest.[7] . . .

Because, following the deposition of witnesses in the court set up in judgment against Arnaud by the lord bishop, it did not seem to the lord bishop that Arnaud had fully confessed the truth about himself and others, but rather that he had concealed a great many grave matters despite his oath, the bishop therefore admonished and warned him according to the law to confess the truth about both himself and others. He bound him over until the following Monday, which will be the twenty-eighth day of the present month [June]; in the meantime, the lord bishop wanted to inform himself and inquire about Arnaud more fully and completely concerning those crimes and other matters touching the Catholic faith.

Arnaud of Verniolle confessed and testified the preceding in the presence of the lord bishop, in a place, year, and day noted above, in the presence of the friars Gaillard of Pomiès and Arnaud of Carla, Dominicans

---

7. The rest of the testimony deals with Arnaud's posing as a priest.

of Pamiers; Bernard ofe Taix, a Cistercian of Fontfroide; Master Guillaume Nadini of Carcassonne, notary of the king of France and of the lord bishop in cases relating to the Inquisition touching the investigation of heresy; and Jean Strabaud of Sautel, notary of the city of Pamiers, who at the bishop's order received the preceding confession which I, Jean Jabaud, clerk, faithfully transcribed and corrected from the original.

On June 28, which day in the preceding acts had been set aside for Arnaud of Verniolle's full confession to testify about himself and others about the crime of heresy, sodomy, and other things of which he was very much suspected and which he had not yet, so it appeared, fully confessed, he was led to the presence of the lord bishop in an upper chamber of the episcopal see of Pamiers. In a court established there he swore again to tell the whole truth and nothing but the truth concerning the aforementioned crimes relating to the office and business of the investigation of heresy, about himself and all others living and dead. After this oath, he was asked if he wanted to confess more fully and completely and to reveal the truth about himself and others regarding those matters touching the office and business of the Inquisition involved in the investigation of heresy; he replied in the negative, because he knew nothing more, so he said.

The lord bishop then ordered that Arnaud should be taken to and placed in the prison of the castle of Pamiers.

These acts were set down on the year, day, and place noted above, in the presence of the lord bishop, the Dominican friars Gaillard of Pomiès and Arnaud of Carla, of the monastery of Pamiers; Bernard of Taix, Cistercian of Fontfroide; and Master Jean Strabaud of Sautel, notary, which I, Jean Jabaud, faithfully transcribed and corrected from the original.

A year later, on August 1, 1324, Arnaud of Verniolle was taken from the prison in the tower of Les Allemans and brought before the lord bishop in the upper chamber of the episcopal see of Pamiers, in a court set up in the bishop's presence. He swore again to tell the whole truth and nothing but the truth concerning heresy and sodomy, about himself and all persons living and dead; when this oath was completed, he was asked if what he had confessed to the bishop on June 23, 1323 was full and complete and true. When this was read to Arnaud, the bishop suggested that he consider whether he did not remember his confession. Arnaud replied that everything in his confession was true and complete and that it was entirely factual and that he needn't read the confession since he remembered it.

Asked if he wanted to add or subtract anything in his confession, concerning himself or others living or dead, he replied in the negative. Asked if he ever told anyone or he believed that sodomy with men was a lesser sin than simple fornication with a prostitute, and especially if he had shown anyone that this was written in a book of decretals, he replied to each of these in the negative.

Asked if he told anyone or believed that because his nature required him to satisfy his lust either with a man or a woman it is not sinful to have relations with men or women, or that these may be minor or venial sins, he replied that his nature inclined him to commit sodomy, although he always believed that sodomy is a mortal sin. Nevertheless, he held that sodomy is as sinful as simple fornication and that illicit deflowering of a virgin and incest may be graver sins, and in any case the same as men carnally knowing other men. And he had indeed told this to Guillaume Roux, son of Pierre Roux of Ribouisse, and Guillaume Bernardi, son of Jean Ioc of Gaudiès in Mirepoix, with whom he committed sodomy. But he had not told them this in order to induce them to consent to perpetrate that sin with him lest they not do it. He told Guillaume Roux that the sin of masturbation is equal to the sin of simple fornication and to the sin of sodomy. They were equal, so he said (and, so he said, he had believed this in his heart at that time, from the feast of All Saints just past until he confessed), even if that sin of masturbation was committed on purpose and deliberately.

Asked if he had told anyone or believed that he, a subdeacon, could sacramentally absolve penitents of mortal sin so that they were completely absolved by him of all their sins and that it was not necessary for them to again confess to another priest, he replied that he had indeed told others that he could absolve them of their sins. . . .

Bibliothèque Nationale, Doat 23, *fols. 71ʳ–76ᵛ*

In the name of Our Lord Jesus Christ, Amen. It has been established as a result of written confessions made in court before us, the bishop and inquisitor, that Arnaud of Verniolle, subdeacon of the city of Pamiers, apostate from the Franciscan order, whom we have first decreed must be deposed from orders as subdeacon and cleric, from every tonsure and clerical privilege, and degraded on this day and place, in order to receive penance from us and hear the definitive sentence peremptorily imposed upon him, must undergo the salutary penance of life imprisonment.

You, Arnaud of Verniolle, have fallen into the horrible and damnable crime of sodomy, as is noted above in your full confession, and because of which you are to be gravely and harshly punished. . . . You should therefore be degraded and placed in iron chains in the strictest prison, to be fed a diet of bread and water for life . . . so that no one may grant you grace in the future, neither the bishops nor inquisitors who succeed us. . . .

After this, the lord bishop, dressed in his pontifical robes with his pastoral staff and his cap without a mitre, deposed the aforesaid Arnaud of Verniolle, a subdeacon dressed in his subdeacon's garb, from his office, degrading, stripping and depriving him of his position.

Gerard Cagnoli (d. 1342) and the Exorcism of Lust

Gerard Cagnoli was a Franciscan saint active in the regions of Pisa and Sicily. After his death, friar Bartholomeo Albizi traveled the countryside performing miraculous cures by using the saint's relics, his portrait, holy water, and other means. In order to encourage the establishment of a cult, Bartholomeo duly recorded the testimony of those persons who had known the dead friar personally, or had been the recipient of or witness to his miracles. The following two cases indicate how sexual nonconformity could threaten a family with the badge of infamy and social exclusion. Only divine intervention was perceived as a sufficient antidote to the poison of prohibited lust which had infected a member of the family.

Source: Filippo Rotolo, ed., "Il trattato del miracoli del B. Gerardo Cagnoli, O.Min. (1267–1342) di Frà Bartolomeo Albizi, O.Min. (†1351)", *Miscellanea Franciscana* 66 (1966): 128–92; ibid., "La Leggenda del B. Gerardo Cagnoli, O.Min. (1267–1342) di Frà Bartolomeo Albizi, O.Min. (†1351)," *Miscellanea Franciscana* 57 (1951), 367–446.

Bibliography: Eva Cantarella, "Homicides of Honor: The Development of Italian Adultery Law over Two Millennia," in *The Family in Italy from Antiquity to the Present*, ed. David Kertzer and Richard Saller (New Haven, Conn.: Yale University Press, 1991), 229–44.

*   *   *

There was a well-known secular youth who had a brother in the order of St. Francis. In 1344 he was so occupied with an accursed woman that he wasn't strong enough to cease his adultery. His brother invoked St. Gerard, fasted, and placed a candle [in the image?] of the saint at the head [of the bed] where the youth slept. Wonder of wonders! The youth's lust (*libido*) eased, he expelled the accursed woman, and he began to reform both his house and family.

I have a son in the village in which we live who is twenty-one years old. He has been bewitched and taken away by a woman who has been unfaithful to her husband, and for the past two years my son has commingled with her. When the affair became publicly known in the town, her husband became very indignant, and we, his father and mother, were much distressed by our son's great deviation. As a result we summoned him, and began to warn him; but our interference wasn't the least bit effective. Our son and this woman, preoccupied with evil, seeing this, thought of fleeing, and of continuing to sin together. Learning of this, I began to cry about the danger to my son. Since we could find no remedy for the situation, I turned to Gerard, whose fame had grown greatly, as my patron. One evening, totally preoccupied with my son's misdeed, I vowed to St. Gerard to go barefoot to him at Pisa and offer a waxen candle and three pounds [*librae*], and another one should he succeed through his grace, and should God free my son from such snares of the Devil, returning to the authority of his father and mother. For he had become totally rebellious and insolent toward us in everything. All night long I tearfully invoked St. Gerard, asking mercy for my son. In the morning, having secured virtue from the saint, this branch of rebellion turned into an obedient son.

Bridget of Sweden (d. 1371)

The following selection illustrates how witchcraft and the Devil were often regarded as the cause of sexual disorder. It is taken from the canonization protocol of Bridget of Sweden, whose pastoral activity focused on a region where pagan practices had presumably survived longer than in the south.

Source: Isak Collijn, ed., *Acta et processus canonizacionis beate Birgitte* (Uppsala: Almqvist and Wiksells, 1924–31), 513.

* * *

The witness heard from mistress Bridget and from a certain good priest in Sweden named John that when he was a parish priest at Rinna in the diocese of Linköping, as a priest he was so bewitched by a sorceress that he burned with carnal temptation like a fire, so that he could think of nothing except foul carnal thoughts; nor could he pray according to custom. After he had been driven out of his senses, but not wanting to lose the continence and chastity he had preserved so long, he asked mistress Bridget (who was then residing at the monastery of Alvastra) to free him of such evil temptation and to beseech God to grant him his goodness. After mistress Bridget had prayed for him, Christ said to her, "You know that the sorceress possesses three things which are used in her incantations, namely lack of faith (*infidelitas*), an obdurate heart, and avarice (*cupiditas*). The Devil therefore dominates him who drinks from the excrement of his bitterness; and you know that her tongue will be her end, and her hand her death, and the demon the author of her testament." All of this actually happened, since just as the witness said, on the third night the sorceress bit her own tongue, took a knife and cut her own groin with it, and shouted to all who were listening, "Come, my Devil, and follow me." And thus with such a horrible cry she put an end to her life in a wretched way. The aforesaid priest, freed of temptation, immediately entered the Dominican order, in which until the end of his life he returned the fruit of divine grace, as the witness said.

Third Lateran Council Decree on Lepers (1179)

The lepers occupied a somewhat different position from other marginalized groups. On the one hand, they suffered legal liabilities, were excluded from civil society, and were feared and isolated. Their condition was regarded as the product of sin. On the other hand, they were provided with religious services and minimal living conditions and became the objects of penitential interest on the part of such saints as Francis of Assisi. The highest incidence of leprosy seems to have been during the central Middle Ages, and by the fourteenth century, their numbers appear to have dropped considerably, so that some leprosaria were depopulated.

Source: Joseph Alberigo et al., eds., *Conciliorum oecumenicorum decreta* (Bologna: Istituto per le Scienze Religiose, 1973), 222–23.

Bibliography: Peter Richards, *The Medieval Leper and His Northern Heirs* (Cambridge: D. S. Brewer, 1977).

* * *

23. Despite the fact that the Apostle [1 Corinthians 12.22–23] says that great honor should be accorded to the weaker members, there are some ecclesiastics who, more desirous of what belongs to them than what per-

tains to Jesus Christ [Philippians 2.21], do not allow lepers, who cannot live with healthy persons and gather together with others in churches, to have churches and cemeteries or to be aided by the ministry of their own priest. Since it is clear that this is far removed from Christian piety, we have decided by apostolic charity that wherever some of them are gathered together in such a way under the rule of the common life that they can provide themselves with a cemetery and they are able to enjoy their own priest, they should be allowed to do so without contradiction. They should, nevertheless, beware not to do any injury to the parochial rights of old churches should they exist. This is granted to them for the sake of piety, but we do not want it to lead to the injury of others. We have also decided that they should not have to pay tithes for their gardens or the pasturing of their animals.

Humbert of Romans, *To the Leprous*

The following material was suggested by the Dominican minister-general Humbert of Romans (1194?–1277) as suitable for sermons directed at lepers. It is contained in his collection of *Sermones ad status*, which were intended to assist preachers in the composition of sermons tailored to persons of different ages, sex, social status, professions, and so on.

Source: Humbert of Romans, *De eruditione praedicatorum* VII.9 (series II, cap. 93): *Ad leprosos*, ed. Nicole Bériou and François-Olivier Touati, *Voluntate Dei leprosus: Les lépreux entre conversion et exclusion aux xiième et xiiième siècles*. Centro italiano di studi sull'alto medioevo (Spoleto, 1991), 160–63 (Testi, Studi, Strumenti, 4).

Bibliography: Edward Tracy Brett, *Humbert of Romans: His Life and Views of Thirteenth-Century Society*, in *Studies and Texts* 67 (Toronto: Pontifical Institute of Medieval Studies, 1984), 151–66.

*   *   *

Since these sick persons never come to hear sermons along with other people, it is regarded as an extremely pious act to visit them from time to time or even, when one finds them in a place where one is praying, to talk to them about God, altogether or in a group. But since they have invariably shown themselves incapable of patience, whoever is talking should take care not to make reference to their disease by its proper name of leprosy, since that is very displeasing to them, but rather to talk about it in a general way.

One should always avoid anything which might make them angry, but rather to address them with sweetness and compassion.

This is what one ought to say to them. One should note that some of them abuse the discipline which God grants them, so that the conditions of their illness lead them to commit many sins. They blaspheme God like persons in Hell as a result of the injuries they have received. They are filled with anger over the behavior of others, whom they curse for having abandoned them. They fight among themselves and sometimes get excited and beat each other. They throw at each other the charity they have received, lacking even the most minimal mutual loyalty. They stuff themselves with food and get drunk as a result of an excess of food. Putting aside any rein on the fires of their desire, they abandon themselves to lust and filthy behavior, which I prefer not to report. They give themselves up to all of this and also to other evils even worse than this, as someone who had acted this way said to God, "Lord, you have deprived me of my body, while I deprive you of my soul." Unfortunately for them, they have nothing left for the Lord, for they have stripped themselves naked, since they have lost their bodies in this world and have lost their souls in the next. They are "oppressed by a double oppression." [Jeremiah 17.18], like Herod, who after the grave illness which had been inflicted on him in his earthly life went to Hell [Acts 12.23].

Others, although they may not do evil, nevertheless do nothing good. They spend their lives in bitterness and grief, barely or not at all thinking about their salvation. Job expresses it in their name when he says, in chapter 10, "I am sickened of life, I will give free rein to my griefs, I will speak out in bitterness of soul, etc." [Job 10.1].

Others make use of this scourge for the good of their souls. Instead of acting evilly when they suffer blows or spending their time in grief, they do everything for the sake of the future, when this disease will come to an end, for the sake of eternal salvation. That is why they renounce their past sins, as is written in Ecclesiasticus 18 [verses 20–21], "Before you fall sick, examine yourself," by which is understood, "your past behavior." They confess their sins to priests, in accordance with the statement addressed to the leprous in Luke 17 [verse 14] "Go and show yourselves to the priests." They avoid performing new sins as a consequence of their disease, following Job's example when he says, in Job 2 [verse 10] "throughout all of this", in other words throughout all the evils he suffered, "Job did not utter one sinful word," not against God, not against his neighbor or against his wife. Furthermore, they suffer everything with patience, again comforted by the example of Job in accordance with the statement in the last chapter of the

epistle of James [verse 5.11], "'You have all heard how Job stood firm.'"
For indeed, such an example should give them courage. If Job, who was
a king, or nearly one, and even rather rich, and innocent in everything,
was able to bear with such patience the loss of so much and of his own sons,
and was able to bear such a painful and horrible disease, "smote with
running sores from head to foot" [Job 2.7]; how much more should those
who are not as well provided as he was, show patience in the face of lesser
trials.

It is again necessary to recall that love of this life provides the occasion
to do evil, as Saint Sebastian showed in his speech before Mark and Mar-
cellinus, when he finished his listing of many great evil deeds in this way, "Is
it not the love of this life which leads one to do all of this?"[1] But this harsh,
hopeless, terrible disease makes all the joys of life bitter, and it should in fact
separate oneself from the love of this life, just as the bitter of the unguent
which is placed around the womb separated the infant from its love of the
womb. The bitterness of this life should also lead us to desire another happy
life which is devoid of bitterness. As Augustine says, "The unpleasantness
which grows in this fragile life makes us desire eternal rest."[2] That is why
those who are immersed in the bitterness of this disease ought to strive
strongly for this happy life. This is what a leprous person who was religious
did, who behaved in a holy way in his disease. One day when he was very
thirsty, turning his soul toward God, he sighed and said, "Whoever drinks
the water that I shall give him will never suffer thirst any more" [John
4.13]. And he immediately received the spirit. This painful disease should
also make one fear future suffering. For if the blow of the staff is hard, how
much sharper will be the blow of the sword when the Lord wields "his
mighty and powerful sword" [Isaiah 27.1]! Oh, how much was this suffering dreaded by Augustine when he said, "Lord, burn me here, injure me
here," etc.,[3] and by the prophet who said, "My lips quiver at the sound,
trembling comes over my bones, and my feet totter in their tracks, I sigh for
the day of distress" [Habbakuk 3.16]. It is very clear that those who know
how to make use of this disease, beside the other goods which they will

1. St. Sebastian was an early Christian martyr. It was later believed that he was martyred
by being shot with arrows, and his wounds became identified with the scars of the Plague, so
he was often invoked against the Plague. See *Passio Sancti Sebastiani*, in Jacques-Paul Migne,
ed., *Patrologia Latina. Cursus completus*, 221 vols. (Paris: J. P. Migne, 1844–55), 17: 1025D–
1026A.

2. This is found in Augustine, *Epistolae*, 14.5, in Migne, *Patrologia Latina* 33: 593.

3. See Peter Lombard, *Commentaria in Psalmum*, in Migne, *Patrologia Latina* 191: 105.
Peter is citing the *Glossa ordinaria*, the standard gloss on Scripture. The person referred to in
the *exemplum* cannot be identified.

acquire, are brought to feel contempt for the present life, to yearn for the future life, and to fear the pains of the world to come.

The theme is Ecclesiasticus 38 [verse 9] "My son, if you have an illness, do not neglect it." It should be known that there are sick persons who neglect their souls and others who do not. In order to understand such persons, one should know that there are some among them, etc., as is written above.

IV

Victims of the Devil:
The Possessed, the Ecstatics,
and the Suicidal

Medieval people were intensely aware of the real presence of an evil force that sought to undermine the foundations of civil society, sow the seeds of disbelief and blasphemy, and lead the faithful away from salvation and into damnation. In some instances, such as the case of Otloh of St. Emmeram, the Devil insinuated himself into the believer's mind, raising doubts about the true faith. In other cases, such persons were classified as possessed by the Devil and were said to have "lost their minds." They were often locked up, bound, and restrained because of the danger they posed to themselves and others. A variety of techniques were employed in order to free them of their affliction and restore them to the Christian polity.

In later medieval theology, the pagan deities had been identified as fallen angels who, along with the archdemon Satan, might gain control of the innocent believer in the battle with God, the saints, and the true Church. They possessed the power of performing what appeared to be miracles, but only the church's authorized agents could identify such fake miracles and free the believer from the Devil's grip. It was claimed that Satan's power and possession by the Devil were more prevalent in the geographical margins — in rural, mountainous, wooded, and uninhabited regions. Therefore, persons who by choice or circumstance found themselves in such marginal areas, such as hermits, woodsmen, sailors, roving mendicants, and the like, would be more subject to the Devil's wiles. William of Auvergne, for example, argued that demons tend to concentrate particularly in the resources of nature, such as caves, distant forests, deserts, springs, orchards, rivers, herbs, trees, gems, and precious stones. These malign spirits may appear as fauns, dwarfs, wolves, and hyenas, and, in order to corrupt the innocent souls they wish to dominate, they employ various tricks and acts of violence. The weak melancholic personality, who might become a hermit, was especially prone to the illusions of the Devil. Like the desert fathers of early Christianity, a hermit such as Pope Celestine V sequestered himself in mountainous and rural areas; he described the appearance of the Devil in the form of scorpions, snakes, unwanted guests, and female temptresses who came to attack his chastity.

As noted in the previous chapter, Thomas Aquinas and others argued that since the corruption of original sin, through which man became the servant of Satan, entered us by means of the act of generation, human lust has become the chief means whereby the Devil can influence humanity. The most frequently noted demonic agent was therefore an incubus or succubus, which takes advantage of uncontrollable sexual urges, particularly in the young, as a means of insinuating itself into the soul of the believer and stealing the host's seed. Through the use of *maleficium*, Satan and his agents can inflame the chaste to lust, kill innocent persons, drive some to suicide, and induce pain, illness, dreams, and visions. Aquinas, Bonaventure, and other scholastics noted that in the natural world God allows demons to spread disease among both man and beast, induce storms and disturbances in the air, make fields infertile, excite the winds, and bring fire down from heaven. To confound the impact of such demons, as, for example, when a storm began to brew as the Gascons were laying siege to Ansouis in 1358, Delphine of Languedoc employed the liturgical formula of exorcism in order to put an end to the tempest.

During the thirteenth century the Christian battle with the Devil intensified. In 1233 the Inquisitor Conrad of Marburg noted the existence of persons who worshiped the Devil and who should be dealt with by the Inquisition. In the fourteenth century the Avignonese papacy mounted a series of show trials against political foes accused of consorting with the Devil and practicing black magic. The Inquisition, which had formerly largely ignored such phenomena, began to systematically persecute persons accused of witchcraft and Devil worship, such as Archbishop Robert Mauvoisin of Aix, Bishop Hugh Geraud of Cahors, and Galeazzo Visconti of Milan. Although such trials received much notoriety because of their political repercussions, a better source for our knowledge of the conflict between God and the Devil among the anonymous laity are contemporary miracle collections and canonization records, which contain detailed accounts of devil possession and exorcism either by the saints themselves or by priests trained in this skill.

As in other cultures, the exorcism ceremony involved both the victim and the audience in a ritualized drama in which certain cultural signs and messages were being conveyed which are as clear to the participants as speech itself. The aim is to restore a marginalized person to both mental health and the community of the faithful. The victim finds herself or himself in a liminal situation, becoming the vehicle for the transmission of certain shared values. The classic exorcism ceremony appears in Mark 5.1–20, where the exorcized spirit is called "Legion" and his expulsion plays an evangelical role of bringing the witnesses closer to the Faith. The medieval accounts confirm both the presence of the Devil and his expulsion by an agent of the Church by noting: (1) the identity of the succubi/incubi that have attacked the victim; (2) the words and or/sounds emitted by the victim; (3) the actions attributed to the Devil, indicating his presence; (4) the words of the exorcist; and (5) the therapeutic means (such as the use of relics, signing with the cross, prayers) employed by the exorcist. Reference to the "natural" means employed prior to resorting to supernatural intercession freed the medical profession of responsibility for the possessed, since medicine cured only those phenomena caused by natural imbalance, and miracle those born of metaphysical causes. The possessed were thereby regarded as marginalized, no longer subject to the regular treatment which traditional medicine could apply. The exorcism thus occurred after all regular therapies had been exhausted. Such phenomena fall outside the normal course of nature, are effected through divine intercession, and serve the necessary evangelical function of confounding heretics and other nonbelievers, strengthening the faith of wavering Christians, and confirming the truth of Christianity. Public demonstration of the liberation of the demoniac from the grip of the Devil represented a particularly graphic display of the victory of the true faith over its leading foe. It concluded with the readmission of the victim to the body of the faithful.

While theologians did not doubt the power of Satan to gain control of the innocent believer, they argued that the demon's power may be impeded, and that the victim's liberation requires the intervention of a saint, his/her surrogate the exorcist, and God. The cosmic conflict between God and the Devil is thus worked out within the soul of every believer gripped by Satan and his minions; the community of the faithful is renewed and strengthened among those who witness the miraculous transformation of the victim undergoing exorcism. Many of the victims report a conversation between the demon and an already dead saint for control of their souls. One such case of bewitchment, that of Yves of Penguennan, is described below.

The interaction between a wider audience of believers and the victim-performer may be seen as a kind of sacred theater in which the recurring drama of the conflict between God and Satan is reenacted. The presence of spectators, including relatives, friends, local parishioners, and curious on-lookers, is a sine qua non of successful therapy. The cult of the Servite saint Joachim of Siena, for example, had been initiated in 1310 with the public expulsion of demons from the afflicted.[1] At about three in the afternoon, on June 7, 1310, during Pentecost, a demoniac was brought before a large crowd that had come to hear a sermon delivered by Nicholas of Siena beside Joachim's tomb. The preacher recounted Joachim's recent posthu-mous expulsion of a succubus. The incubus who had possessed a demoniac named Christianella, who had been brought to the church for the occasion, spoke through her, saying, "The time has now come for my exit and for Christianella's liberation." The demon then explained why he had failed to respond to the therapy offered by other saints, saying that, "God has re-served this miracle for this saint, and it is thus pleasing to dispense the divine wisdom." After being conjured up, the demon said, "When I leave her, I will break a lamp and leave Christianella as if she were dead." After so doing, even though the woman was illiterate, the demon again spoke through her perfectly, saying, "Take the clothes off her back, cut the hair from her head, and hang it on the tomb as evidence of this miracle, lest I have the power to return." A similar announcement of his departure was made by a demon who had possessed a woman in 1345, saying, "Woe is me, because I have possessed you for twenty years, and now defeated I will leave, never to return."

The victim's symptoms are described in great detail in cases of posses-sion. The most graphic and extended descriptions are often found in saints' lives. The characteristic feature of several medieval mystical women such as Christina of Stommeln (d. 1312) (see below) and Christina Mirabilis (d. 1224) was their agonizing battle with Satan. Observers were often con-vinced that their unorthodox stigmatization, scatology, and uncontrolled behavior were evidence of control by the Evil One. Such reports almost invariably state that the superhuman strength of the possessed demanded that the victim be bound or tied in order to prevent violent injury to himself or others until the cure was effected. In one Polish case, even eight men could not restrain a demoniac. Alain Senis, a man of Trelevern in Brittany who was forcibly kept at home, for example, received his food through a small window through which he would also often urinate. Many of the cases suggest that the victims had scratched themselves so hard that they

1. P. M. Soulier, ed., "Vita et legenda beati Ioachimi Senensis ordinis servorum," *Ana-lecta Bollandiana* 13 (1894): 192, 309.

appeared to have been attacked by dogs, or that they would bite anything or anyone who came near them. Some attempted suicide, since in order to control the victim's soul the Devil created the delusions and melancholy which often precede such an attempt. The spirit or demon gains control of the victim's senses, action, and speech, and behaves in ways which are universally recognized as symptomatic of possession, suggesting that such behavior may be learned. Indeed, some of the reports merely state that a particular victim "was bewitched, and did things which demoniacs generally do." This suggests widespread familiarity with the phenomenon. In cases found in the collections of Nicholas of Tolentino and Gerard of Pisa, entire communities of nuns experienced some kind of mass psychosis involving hallucinations, cursing, violent fits, and other afflictions.

A number of universal symptoms immediately identify the victim as a person possessed, and all are documented in the miracle collections. The signs of possession included fever, disorientation, compulsive eating disorders, stench, insomnia, convulsions or trembling, rigid muscles (i.e., catatonia), speechlessness, foaming saliva, memory loss, screaming fits accompanied by grinding of the teeth, and uncontrolled weeping. The "demon" speaks through the victim's mouth, often with a rasping, low voice, uttering obscenities, blasphemies, or insults, or speaking incomprehensibly, and displays aggressive behavior toward himself or others. A thud or *clamor* is traditionally emitted by the victim as evidence that the demon has exited from the host. Bartolomeo Albizi noted a violent aversion to sacred objects, persons, or places as a sign of the Devil's presence, thus requiring the therapy offered by faith rather than medicine. Such victims might refuse to honor God or the saint in word or genuflection; make the sign of the cross; receive or look at holy water, enter a church, take part in the Eucharist service, or recite a Paternoster. At the same time, in moments of lucidity many victims themselves suggest, as Christianella did, a possible cure for their condition such as pilgrimage to a sacred shrine or adhering to a cult. In April 1343 a woman named Massea from the Tuscan village of Santa Maria a Monte, for example, was asked by her husband, Pietro, why she suffered such an affliction, saying: "You break your chains and bonds and have thrown four strong young men to the ground. Is there no remedy or cure?"[2] She became calm, and replied, "There is no remedy nor cure except for the one which someone named friar Bartolomeo [Gerard of Pisa's follower] possesses." A seaman of the parish of Santa Lucia, Pisa, had once

---

2. Filippo Rotolo, ed., "La Leggenda dei miracoli del B. Gerardo Cagnoli, O. Min (1267–1342) di Frà Bartolomeo Albizi, O. Min. (d. 1351)," *Miscellanea Franciscana* 57 (1951): 402.

called for the Devil's help when he had fallen. After other saints were invoked to no effect, he himself asked to be brought before a picture of Gerard of Pisa and to have the sign of the cross made over him with the saint's relics. A thirteen-year-old girl of San Lorenzo in Kinsica first specifically asked to be brought to the relics of Gerard, but then entered the chapel reluctantly before demanding that she be signed with the saint's relics.

In most cases, only one demon in human or animal form takes control. In 1346 a fourteen-year-old boy claimed to be gripped by the soul of a dead priest of Lucca, imitating his gestures and manner; Francesco, the chief prison guard at Pisa, was obsessed by a recently murdered man named Giovanni; at Camboro, a woman who cursed and abused all she met was possessed by two men who had been executed; and a youth of San Lorenzo in Kinsica was gripped by a dead neighbor named Nerone. In other cases, the succubus/incubus is not named but its aims are clear, as with the woman who had been gripped for four years by the Devil, who had appeared as a man who wished to sleep with her, so that it was feared she would take her own life. One girl of a village near Pisa who had just taken a vow of chastity was gripped by an ass with paw-like hands. A four-year-old boy reported that he had witnessed "a black beetle exit from the mouth [of the possessed woman], flying out through the church window," as the shouting woman went through the throes of her cure.[3]

But in the most difficult cases several incubi may be named. A girl of Crack whose exorcism required a long vigil at the shrine of Cunegunda, during which the sisters read from Scripture and the passion of the saints, named the demons as Oksza, Naton, and Rozen. The father of a possessed woman reported seeing six frightening, black demons in human form, one of whom stood above his daughter Donessa's head, addressing the others. The nuns of the Cistercian house of Santa Lucia in Pian di Pieca near San Ginesio were allegedly pursued between 1320 and 1323 by knights and dead murderers. One of the victims allegedly cried out, "Oh Belial, come, come to me and lead me with a thousand knights, because Giovanni Vivibene of Ascoli and Rainaldo of Brunforte are coming against me with many knights."[4] Both men had been local tyrants who had gained a reputation for murder, theft, and pillage in the region of San Ginesio in the late thirteenth century. Philippucia, the afflicted nun, may therefore have remembered fears or even personal acts of violence she had experienced in her childhood.

Sometimes the moment of bewitchment is described in vivid detail

3. Ibid., 403.

4. Nichola Occhioni, ed., *Il processo per la canonizzazione di S. Nicola da Tolentino* (Rome: École Française de Rome, 1984), 136–37, 140, 323–30.

and is attributed to a curse cast upon the victim. The demoniac may become possessed as revenge against some act of sacrilege, as occurred to a Spanish seaman in 1320 who gave a beggar at the shrine of Yves of Tréguier some worthless coin, and then, when the beggar protested, spat in his hand. In other cases, possession occurs after an act of bewitchment, as occurred to Yves of Penguennan, whose case appears in this chapter. But although his mother may have called upon the Evil One, she was herself active in securing her son's liberation, thus displaying a deeply felt faith in the reality of Satan and his power, along with the ability of the Church to assist those in distress.

The specific means of obtaining a cure may include the use of cards inscribed with an invocation or image of the saint such as the kind supplied by Bartolomeo Albizi, or presentation before the saint's portrait, an increasingly common phenomenon in late medieval piety. Among the exercises employed were fasts undertaken by the victim or members of the family, confession, or the recitation of prayers, masses, or the Paternoster by the exorcist or community. The most widespread ceremony involved signing with the cross, relics, or a consecrated candle. Other means included having the victim drink water in which relics had been washed; vow to visit the saint's shrine and provide an ex-voto offering or to join a religious order; or remain several days at the tomb. A bound *furiosus* of Erice in Sicily was brought to the chapel of Louis of Toulouse at Palermo. Gerard of Pisa took a piece of cypress wood, touched it to the portrait of St. Louis, dipped it in burning oil, and then touched the victim's tongue with the stick, invoking the aid of God, the Virgin, and saints Francis and Louis, thereby curing the man.

A classic description of such an exorcism was reported in the canonization protocol of Yves of Tréguier. In about 1301/2 a demoniac named Alain de Senis of the rural parish of Trelevern—who had suffered insomnia and loss of appetite, customarily shouted and tore at his clothes, tried to injure himself and others, and conversed with his demon—was led to Yves's small chapel at Lohanec. He had calmed down on the way, and he made his confession. Yves then engaged the demon in conversation. The demon threateningly said, "Why have you brought me here? Why have you brought me here? Just you wait until tonight, wait until tonight. For you will pay dearly tonight because you brought me here."[5] Yves replied, "The demon lies,

---

5. Louis Arthur Lemoyne de la Borderie, ed., *Monuments originaux de l'histoire de S. Yves* (Saint-Brieuc: Prud'homme, 1887), 168–72, 383–84.

because you will not pay, but instead he will pay, and you will sleep in my house tonight." That evening, Alain slept beside Yves in a straw bed which, like the house, had been sprinkled with holy water, while Yves kept a vigil all night reading the Evangel and other prayers. The next morning, Alain awoke fully rested and freed of the demon who had afflicted him for three years. Yves used this as an evangelical opportunity to extract a promise from the victim to keep the precepts of the Faith, live a good and charitable life, and listen often to masses and sermons, lest the demon return. Alain lived until 1318, and the episode was reported by three witnesses, including his son Guillaume, who was twenty-one at the time of the man's liberation.

As those who experienced or witnessed such a liberation were to admit, their faith had been strengthened by the event. Such scenes often required the mobilization of all those present as a way of both encouraging the victim and strengthening the community of the faithful, and should one without faith be present, revenge might be swift. In April 1346, for example, a youth named Ciuccio of Corliano was cured, but one of the bystanders, who did not have faith in the sainthood of Gerard Cagnoli, remained afflicted. The exorcist Albizi vividly described how he had exorcized a woman of Calci in 1346 whose first symptoms had entailed uttering obscenities: "I called her to come and made the sign of the cross over her with the saint's relics, so that she appeared to be gnawing her teeth. Again and again making the sign and praying, I began to ask the bystanders to pray, and shortly thereafter, the devil exited from her, and she was left in peace. Without delay I had her confess to friar Francesco of Ferrara and provided communion to her with the relics of St. Gerard."[6]

Thus, although word and example (*verba et exempla*) continued as the cornerstone of the official policy of evangelization, the dramatic public exorcism of Satan remained perhaps the most demonstrable weapon of the Church in its battle with evil and of bringing the marginalized back into the fold. In a region such as Sweden, still under strong pagan influence, the superiority of Christianity continued to be proven by demonstrating that the spells of the *incantor* had failed to exorcize demons, while the relics of Bridget of Sweden drove away the Devil. It has been noted that the deep crises of the fourteenth century had in particular encouraged the scapegoating of Jews, lepers, witches, heretics, and others, who were seen as agents of the Devil. The battle against Satan and his agents was to produce many

6. Filippo Rotolo, ed., "Il trattato dei miracoli del B. Gerardo Cagnoli, O. Min. (1267–1342) di Frà Bartolomeo Albizi, O. Min. (d. 1351)," *Miscellanea Franciscana* 66 (1966): 150.

learned treatises and papal decrees and finds its expression in a variety of testimonies detailing the activities of "the Evil One." These fears were described by the monk Otloh of St. Emmeram as devilish delusions aimed weakening his faith. The Devil tried to convince him that: his decision to become a monk had been "improvident and foolish"; Otloh had committed so many sins that God would never pardon him; God is unjust and shows little mercy, since persons who have committed even one evil deed like Judas Iscariot, despite their many good acts, may be damned by Him; God is not omnipotent; and Scripture is so filled with contradictions and multiple levels of meaning that one may not place one's faith in it with certainty. A similar denial of Divine Providence appears in the life of Christina of Stommeln. Otloh suffered periods of sleeplessness and feelings of physical weakness, and his sight and hearing were impaired due to the Devil's machinations. Writing down these confessions of doubt and suffering seem to have offered some kind of therapy.

The reports which follow provide perhaps the most authentic voice of Satan's alleged power among those who sought the therapeutic aid of the faith against what were perceived as the wiles of a supernatural, diabolical power. The modern observer may be easily tempted to see in the behavior of the possessed, which in the Middle Ages was regarded as supernatural in origin, some of the neurophysiological and psychological symptoms which both anthropologists and psychiatrists have observed among those experiencing either altered states of consciousness, or an emotional disorder. Some of the modern clinical characteristics of depression, schizophrenia, epilepsy, Tourette's syndrome, hysterical neurosis, and the influence of psychotropic plants, herbs, or drugs may be observed among those persons lumped together as demoniacs. What moderns would characterize as disassociation, or the process whereby one's self-identity and memory are disturbed, is a central characteristic of the *demoniacus*. The person so possessed may appear to display many of the characteristics of the split or multiple personality found above in Christianella, and the exorcist/saint engages in a conversation with the evil spirit prior to its expulsion. The drama of exorcism resulted in the restoration of the victim to the community of the faithful and his or her rescue from distress and marginality.

Nevertheless, we must free ourselves from the temptation of present-mindedness, since the medieval sources cannot clearly confirm the hypothesis that we are dealing with contemporary clinical disorders. The descriptions are often incomplete and selective, peppered with religious ideology, and clearly intended to praise the therapeutic value of the Christian faith and its practitioners. Even medieval observers sometimes voiced skepticism about such reports and feared that the naivete of believers was being exploited by unscrupulous persons. The Cistercian abbot Philip of Clairvaux, for example, undertook an investigation into the stigmata first displayed by Elizabeth of Erkenrode in 1264, while Peter of Dacia's visits to Christina of Stommeln, reported below, were prompted by similar doubts.

Otloh of St. Emmeram (1010–after 1067), *Liber de tentationibus suis*

Otloh was born in about 1010 in the diocese of Freising, and died sometime after 1067 on November 23 at Regensburg. The scion of a noble family, he entered the monastery of Tegernsee as a child and was attached to its *scriptorium*. At fourteen, in 1024, he was at Hersfeld, attached to Bishop Meinhard of Würzburg as a copyist. As a result of conflict with an archpriest named Weiginher, he retired to the Benedictine house at St. Emmeram in Regensburg in 1032, where he stayed until 1067; he attributes his conversion to a terrible vision he had after reading Lucan. As dean of the monastic school, he visited the great abbeys at Monte Cassino and Fulda, profiting from their libraries. Otloh reports having been attacked for some unstated vice by an archpriest of Freising. In addition to this report of his "temptations," doubts, and mental conflicts, he wrote several doctrinal and hagiographical works and a collection of visions. Such self-awareness is unique, and rivals Augustine's *Confessions* in its frankness. Having been a proponent of classical literature, Otloh became an enemy of worldly learning, a tendency which finds voice in the following selection. He describes how for several years, although he seemed to sleep soundly, on awakening he would feel bodily aches and intense tiredness. This is one of the symptoms of *accedia*, or sloth, a vice regarded as widespread among the cloistered, a condition of torpor brought on by monastic exercises, such as fasting. Otloh experiences the "dark night of the soul," which has been a common feature of the mystic's odyssey, as he is buffeted by self-doubt, anxiety, and depression prior to reaching enlightenment.

Source: Otloh of St. Emmeram, *Liber de tentationibus*, in Jacques-Paul Migne, *Patrologia Latina. Cursus completus*, 221 vols. (Paris: J. P. Migne, 1844–55), 146: 38–58.

Bibliography: Irven Resnick, "'Scientia liberalis,' Dialectics and Otloh of St. Emmeram," *Revue Bénédictine* 103 (1987): 241–52.

*   *   *

There was a certain cleric who was steeped in all kinds of vices, who was often admonished by God to reform his life. He came as a *conversus*[1] to the monastic profession unknown to his friends. In the monastery where he was a monk he found all kinds of men, some reading the books of the Gentiles, others reading Holy Scripture. As a result, he began to imitate only those who read divine literature.

But the more he read, the more he felt himself falling prey to devilish temptations. Trusting the Lord and binding himself to the Lord's grace he determined to persevere in his sacred studies with the same diligence. After a long time he was rescued from temptation. Thinking that what he had experienced might edify others, he recorded not only the temptations he had suffered, but also the words of Holy Scripture, which led him by divine inspiration and served as a shield against devilish fraud. Thus, he began to write about his temptations.

Both awake and asleep I suffered devilish delusions, more than I can recall; some, which remain in my memory, I will report as best I can. The first fraud perpetrated upon me, which I suffered both before and after my monastic profession, was that the will to convert [*conversio*] had been very improvident and foolish. Contrary to Scripture, which says, "Do nothing without counsel" [Ecclesiastes 23.9], in the full fervor of youth and without the advice of parents and friends, I wanted to enter religion; but it would have been unwise for a person such as me to undertake such a dangerous vow. It would have been much better to wait until I was older, when, possessing every virtue, I would then make the decision to convert of my own free will. I suffered these and similar devilish delusions under the misnomer of compassion and good advice.

It was by means of such wiles that the most evil tempter tried to seduce me. Because, with God's help, he had failed to arouse me to iniquity, with his customary artfulness he tried to trap me into despair, suggested that it would be vain to turn back, as I had been implicated in such crimes that not only rulers, but others, including my parents and relatives, would detest me. "Do you think," he said, "that such an evil man can be pardoned by God, the strictest judge of all? How is it possible, since it is written, 'Scarcely the just will be saved' [1 Peter 4.18]. Stop wanting what ought not to be desired, but rather strive for what is attainable. If, as you zealously believe, the right to enter the heavenly kingdom has been granted to all

---

1. A candidate for the monastic life.

kinds of persons, whether perverse or just, then Paul, the greatest of the Apostles, would not have said, 'Not all men have faith' [Romans 10.16]. The Savior and truest Author gave these principles to the whole world, saying, 'He who is able to do so, let him receive it' [Matthew 19.12]. He therefore left a doubt that not everyone is good." Since I was tortured with such delusions, what do you think was my state of mind at the time? I could only weep; as the Psalmist says, "Day and night, my tears were my bread" [Psalms 41.2]. I admit from the bottom of my heart that no one can prevail [over Satan] except with the aid of God's grace.

Therefore, that insidious troublemaker, failing to draw me into desperation, urged me with the aid of fraudulent arguments to blaspheme divine justice. He did not do so by means of fear and reproach, but rather by consoling and taking pity on me in my affliction, insinuating such thoughts into my heart: "Oh pitiable youth, whose grief is of concern to no one. Who can imagine how great is the depression you suffer? You therefore ought not to credit it to them; since they don't know, they cannot help. Only the Lord knows everything. Only to Him can one credit what appears to be foolish and disordered. Since He knows and can do all things, why can't He help you in your tribulation, since it was for His sake that you first abandoned the world and have already sustained inestimable suffering? I ask, what is the reason for this strictness, which torments those who cry out to Him? Do what you can. Cease those useless prayers and lamentations, since He maintains the same severity which always characterizes Him. For it is very foolish to pray for what you know is impossible to attain. Nevertheless, do not fear, because the injustice of one powerful person does not allow all to perish. How can it be that a man deserves to suffer all the time? Who among mortals ought to be without sin from the beginning to the end of the world? How can the innocence of a child be acquired in old age? As Christ teaches, "Unless," he says, "you turn around and become like children, you will not enter the kingdom of heaven" [Matthew 18.3]. Haven't you taken note of the threatening words of Ezekiel [18.4, 18.20], "The soul that sins shall die"? If indeed anyone who sins must die, then who will be saved, because no one can be found who is without sin? Does your mind not take heed of the terrible remark made elsewhere by the prophet, who said, "If a righteous man turns away from justice and does wrong, the righteous deeds that he has done will not be taken into account" [Ezekiel 3.20]? Take Judas, the Lord's betrayer, as an example. After he had committed the crime of betrayal, despite many just deeds, he was damned. Take note of this and of two other examples in which our statement can be proved and tested. It is written in the book of Exodus [33.19], where the Lord says to Moses, "I will be gracious to whom I will be gracious and I will have compassion on whom I will have compassion." It is also written in the Gospels that when a certain disciple wanted to follow Him, he said, "I will follow you wherever you go" [Matthew 8.19–20; Luke 9.58–59]. He was repelled by the Lord, who said, "Foxes have their holes, the birds their roosts; but the Son of Man has nowhere to lay His head." Oh indiscriminate austerity! Oh wretched justice! He follows the decision of His own will and refuses to shelter those who flee to Him. Such a discipline is definitely intolerable and unworthy of commendation." All these delusions disturbed my thoughts, which proved that my mind was subject to great dangers.

I want to make reference to something which seemed to have pointed to these same delusions. It often happened when I was about to get up at the first sign of matins, as the holy rule teaches. Long before rising time, I was aroused by some fantastic sign, and quickly went to church. For a long time I believed that this was the work of God, until this lack of sleep forced me to sleep at unsuitable times. For several years I suffered at night in the following way: although I slept in my bed in a healthy way, when I got up in the morning to sing *Laudes*, my limbs felt weak, as if tied in chains; I would therefore come to church shakily and with halting steps.

At this point one particular temptation and delusion should be noted. I report it with great difficultly, since I have read or heard about it with respect to no one else but me. Having been attacked by the aforesaid and other temptations (many of which I can barely remember or, so as not to tire the reader, I would prefer not to report), and although I never lost my faith (by the grace of God) or the hope of help from heaven, I felt tormented for a long period of time by doubts concerning the knowledge of Holy Scripture and even the very essence (*essentia*) of God Himself. Although in the course of other delusions I experienced a moment of peace and a refuge of hope, in this case I experienced scarcely any solace for many long hours. In the past, I had been strengthened by Holy Scripture. I had been aided against the arrows of death by the arms of faith and hope. In this case, however, I was surrounded by every doubt and blindness of mind, so that I was unsure whether there was any truth whatsoever in Sacred Scripture, and whether God was in fact omnipotent. Concerning other matters, the siege was bearable and moderate. But in this matter, the violence of the attack was so great that both my spiritual and bodily senses were sapped of all their customary strength. Sometimes it seemed to me as though my senses of sight and hearing were so impaired that I could no longer see or hear with my usual ability. At the same time it seemed to me that I heard lips whispering in my ears, addressing me in the following way: "Why are you wearied by such a vain task? Where are the hopes that up until now you have invested in Scripture? Oh most foolish of mortals, can't you prove from your own circumstances that both the evidence of Scripture and the imagination of every creature lack both reason and order? Haven't you noticed by experience that, on the one hand, the reports found in divine books and, on the other hand, the lives and behavior of men contradict each other? Do you actually believe that those thousands of men who neither observe nor accept Holy Scripture are in error, as a person like you has seen so far?"

I weighed these matters often in my heart, asking myself and arguing, "If this is the case, why are almost all these divinely inspired Scriptures in agreement concerning God the Creator and the observance of His commandments?" It seemed again as though a reply came to me, saying, "Idiot! Those Scriptures in which you put your trust concerning the person of God and many religious questions merely provide explanations about how those who composed the Scriptures once lived. People lived in those days as they do today. As you know, upright religious persons today say one thing and do another, in accordance with human expedience and weakness. Don't you see this every day? You can well imagine that the authors of ancient writings composed upright and religious words, but they themselves did not live in accordance with those principles. You should therefore learn that all books dealing with religious issues possess an outer quality of piety and virtue, while inside they display a different reason and understanding. Therefore, in many matters, but particularly when dealing with divine subjects, the sentence says one thing in the letter, superficially, but has another meaning. I will prove this by means of Paul's remark, 'The letter killeth, while the spirit,' that is, the real sense, 'giveth life' [2 Corinthians 3.6]. Don't these words of the Apostle clearly prove that, by following the words of Scripture, you will suffer great dangers? God's essence should be understood in the same way. If there were such a person as God and if He were omnipotent, this kind of confusion and diversity in all matters would not exist. Problems of this kind would not weigh you down, and you would not be so threatened by the doubt you now experience."

I was attacked by such delusions in an unbelievable way. Because of the unprecedented nature of these attacks, I was embarrassed to report them openly to my brethren, assuming that they would neither believe me nor even entertain such matters. As I lay prostrate alone, I took long embittered breaths, collecting all my strength of mind. Out of the depths of my heart I cried out in this way, "Who are you, Omnipotent One? If, as I have read often in many books, you are to be found everywhere, please show me who you are and what you can do by quickly snatching me from imminent danger, since I can no longer endure such pain." Without any delay not merely was I freed by God's grace not only from the slightest shadow of doubt, but such a light of knowledge shone in my heart that I was never again to suffer the deadly darkness of doubt; I also began to understand those things which I only vaguely perceived before. The grace of intelligence so grew in me at that time that I could hide it with difficulty. Having been aroused by a certain unequaled instinct and unaccustomed fervor, I was excited to undertake a certain deed for the sake of the grace that I had acquired. Since I could say absolutely nothing about the grace of understanding nor demonstrate it in a reasonable fashion, I began to discuss it in the hope that by chance, through speaking and writing, that same fervor which had been instilled in me could be communicated to others. In this way, occasionally undertaking to write, I reported those things about the diabolical delusions which I have noted above, writing out of divine inspiration.

Christina of Stommeln, *Epistolae* (1272)

Christina of Stommeln (1241–1312) was a beguine of Cologne, a member of an informal community of women (most of whom lived in the Low Countries and Rhine Valley), often engaged in handicrafts, who were largely brought under clerical control by the mid-thirteenth century. Such women beginning in the late twelfth century sought to lead a more spiritual life as hermits, on the peripheries of a convent or monastery, or within a voluntary community stressing asceticism and devotion.

Because of their unconventional life, their high spiritual and intellectual aspirations, and their unwillingness to accept strict ecclesiastical control, they were sometimes accused of heretical tendencies, although they were in the forefront of many of the lay mystical movements of the period. Christina suffered throughout most of her life from hallucinations, possession by demons, and suicidal episodes. Although she joined the beguines at the age of thirteen, in 1259 she returned to her parents' home because of her uncontrollable, unorthodox behavior. Her suffering is recorded by Peter of Dacia (d. 1289), Dominican lector of Skänninge and Västerås, who first met the German mystic in 1267 and produced a life and a series of letters describing her extraordinary experiences (including stigmata), many of which appear quite scatalogical.

Source: *Acta Sanctorum*, ed. Socii Bollandiani, 69 vols. (Paris: V. Palme, 1863–1940), 22 June V: 257–62.

Bibliography: Ernest W. McDonnell, *The Beguines and Beghards in Medieval Culture, with Special Reference to the Belgian Scene* (New Brunswick, N.J.: Rutgers University Press, 1954), 344–55.

*   *   *

From Letter II (May 1272), Christina to Peter of Dacia, while he was at Paris

You ought to know that since the feast of John the Baptist [June 24] I have been unable to pray or confess since a demon has burned me with a hot iron, producing sores on both my mouth and face, both inside and out. I believe this lasted until the Assumption of the Virgin [August 5].

From Letter III, her confessor Gerard Gritone to Peter while he was at Paris in 1272

You ought to know that after you left, until the octave of the Holy Trinity [May 27], your beloved Christina was well and, according to the course of her life, she was sufficiently quiet in both flesh and spirit and rested tolerably. After that she suffered from tertian fever[1] for almost three weeks and was gravely afflicted. That nasty old perpetrator of evil cruelly molests her with all manner of affliction. When she wants to pray, contemplate the good, or confess some small errors, he appears to her in a terrible way, menacing and threatening her with lances and knives, and everything good becomes irksome. This occurred recently when she was sitting before the chapel with several others. She tried to pray and contemplate something, but the devil came and stuck a lance in her mouth, so that those who were present saw a great quantity of blood issuing from her, as if streaming from a new wound. It was so terrible that it seemed as if God had utterly abandoned her. Already on several occasions she has failed to experience the customary pleasures of communion. Since she suffers fiendishly from this, I ask you to pray for her as much as possible; which, I believe, you will do.

---

1. A fever recurring every third day.

From Letter IV, Christina to Peter of Dacia

Sometimes when I am about to take communion, I suffer severely at night from the terrible sight of a demon whom I believe has made me sweat drops of blood. This once lasted for fifteen days. Afterward, I didn't enjoy hearing mass, nor the Word of God, nor did I speak of God, nor could I pray in any way without fear of burning iron. When I went to the customary place in order to partake of the Lord's body, my heart remained completely unconsoled; whence this tribulation was so great to me and it occurred at every communion until that feast.

The outside of my face was so visibly burned that white pustules appeared around my chin; but I was never in rapture the entire time. This burning lasted a certain amount of time and then I was cured; at other times my ears burned all night long. When this was over, my eyes and brow burned. I appeared wretched in my friends' eyes, since my eyes were fouled by a wound and the pustules were large. My nose was afterward stanched in a dish in the presence of the brethren William Bonentant and Godefrid Werde. My body suffered so much that my heart was also tempted. A demon advised me to deny my God and said that I was like other persons. When I suffered this affliction of heart and body, and God's consolation was lacking, I was so desolated that it sometimes appeared to me that I was totally abandoned by God, so that I couldn't control myself at all, as you have sometimes seen. On other occasions, when I was supposed to pray or confess, my body seemed to be aflame, along with the book I held and the priest to whom I confessed. When my sister Gertrude was sleeping in bed with me, her nose began to burn one night, so that she stopped sleeping with me on the succeeding nights. Last night, from the first sound of the cock until morning, a little before daytime, I was locked in a terrible battle with a demon who pierced my ears with a hot iron. Holding the iron in my ears, he asked whether I wanted to deny my God. He wanted to kill me immediately, since he had the power to do so . . . saying that I should be ready to die a thousand deaths for Christ. The fire came as if from a furnace, scalding my entire face, whence I lay down not knowing where I was all night; my whole head was aflame, and my throat was infested with sores. . . .

That same night four demons appeared standing before me like an apparition. One of the demons gave his name. Their names reveal the pains[2] which I suffered at the time. When asked, they said that God gave them the

2. The term used here is *poenae*, which also suggests punishment.

power and they praised God a great deal, and because of this great pain they were to be followed. Undaunted, I said, "Apparently God wants to purge my senses before the feast day." When they began to praise me, I returned to my prayer. They seemed to start to cry, and, with a great roar, turned their backs on me and departed. The next day my face appeared to be burned all over: hair, eyes, nose, and brow. The sores were so large that it appeared to everyone as though I didn't have a face, but I rather looked like a leper, injured by God. . . .

One demon appeared in two places in the form of a beghard.[3] I asked what he wanted, why he pursued me. He replied, "I pursue you in order to provoke you to anger and other sins. You, however, immediately raise your hands to God and ask remission of your sins. He mercifully grants you indulgence, and thus I labor in vain." On the Thursday after the feast of the Exaltation of the Cross [September 14], when I intended taking communion the next day, he came to me in the guise of my brother who was at Cologne. On his chest was a burning candle, and he appeared above the chair beside my bed, wounded and covered with blood. He said to me, "Don't be afraid, my dear sister. Whenever I come to you, as I have done in the past, my enemies come and injure me. Help me to bandage my wounds and keep it a secret, lest my mother know." I answered, falling to the ground and knowing that it was the demon, "Oh cruel beast, why do you pursue me?" He replied, "I see there is some design in you." He then disappeared. . . .

From Letter VII, Christina to Peter

You ought to know that for fifteen days before the feast of All Saints [beginning October 18] I experienced a certain temptation. It appeared to me that I prayed in the name of a demon, which was a great tribulation to me. The demon spoke, as you know, in a tempting way. At the raising of the host, I couldn't see the Corpus Christi [the Body of Christ]; but another demon appeared before my eyes, saying "Lo, you see I am your god." When I was supposed to genuflect, he threw me down on my knees, and I couldn't get up. On the Wednesday before the feast, when I was in church, the demon came and took two herring, fouled [them?] with a knife, which he had dropped in feces at the entrance to the hermitage. He told me that within the enclosure of the hermitage he had stolen ten *solidi* of Cologne from a certain old beguine, my rival, and he brought it to the sewer of the Domini-

3. A beghard was a mendicant who had not taken formal religious vows; some were regarded as heretics.

can house. She found it there afterward. That night I remained in church with my father and friends. He broke all my limbs and removed a shoe from my foot which he afterward threw at a servant's head in my father's house. He broke a window so frightfully in the house that my brother almost went insane. When I prayed, he wounded me in the nose with an iron, so the blood flowed. On the vigils of All Saints [October 31] he departed with a great noise after having fouled the hermitage in the presence of Hilla de Engindorp and the recluses. To those who heard he called himself Berlabam and left. On All Saints' Day I remained abandoned by God, and was thereafter rarely consoled. . . . Afterward he threw a terrible stone at my father's head, and inflicted two wounds on his arm. He injured the priest's sister Gertrude horribly in the face. He threw a big stone at the head of a certain Jewish woman who had come. She had not taken care, and had spoken to him in an unsuitable way.

Pope Celestine V (1212?–1296), *Autobiografia*

Critics are divided concerning the authenticity of the so-called *Autobiografia* of Peter of Murrone, later Pope Celestine V (d. 1294). He was elected pope on July 5, 1294, was consecrated on August 29, 1294, and abdicated on December 13, 1294, dying on May 19, 1296, the date of his feast day. Several weeks after the pope's death, Cardinal Thomas of Santa Cecilia ordered a private inquiry into his life among the members of the Celestinian order. His action probably led to the composition of the earliest biographies. Since much of the autobiographical account is written in the third person (with occasional lapses into the first person, suggesting some reliance on the direct testimony of the saint), the text may not have been penned by Celestine himself. Rather, like the *Dicta*, or exemplary deeds and sayings of Francis of Assisi and the earlier *Vitae patrum* (the lives of the early Christian hermits), it may represent a compilation of oral traditions concerning the saint's formative years, heard and taken down in Celestine's lifetime by his faithful followers. As other contemporary biographies stated, the saint often sat with his disciples and provided them with insights into Scripture and the lives of the saints and the fathers. The life (ca. 1300) by his disciple Thomas of Sulmona makes explicit reference to an autobiography "written by his own hand." While the first poetic life of Celestine by Cardinal Stefaneschi, the *Opus metricum* (ca. 1296), makes no mention of the work, the second version (after 1319) does. Since the work ends abruptly when Celestine was thirty, it remains difficult to determine when it was written. These facts, coupled with the allegation that Celestine knew no Latin, suggest that it was in fact composed by his followers after Celestine's death based upon his own oral recollections. In addition, many of the episodes are rather stereotypical, in keeping with a long tradition of eremitical hagiography.

Nevertheless, the report of a nocturnal emission (possibly unique in such documents), in which the saint finds the solution to the problem of whether to celebrate communion following a ritual pollution through a divinely sent dream, is so unusual that it seems unlikely a "pious forgery" would contain such embarrassing material; only Celestine V could have provided direct evidence for such a work, even if he was not the author. Similarly, the contemporary *Confessions* of Angela of Foligno, although penned by her confessor, were based on direct contact with the saint. The rather simple fashion in which it is written, the evocation of peasant life in rural Molise and the Abruzzi, the details of childhood naïveté and piety perhaps suggest faithful adherence to Celestine's own memories, along with some effort by his followers to eulogize the saint's personal contact with the sacred. The text is divided into four sections dealing with different parts of his early life, each beginning with a miracle: Celestine's youth, his eremitical life, his ordination, and his life among his early followers.

If a birth date of 1209/10 is accepted, the work deals with the period up to about 1240. In about 1231 Peter made his profession at the Benedictine house of Santa Maria at Faifoli. The Benedictines were perhaps the most prosperous order in the region of Molise. He then apparently intended to journey to Rome, but instead spent about three years at a cave near Mt. Palleno (today called La Porrara) at Castel di Sangrio in the Abruzzi. After making his priestly profession at Rome, he became a hermit at Sulmona. In the late 1230s or early 1240s he settled at Mt. Murrone in a place formerly occupied by another hermit and later moved to Maiella, where the cloister of the Holy Spirit was founded. He was soon surrounded by a corps of followers, whose ascetic life combined elements of the Benedictine and Franciscan rules; a rule was confirmed by Pope Urban IV in 1263. By about 1275 the community may have numbered over one thousand members and had been joined by a lay confraternity.

Celestine's unprecedented resignation from papal office in 1294 led to a two-year interregnum, followed by the election of Pope Boniface VIII, whose selection was regarded as illegitimate by radical Franciscans. The troubles experienced by the church were seen as a sign of the Apocalypse by heretical sects, who looked on Celestine as an angelic pope, while others, including Dante (who placed the dead pope along with Pontius Pilate in the bowels of Hell due to his abdication), viewed him with scorn.

The following text contains many elements stereotypically found in the lives of hermit saints since the days of the desert fathers. Hermits sought solitude and isolation in the desert or mountains in order to flee the temptations of the city or of family life. According to the account, the Devil was Peter's constant companion, attempting to test his faith and resolve. When Peter was a child, Satan appeared in the form of his brothers, who complained that he was needed to help support the family and should not waste scarce resources on his religious vocation; he also appeared as a rich man who wanted to make Peter his heir and as playmates who tried to lead him into sin. As Peter grew older, new temptations appeared: false monks, whose lives did not conform to the rule; nightmares and illusions of a sexual nature; intrusive visitors. At the same time, he was likened to the biblical Joseph, he was the son of a pious mother, and his odyssey was accompanied by miracles and heavenly visions that guided him forward and strengthened his faith. This included a childhood vision in the local chapel, his mother's dream confirming that he would be a shepherd of men, miraculous cures, the appearance of a dove at his hermitage, and the heavenly music that surrounded his mountain retreat. Despite the hagiographical character of this text, specific local details provide us with a closer look at the rural environment in which Peter lived, in which poverty, famine, food shortages, inclement weather, and dangerous and wild animals threatened rural tranquility.

Source: Arsenio Frugoni, ed., "'L'Autobiografia' di Pietro Celestino," in idem, *Celestiniana* (Rome: Istituto Storico Italiano per il Medio Evo, 1954), 56–67.

Bibliography: George Ferzoco, "Church and Sanctity: The Hagiographical Dossier of Peter of Morrone," in *Normes et pouvoir à la fin du moyen âge*, ed. Marie-Claude Déprez-Masson (Montreal: CERES, 1990), 53–69.

*   *   *

Here begins the life of the most holy father, brother Peter of Murrone, or Pope Celestine V. The tract first deals with his life and was written by his own hand and was left in his own cell.

Come, listen to me and I will tell you, all who fear God, what He did to my soul. May God purify my heart and renew the upright spirit in my loins.

May the Lord open my lips and may my mouth proclaim his praises. May whatever we say enhance praise of God and the edification of those close to Him, as is written in Scripture, "Let your good faith and loyalty never fail, but bind them about your neck, and guard my commandments in your heart" [Proverbs 3.1–3]. And elsewhere [it is written], "A lying tongue is a man's destruction" [Wisdom 1.11]. Therefore, everything I am about to say, I speak the truth in [the name of] Christ, and I will not lie.

I will first say something about my parents, whose names were Angelerio and Maria. I believe they were both just in the face of God and were much praised among men; simple, upright and God-fearing, humble and peaceful, not returning evil for evil, they freely gave charity and hospitality to the poor. Like the patriarch Jacob, they bore twelve sons, always giving thanks to God like true servants of God. They devoted their second son to literary studies. When he grew up, he was handsome and good in accordance with the standards of the secular world, but he did not interest himself in the service of God, as his parents had wanted. When my father died at a ripe old age, he left his wife with seven sons, since some had already died. The good woman, seeing that this son would not be a cleric, as she had desired, grieved and said, "Woe is me, a wretch, who has reared and nurtured sons, none of whom I will see as a servant of God."

The eleventh son was then five or six years old, and God's grace was shown in him in a miraculous way, since he well understood what he heard; that is, he stored it away in his heart, and often said to his mother, "I want to be a good servant of God." She considered all his words, and said to herself, "I will give this son to literary studies, and perhaps God will grant him greater favor than the other son; and should one die, the other will remain." And what she said came true, since the one who had been a monk died a short time thereafter, and this one survived, although he thus far possessed little learning. But the Devil, always acting against the good, fought first one, then the others. First he tempted the boy not to want to study, then the other brothers so that they should not permit it. They came to their mother and said, "It's enough that one doesn't work." For in that *castro*[1] the clergy didn't work. The Devil tempted a certain rich man of the region to flatter the boy by saying, "I want to make you my heir." The demon even appeared, or so it appeared to me, although I was a mere child, saying that he was divine, and he said to my mother, "What have you done? Take him away from study, and teach the younger son, since he will not be a servant of God, as

---

1. A *castro* is a castle with a residential and commercial quarter.

you believe, but will soon die." My mother was much saddened by these words, but nevertheless she did not cease doing what she wanted to do.

Something that happened at his birth is reported. As she said, when the boy came out of his mother's womb, he was dressed in religious garb. It is also reported that, on the first day that he began to read, a man appeared to his godmother and said, "My wife decided that our son should study. How good this is for me, for her and for many others! Tell him from me that if he loves me, he should do the best he can, and complete what he has begun." Contrary to the other sons' desires, his mother took some of their property and gave it to a teacher to teach her son, whom God favored, since in a short time he learned the Psalter. Since at the time the child was unlearned [*simplex*], he didn't yet recognize the Virgin Mary and St. John, who are portrayed at the Crucifixion. He saw them coming down from the Crucifixion and grasp the book which the child was reading, and both the Virgin and John sang sweetly. The boy reported the matter to his mother with great pleasure. She said, "Look, my son, don't tell anyone about it." When he went to play with the other children, he was tempted by the Devil to say those words which he had been forbidden to say, and which he didn't understand. The following night he dreamed that he was in the church in which he studied by day, standing before the altar. While children stood about threateningly, the angels descended from on high, saying, "Why did you say such things? Beware lest you say such things again!" One said to the others, "Hit him! Why did he say those things?" Nevertheless, no one hit him.

He often saw these and other good things in visions, which he reported to his mother. She ordered him not to tell anyone, and he didn't. His mother dreamed that he was a shepherd tending many white sheep, which grieved her. When she got up she was much saddened. But the next day, when she was with her son, who was already twelve years old, she said to him, "I had a dream about a certain cleric." The boy immediately replied, saying, "He will be a shepherd of good souls." She heard this and was overjoyed, saying, "My son, it is you. Take comfort in the Lord."

God performed many miracles through the agency of his mother. A speck of grain got caught in his eye and was so hidden that no one could find it. For several days he roamed about looking for help but couldn't find any. He therefore cried out in pain day and night. His mother sadly beseeched the Virgin one night, saying, "My mistress, give my son his eye back, as you did to another son." At daylight the clerical son looked in his brother's eye, where the speck had reached the center of his eye, sticking out. He pulled it out with his middle finger. Also, at a time of great famine, no refuge could be found. One night she turned to God, asking him to take pity and provide for her sons, lest they die of starvation. In the morning, she said to one of the sons, "Son, take a sickle and go to the field and look. Perhaps the Lord has taken pity on us so we won't die of hunger." It was close to harvest time. The son refused, and did not want to go, saying, "Why should I go? The hay is green, and I won't find anything." Nevertheless, he went to the field and found in the middle dry white grain, as much as was needed. He collected and threshed it the same day and brought it to the mill, giving thanks to God. His mother gave great honor to the saints, celebrating all of their feast days. On the day after the feast of the Decapitation of St. John [August 29], she was supposed to make bread. She wanted to prepare the dough and began to mix the flour with water, and suddenly saw that the flour was filled with worms. In terror, she fell to the ground, praying to God, saying, "Woe is me," and the flour immediately returned to its former state.

The child aspired more and more to serve God, and especially in a hermitage. He didn't know that he could also be a hermit with a companion, but rather thought that he would always have to be alone; he especially feared the night because of his nightmares. He was thus in a quandary and didn't know what to do. Nor was there any servant of God in his region [*patria*] with whom to consult. In this way he passed his time until he was just over twenty years old. The youth then had a friend who was older than he and of higher station, who said to him, "What shall we do? Let's leave our homeland and travel afar in order to serve God; but let's first go to Rome and do everything on the church's advice." He agreed, and they began to walk; after one day's journey, the older one relented and said, "Let's go back; let's not abandon our home and families." Inspired by God, the other one said to him, "I place my trust in God, because if you leave me, God will not abandon me. I will not go back again." He remained by himself. After a day's journey he reached the region of Castro Sangre at nine o'clock at night. At the moment he entered the castro, the air became turbulent, and there was a heavy wind, rain and storm. Before he could reach the castro itself, it would be midnight. But he wanted to go further. He came to a bridge which was just outside the castro. While on the bridge, a strong wind blew toward him and he was gripped with fear, so he was forced to turn back. At the foot of the bridge, there was a church of St. Nicholas,[2] which he entered, and he beseeched the Lord and St. Nicholas to

---

2. St. Nicholas of Myra or Bari was one of the most popular saints of the region.

help him. Comforted by God, he remained there for several days. While there, someone reported to him that there was a hermitage situated on a mountain near the castro. Overjoyed, he went to the spot, but before he could arrive the Holy Spirit prohibited him from telling his secrets. He therefore approached the hermit, but before he could enter his cell, God showed him the man's dishonest life, and [warned him] that he should say nothing to him, except that he was on his way to Rome. . . .

On another day he brought two loaves of bread and some fish and went into the mountains. When he was near that spot [in which he was to remain], two beautiful women approached him; they grappled with him, grabbing him with their hands, saying, "Don't go since there's no hermitage there, but rather come with us." He could barely get away from them. When he reached that spot he found an open cell, fire, and water, and, bringing his two loaves and fish, he found no one there. This was in January, and there was a heavy snowfall. The Holy Spirit was with him at that time, and he began to think, saying, "Remain steadfast, and you'll see what God will do to you." But he was filled with doubt and fear. He remained awake for awhile during the day until he fell asleep on the ground. Behold, in his sleep a great crowd of angels and saints stood around him, so clearly that it seemed to him that he was awake, and all had red roses in their mouths, and they bloomed so beautifully. Afterward, he awoke and heard a song which lasted as long as it would take for him to say a Paternoster. He was then more joyful than he could say, safe as could be, and remained there alone for ten days, with two loaves of bread, filled with pleasure and joy.

After this the Lord showed him a spot in another mountain, in which he found a large boulder; he dug a bit under it, so he could scarcely straighten up or stretch, and remained there for three years; in this place God showed him many good things. Every night he would hear a certain bell making a great sound. Someone came out of a nearby hermitage, saying, "Since this brother has a cock which sings at night, why don't you?" A certain woman was then present, who said to him, "I have a very beautiful cock; if you want I'll bring it to you." He, an unlettered man [*simplex*], replied, "I want it." And so it was. But the cock never sang, and the sound of the bell disappeared. He considered why that was the case. . . . Often, when he prayed at night, he would see two handsome men beside him, dressed as bishops singing mass, and it seemed to him that they recited psalms with him. At the beginning of his conversion he suffered many temptations both in his waking hours and while asleep. Two demons took the form of women whom he had seen earlier in the world, and they were very attractive. They appeared often to him and were pleasing to his eyes. As he slept, one lay naked beside him on one side, while the other spoke to him on the other side. In this way they would argue with him. When he was awake, he would bolster his feet up with his tunic, as the demons would forcibly pull the bits of cloth away from under his feet, and cling to his body. There were also snakes, serpents, scorpions, and lizards there. Sometimes, when he was asleep, what are locally called *crapolli* [probably toads] would climb on his chest and cling to his flesh, since he didn't have any clothes except for the hooded tunic with which he covered his head. They therefore clung close to his flesh when he slept. Even after he got up, sometimes he didn't feel them, would say matins, and would genuflect many times; when he felt their presence, he would bend from his waist and they would fall to the ground. He was surprised that he thought nothing of it, but after they had fallen at his feet, he trampled on them, water would spew forth from their mouths, and he then knew what they were. Many good and bad things happened there. I will therefore turn to other matters.

After spending three years in this place, everyone persuaded him to become a priest. At that time he went to Rome, and there was made a priest. He then came to Mount Murrone, where he found a cave that pleased him very much. After entering, he sat down. A great snake appeared and then left. During a period of five years, God did many good things to him there. Although he always sought solitude and poverty, he sometimes thought that, with the pope's agreement, he ought to celebrate the office of the mass. It was winter, however, and since a heavy snow covered the mountain, he could not descend. He suffered temptation for several days until he could take the road to Rome. At night he had a vision that he was on the road to Rome, but went in the wrong direction. As he looked about, two friars approached him whom he queried about the road. They said nothing, but joked about him among themselves; he sat down and grieved sadly. A woman then came by whom he also asked about the road, and she answered, "You should ask God when you are in the cave," and said nothing else. He knew that he should not make a prayer about this. He beseeched God, and that night a certain abbot (that is, the one who had conferred the religious habit on him) appeared to him in a vision in the same way. He appeared to be standing before an altar, and appeared afterward dressed in a very white robe, saying to him, "My son, pray to me, and you will remain with God," and he wanted to depart. But he grabbed him by his cloak and would not let him go, while the abbot said, "Let me go, my son, let me go." Peter replied, "I swear to you by the living God." And he said, swearing by the Holy Trinity and other saints, "you should tell me what I should do about this." He said to him, "You should recite the mass, my son, recite the mass." And Peter said, "John the Baptist and the blessed Benedict and many other saints did not want to partake of such a mystery. How should I, who am such a great sinner and am unworthy of performing such a task?" The abbot said, "O my son! Worthy? Who is then worthy? Say the mass, my son; but say it with fear and trembling." And he disappeared immediately. On the same day a holy monk, to whom he customarily confessed, came to him. He said the same thing that the abbot had said in his vision.

On another occasion he experienced great temptation, when he experienced a [nocturnal] pollution and didn't know whether he should celebrate the mass on that day or not. He asked the advice of many monks; one said yes, and another no. He was thus subject to great doubt, not knowing what to do. He therefore beseeched God's help. And lo, that night as he slept [he dreamed] that he went up to a castle situated on a mountain. As he ascended he saw a great cloister, and the castle gate was situated in the middle of the castle. There was a great palace. Surrounding the cloister there were many cells in which there were monks dressed in white robes. He wanted to enter the palace, but he was accompanied by a certain ass whom he couldn't get rid of. He began to climb the steps to the palace, and the ass likewise ascended slowly. After taking two or three steps, the evil ass began to foully defecate, as though he had eaten hard herbs. Seeing this, Peter stopped in his tracks, sad and grief-filled, not daring to continue his climb. At the top of the stairs, at the palace entrance, he saw three similar and equal persons, so that they appeared to be one, and they all looked at him. The one who appeared to be Christ said to him, "Climb, climb. Why don't you climb? Because that ass behaved as he habitually does? What is that to you? Climb, climb." He immediately awoke, filled with great joy and pleasure, praising and blessing the Lord. Many good things which cannot be reported happened to him in that place in the course of five years.

Because he always sought solitude, and as all the forests in the region had been destroyed and cut down, he left that place and went to Mount Maiella, where he found a large cave that pleased him very much. But it pleased neither his two companions nor his friends. They were all opposed, except for one, so he remained there alone. A few days later his companions followed, because they loved him. They gathered branches and surrounded the cave in such a way that they could then live there. Since it was a hot summer, that is, the month of June, the branches were very dry. The tempter was present one night, and took note of how he could burn down the whole cell. Peter called to the brothers, saying, "Get up quickly, and throw everything outside." They got up and saw that the cell was afire. They quickly collected what they could, ran outside, and began to complain because he [i.e., Peter] had come to this place. They believed that the fire had come down from the mountaintop. But he was comforted by God and said to himself, "Even if my whole body should burn, I won't leave this place." And the fire ceased completely, as if they were in a dream.

Many devotees came and argued with him about the place, saying, "Everyone talks against you and blames you. They fear you, otherwise they would complain in your presence. You ought to know this, because we love you. We are very exhausted and can scarcely get here, as the road is long and arduous. Even those from the nearby castro don't want to come." He replied with humility and restraint, saying, "Dear ones, depart with God's blessing, and you may come when you are filled with great desire." But shortly thereafter one of them asked that he admit him as a brother, and he did. Many eventually began to abandon the world, and they came to him. As much as possible, he refused to accept them, saying that he was a simple man and that he always wanted to remain alone. But overcome with charity, he agreed as often as he could. Many great signs appeared there, whereby God showed that the place had been selected in honor of the Holy Spirit. In the beginning, when the brethren began to inhabit the spot, a dove appeared which always seemed to feed in the same place where the altar was later built, and so would move about among the brethren as if he had been fed by them. After a small oratory had been set up, this dove was always there, even when they recited the office, so that when some thieves were present in the oratory at mass and the dove was among them, and although it was caught by one of them who wanted to capture it, he couldn't. And so that dove appeared there for two or three years.

Afterward a beautiful oratory in honor of the Holy Spirit was built. Many came from afar with great devotion. One day people came from the region and the brother sat with them speaking about the Word of life. Four men arrived unexpectedly from another region. They turned to that brother, and he was filled with such a spirit of charity and ardor that he could scarcely contain himself. He immediately left the local people by themselves, remaining with the others and with the brethren. At nine o'clock he said to them, "First let us sing the praises due to the Lord, and afterward we will be consoled." They entered the oratory, began to recite the office, and began to hear the sound of great bells. But as the spot was so far away from all human habitation that no bell-ringing could be heard there, they were surprised by the sound. When they left the oratory they turned their eyes and ears to heaven and cried out. After they completed the office, the brethren came to the brother [Peter] fearfully in tears, saying, "Where is the place in which it is ringing?" The brother heard their words, and knowing the reason, said to them, "It is not very far away." And so he expressed himself in other words. They sat discussing many good things until vespers, and then the office began. Again they immediately heard the sound of great bells until three o'clock, when they departed. And so whenever they were outside the dwelling of the seculars they heard the sound come from God. One of them had suffered the following great infirmity: when he slept he would suddenly wake up, shout, and run about from place to place, hiding himself in whatever hole he could, so that no one could catch him. But from that day onward this never happened. Another one suffered an infirmity of a spiritual kind, so that every night he polluted himself at least three times. From that day onward he was freed of that sin and never again suffered from it; although every night for a long time the demons battled with him, by the grace of God they did not prevail. All four of those brethren devoted themselves to God, undertook the religious habit, and gave all their possessions to the poor. Two of them, who were youths, led such lives that God demonstrated many good things in their lives for many years, and they rested in peace.

After those four, many men heard the sound of those bells in that place. And after they heard them there, they heard them everywhere, except in the city or the castro. Once, from one city there were twenty who heard the sound, and from other regions many lay and secular folk, but no clerics or religious, which was surprising. The brethren who were there all heard it, but not all equally well, since one was more willing than the other, and there were many different kinds of bells. One brother heard one that gave out a sweeter sound than the others, and it rang when he raised up the Corpus Christi. This bell was always heard in the same place on the mountain, while in another place there were two bells, and in another two. Doves appeared in the air above that place; and one person might hear it less, others more, and vice versa. The sound might even fill the listener so much that he could scarcely bear it.

A great singing of the office was often heard sometimes in the oratory, and sometimes in Peter's cell, and they would understand what was said. When the office was being recited, one of the brethren would often hear sweet voices mixed with those of the brethren; so that when they stopped singing, those voices were heard even better. On the feast of St. Stephen [August 20, 1231, 1236, or 1242] in the evening Peter said to his brethren, "Let's recite a good office tonight in honor of St. John, and in the morning I will give you food." This was on Saturday. They got up on time for vigils, and the brethren recited the office in their cells. Peter returned to the cell and prayed as long as he wanted; afterward, he lay down on the bench on which he slept and, immediately awakening from sleep, began to hear the office in the oratory. Suddenly aroused, he paid close attention in order to hear clearly, even though his cell was situated ten paces from the oratory. Many recited the office, including youths. One of them stood out above all the others, and his voice rang like a trumpet. After the office had been said, they left the choir, standing before the cross. They began to say many good things, especially about the place. Afterward, their leader turned to the brother's cell and said in a loud voice, "Peter, be abstinent, be abstinent," and immediately vanished.

Likewise one day after matins the brother lay asleep on his bench; it suddenly seemed to him that he was in the oratory, and was supposed to say mass, but he didn't know how. He saw a few men in the oratory, and it was then filled with men dressed in white robes. One appeared on the right side of the altar, saying the mass. He looked like this brother's abbot, but he didn't recognize him. Afterward he was excited since he appeared to him to be the Holy Spirit. Everyone stood nearby very reverently. This brother stood on the right side of the abbot. When the host was raised, the bell sounded in such a way that its splendid sound miraculously attracted to the altar those who stood by. He then woke up and found his head to be where his feet had been before, and he heard the glorious sound even after he got up. At another time at dawn, he sat in his cell reading a book. The window was open. Outside the cell beside the window there suddenly appeared many persons in glory, saying to themselves, "Let us lift this cell up." They began to recite the office of dedication, making a circuit around the cell. The brother recited the office with them, a fact which startled him, as he said to himself, "What is this? Am I asleep?" He looked at the book, placing his hand on his bed of straw, since it was already daylight. When the office was over, he felt as though he had taken off the finest clothes, something he had not felt when he got dressed; and they immediately vanished.

One Sunday a certain brother of that place had a vision of a handsome man who said to him, "Note that this oratory has been dedicated by God, and I will give you a sign. In the morning when you enter the oratory, the lamp standing before the altar will move back and forth." This is what happened, for all the brethren to see; namely, when the lamp was filled with oil, no oil oozed out of it although they saw it move to and fro. At times some of the brethren saw a great throng of demons in the forest around this spot, jumping up and bleating like sheep wanting to enter the area. On the other side there was a large crowd of good spirits who fought against them, and they did not permit them to enter. Once during Pentecost the brethren dedicated themselves as much as possible to abstinence, prayer, silence, and other good deeds. Although the devil tempted their hearts, he could accom-

plish nothing. On Passion Sunday, once at night, before the brethren arose
for vigils, while they were still in their cells, he gripped four brothers with
great fear, so that when they got up for vigils, they cried out and said, "Help
us, help!" One of them spread out both hands, although all the fingers of
both hands were twisted, and all the brethren who were present saw foul
demons in the choir, the church, the air, and everywhere; so all ceased
reciting the office. But the brother, who was in his cell, become aware of
what was going on and said that those who could should not cease saying
the office. In the morning, when this was over, all the imaginary spirits
disappeared. All the aforesaid occurred during a three-year period, when he
was living in the small oratory. Afterward, these things rarely occurred and
only to a few people. So ends the life of the beloved holy confessor Peter of
Murrone, which he wrote by his own hand and left in his cell.

Giacomuccio Fatteboni (1325)

Suicide was regarded as one of the manifold means employed by the Devil
in order to gain control of his victims, often described as melancholics who
suffered from *desperatio*, or loss of hope. The suicide's family suffered infamy, and the victim, who could not be buried in consecrated ground,
suffered eternal damnation. Judas Iscariot and Pontius Pilate were the prototypical suicides, a warning to all those so condemned. In secular legislation, suicide was regarded as a form of homicide. The following case of an
attempted suicide, which comes from the canonization acts of Nicholas of
Tolentino held in 1325, illustrates faith in divine intervention as a means of
allaying the consequences of emotional turmoil. Village life in medieval
Italy is here graphically described, as each of the witnesses gives his or her
own version of what had transpired.

Source: *Il processo per la canonizzazione di S. Nicola da Tolentino*, ed. Nicola Occhioni
(Rome: École Française de Rome, 1984), 278–84, witnesses nos. 96–99.

Bibliography: Michael Goodich, *Violence and Miracles in the Fourteenth Century: Public Grief and Private Salvation* (Chicago: University of Chicago Press, 1995), 79–85.

*   *   *

Giacomuccio Fatteboni, alias Rubei of Belforte in the diocese of Camerino,
aged sixty or more . . . was first asked if he knew friar Nicholas, and replied

that he did not. Asked if he was melancholic, or subject to deception by the Devil because of which he had hung himself, he said that he did not remember. But he heard his neighbors in the *castro* of Belforte say that he had once been found by his neighbors hanging in his house in the castle quarter of the castro of Belforte. He said that he didn't remember if this was the result of devilish temptation or for some other reason. Asked from which neighbors he had heard about it, he replied: from Simonet's wife, Margarita, from his own daughter Pianucia, from Mathiola Andrea of Campolarzo, and from his own sons, Pietro and Vanne. Asked when it had happened, he said that it was reported throughout the whole neighborhood that it had happened five years earlier, although he had heard about it and didn't remember. Asked if he believed that he had been freed due to the prayers and merits of Nicholas of Tolentino, he said that he had, and had heard it so said. Asked if he had heard that he was dead and that he was found hanging, he said that he had. Asked from whom he had heard this, he replied from the aforementioned persons and from all who dwelled in the castro; that it was reported in the churches and piazzas and other locales of the castro; and that it was widely reported that he had been revived due to Nicholas's merits. Asked the basis of his knowledge, he said that such was the public opinion and understanding [of the matter, which was] voiced by all.

Mistress Margarita, wife of Simonet of Belforte, aged twenty-five or more, said that . . . the blessed Nicholas had performed a miracle in the person of Giacomuccio Fatteboni of Belforte. Asked what the miracle was, she said that he had been sick and appeared to have lost his mind and didn't know that he was being controlled by an evil spirit, or that for some other reason he hanged himself in his own home on a cross-beam with a rope around his neck, just as men are generally executed by hanging. Asked how far the lintel on which he hung was from the ground, she replied twelve feet or more. Asked if he was able to rest his feet and stand up so that, although suspended, he could evade death, she said that he couldn't. Asked how she knew about this, she replied because she was a neighbor who lived near Giacomuccio's house. When she heard the outcry made by his former [deceased] wife, Bionda, who had discovered that her husband had hanged himself, the witness rushed in and found him. Bionda climbed up to the arched ceiling to remove the rope from around his neck. The witness and another neighbor, Piana, wife of Deutaleve, raised the body up, and lowered it, laying him down on a bed. He appeared dead to them because he was black, and his black and swollen tongue stood out stiffly from between his teeth. Giacomuccio himself was all black and swollen, like dead persons who have been hanged. Asked if she had been present when Giacomuccio had hanged himself, she said that she had not, except after his wife's outcry, as said above, and believed that no one had been present when he hanged himself, since no one would have allowed him to do so. Asked where Giacomuccio's wife had been at the time, she said that she was at the [communal] oven. Asked how far the oven was from Giacomuccio's house, she said six houses away. Asked how she knew, she said that she had seen her entering and leaving the oven. Asked if any other persons were present at the time, she said not when he had been taken down, but many others were there afterward. Asked who was present, she said Piana, Giacomuccio's daughter, and many men and women of Belforte. Asked how long he was dead, she replied that he had been found hanging in that way at midday, and had been placed on a bed by the witness and the other women (that is, his wife and Piana) until vespers [about 3 p.m.], when he revived due to the prayers and merits of Nicholas of Tolentino. Asked how she knew, she replied that right after he was found in that way, his wife, Bionda, began to cry out, tear her hair, rip her clothes, and lacerate her cheeks, continually wailing and beseeching the blessed Nicholas of Tolentino, saying, "Oh Nicholas, ask God for his sake, that he not die in such a scandalous way. Don't let Giacomuccio lose his soul, and don't allow either him or his sons to be disgraced. Bring him back to life so that he may at least do penance through your prayers and merits. Oh blessed Nicholas, I vow and promise that if you do me this favor, I will bring a cart-load of grain [to your shrine]." She and the others pleaded in this way with St. Nicholas. After the vow had been uttered by the woman with great reverence and tears, at vespers Giacomuccio began to touch himself, to move his eyes, hands, and feet. The next day he got up and went to Tolentino to the blessed Nicholas' tomb, and with his wife brought the grain she had promised. Asked about the source of her knowledge, Margarita said that she had seen him and his wife on their way, saying that they were going with the seam of grain. Asked when the miracle had taken place, she said five years earlier, on a Thursday. . . . Asked if she had known him before, she replied that she was acquainted with Giacomuccio, since she had married in the castro two months before the event. Asked if she knew said Giacomuccio to be a healthy man, and for how long after the miracle, she said uninterruptedly already for five years until now, and that he was in better shape than before. Asked what had prompted his wife to have recourse to a vow to the blessed Nicholas, she said because the saint had a good reputation in the castro of Belforte for the miracles which God had demonstrated and performed due to the merits of said blessed Nicholas, and because the bystanders had advised her to make a vow to that saint. . . .

Mistress Mathiola, wife of Giorgio Bartolomei Alexandrei of Belforte, in the diocese of Camerino, aged twenty-five or more . . . said that . . . five years earlier, on a certain Thursday in the month of April, Giacomuccio Fatteboni of Belforte hanged himself from a cross-beam in his home with stable rope tied in such a way that he was dead. Asked how she knew, she said that she was Giacomuccio's neighbor, and when she heard mistress Bionda, Giacomuccio's wife, she was drawn by the outcry to Giacomuccio's house, and found his wife tearing at her clothes and face and pulling out her hair. Along with her she found among others mistress Margarita, wife of Simonet of Belforte wailing and crying out that said Giacomuccio had hanged himself, as she said, with stable rope from a crossbeam in their house. . . . She had seen him lying dead in his house in bed, his blackened tongue sticking out stiffly between his teeth; he was black and swollen and his wife, Bionda said in her grief that she was more saddened by the perdition to Giacomuccio's soul and the scandal which she and her children had suffered, because she had to take him to a pit to be buried. . . . She saw him dead for an hour, remained a bit, and returned home. . . . On the same day after vespers, but before sunset, she came back in order to visit his wife, children, and others in the house and found him revived and alive due to the merits and prayers of the blessed Nicholas, as mistress Bionda and mistress Margarita reported. . . . Mistress Bionda had vowed to God and the blessed Nicholas that, if the saint would free and revive her husband, he would not lose his soul, she and their children would not suffer the scandal due to such a foul death as her husband's, and that she would go to Tolentino and take her husband with a seam of grain; and this is what happened . . . the next morning. . . . She heard his wife say that a little before he had hanged himself, she had returned from Tolentino . . . from the market which is held there every week on that day. When she returned she had found her husband alive, and he had said to her, "Make a calzone for my children who have gone outside to work so that they'll have something to eat this evening." She had followed her husband's orders concerning the calzone and brought them to the oven to bake, which is situated six houses from Giacomuccio's house. . . . Asked if she had been acquainted with Giacomuccio before the event, she replied that she had for eight years or more, since she was his neighbor. . . . Asked why he had thus hanged himself, she said that she didn't know, except that she believed that he was filled with fantasies.

Pianucia, daughter of Giacomuccio Rubei, wife of Andrea Francesco of the castro of Belforte in the diocese of Camerino, aged over thirty . . . heard from a person named Bruneta of castle Belforte that while friar Nicholas was alive, when Bruneta had gone to Tolentino in order to confess her sins and brought a chicken to friar Nicholas, the friar had kindly received her and heard her confession; but refused to take the chicken, saying, "Go, daughter, and may you be blessed, bring this chicken to some infirm poor person who needs it more than I do, because I don't need such food." And she said that no one heard anything bad about him, only good things.

Asked about his miracles, she said that on a Thursday her father Giacomuccio had hanged himself from the cross-beam of his house with a stable rope while his wife, mistress Bionda, had gone to the oven in order to have calzone baked. When she had left the house her father was sitting alive on a bench, and had sent his wife to the oven in order to have the calzone baked for his children, their family, and his wife's brothers; when she returned to the house, she found her husband hanging from the crossbeam. His wife began to wail, cry, prostrate herself, and tear her clothes, so that the neighbors heard. A woman named Rosa, wife of Francesco Violente, came to the house of the witness and said, "What will you do, Pianucia, since your father Giacomuccio is dead?" The witness began to wail and said, "How can he be dead, since a short time ago I left him perfectly healthy at home? Who has killed him?" Rosa said, "Because he has hanged himself." The witness went immediately to her father's house, and he was considered completely dead from the stable rope; he was lifted up and placed on the bed by his wife, mistress Bionda, and Margarita, wife of Simonet Giraldi. When she saw that her father was dead, and was so regarded by everyone, his tongue stuck stiffly out of his mouth from between his teeth, swollen and black. Giacomuccio was black and swollen and smelled terribly. She didn't touch him in any way since he was dead, but tore open her clothes, pulled her hair out, cried out as strongly as she could both because of her father's death and the infamy. Asked how she knew that he had hanged himself and had been taken down by some women, she replied that she didn't know, except that she had heard it from those women who told her that they had found him hanging, had lifted him up, and had placed him on the bed, as she said above. While the witness was there, her stepmother Bionda, Giacomuccio's wife, began to beseech the blessed Nicholas of Tolentino, saying with great reverence, "Oh blessed Nicholas, ask God, because of your merits and the service you did to Him in your lifetime to revive and free my husband, that he should not lose his soul and not die with such infamy and scandal; because I promise and vow that should he be freed and revived, I will take him to Tolentino with a seam of grain." The witness and the others present asked God to revive Giacomuccio because of the prayers and merits of St. Nicholas. Asked how she knew, she replied because she heard and was

present when her stepmother made the vow, and prayers were uttered by
the witness and others present. Asked who was present when said vow was
uttered, she made mention of the witness herself, Margarita, and many
others, but that she was so filled with grief that she didn't think of who was
present at the time. Asked when this all happened, she said five years ago in
the month of April, on a Thursday, although she didn't remember the day
of the month, but that it was the day before the feast of St. Mark [April 24,
1320]. Asked where the miracle occurred, she said in the castro called
Belforte, near the walls of said castro. Asked at whose invocation said miracle had occurred, she said at the invocation of Giacomuccio's wife and the
prayers of the witness and the others who were present. Asked the words of
that vow, she said as testified above. Asked if she had seen him hanging, she
replied that she hadn't, but had heard it said by the aforementioned women,
as said above. Asked how long before he was dead she had seen him alive,
she replied a short time before she had left him alive in his home. Asked
how long he lay dead, she said from after nones [3 p.m.] until vespers or
thereabouts. Asked if she had been present when he revived, she said that
she was there along with many other persons. Asked how long Giacomuccio survived after the miracle, she said from that day until now. Asked if she
firmly believed and held the belief and faith that her father had revived due
to the prayers of the blessed Nicholas, she said that this is what she and
everyone else of Belforte believed. Such was the commonly held view in
Belforte. Asked what "the commonly held view" is, she said that it is what
all the people say. Asked why her father had hanged himself, she said that he
was sometimes foolish, and filled with fantasies, and not of very good sense.
She believed that it was the work of the Devil.

Yves of Penguennan (1330), Follower of Yves of Tréguier (d. 1303)

The following case, which deals with family conflict, suggests the conten-
tious and complex ties that link family members. It describes the case of a
"demoniac" (perhaps the victim of suggestion) in a small rural community
in Brittany, in which pagan belief appears to have survived. The canonization trial of Yves of Tréguier (d. 1303), from which this text comes, was
held in 1330. Yves is the patron saint of lawyers, due to his willingness to
take on cases for free. The testimony of the victim, who was allegedly
bewitched by his own mother, is expanded by remarks taken from other
bystanders.

Source: Louis Arthur Lemoyne de la Borderie et al., eds., *Monuments originaux de S. Yves* (St. Brieuc: Prud'homme, 1887), 257–62.

Bibliography: Richard Kieckhefer, *Magic in the Middle Ages* (Cambridge: Cambridge University Press, 1990), 56–94.

*   *   *

Yves, son of Yves André of the parish of Penguennan in the diocese of Tréguier, aged twenty or thereabouts . . . stated that one evening when he was in the parish in front of the home of Jean Portavitalha, his mother approached and, addressing him in an ironic way, said, "Was it you who have defamed me, and should you have said what you said before?"

She then stretched her hands out and withdrew her breasts from where they were hidden, saying, "I give you my curse and the curse of my breasts which suckled you, and the curse of my loins which bore you. Whatever I may possess of you legally and can have, I utterly relinquish and give to the Devil."

Immediately after she uttered these words, he fell to the ground, so disturbed in heart and body that four men could barely hold him down. After being laid down in the bed in Jean Portavilha's house, that night he saw two goat-like black and ghastly demons hovering over him as big as towers, saying, "You belong to us. You belong to us because your mother has given you to us."[1]

[St.] Yves then appeared perched above his chest, saying, "Yves, are you asleep?"

He replied, "I'm not sleeping. Lord, who are you?"

St. Yves replied, "Don't be afraid, since last Monday you visited my tomb and called out my name, I've therefore come to save you, since your mother can't give you to the Devil because she has nothing legally of yours except a sack in which grain is taken to the mill."[2]

After the saint had spoken, he disappeared, and Yves slept until daybreak the next day. Aroused from sleep [at cockcrow] he asked his father and a certain Jean Doliga[3] to take him to St. Yves. His mother followed

---

1. His father Jean André says that he called out. "Protect me, protect me from those scoundrels, thieves and goats." His father then said, "Lord Saint Yves, I commend him to you."

2. One witness, Juliana "called the priest's daughter," claimed he shouted, "St. Yves, help me, St. Yves. Help me and protect me from the goats and scoundrels who want to take me."

3. Jean Doliga, age 25, was one of the witnesses. He had been ill in bed, but was aroused by love of his friend Yves André to get up and see what was happening.

them on the road, and the moment he sensed her presence he became agitated and shouted, "Take her away, take her away."[4]

After his father had made her return home, his agitation ceased, but when he reached the tomb of St. Yves in the church of Tréguier, he was again seized with the same difficult agitation as before, suffering until vespers [5 p.m.]. Around vespers his father made him kiss the headstone above the tomb of St. Yves and he immediately felt cured of his disturbance. He removed his purse and his belt and afterward slept a bit. The sacristan asked him in honor of St. Yves not to leave Tréguier until the miracle had been publicized. He therefore tarried for about nine days and returned home sound and healthy.

4. The father reported that she also then said, "My son, I commend you to Saint Yves."

V

Christian Heterodoxy

Following Jewish precedent, the early Christian community reached the conclusion that in order to guarantee unity in the face of persecution the exclusion of certain opinions was necessary. Ecclesiastical authorities (largely the bishop) possessed the legitimate right to separate those espousing unauthorized or heretical views from the orthodox. In addition, several other categories of religious error were defined: the apostate was one who had abandoned the Christian faith entirely; the infidel had never possessed Christian faith; and the schismatic held orthodox theological views but did not accept the duly constituted authority of the Church. Following the adoption of Christianity as the official religion of the Roman Empire in the fourth century, state power was employed to guarantee uniformity of belief and practice. But despite such efforts, often with the cooperation of secular rulers, Christianity has continued to be characterized by sectarianism, messianism, religious revivalism, evangelism, and apocalypticism. Early Christianity was often sharply divided over the most basic dogmas of the faith, such as the definition of the Trinity, the relationship between Judaism and Christianity, the structure of the Church, the role of the clergy, and the nature of the sacraments. Many of the early councils therefore attempted to achieve some consensus in the face of the continuing attacks of sectarians and to find some formula that would ensure the unity of the faithful. Since Christianization was often accomplished through direct appeal to the ruler, as in England, periods of pagan reaction were common, and the Church was often forced to tolerate the survival of pagan practices.

Although Augustine took note of more than one hundred and fifty Christian sects and although many of the polemical treatises dealing with the early medieval doctrinal disputes have survived, there does not appear to have been any consistent, organized attempt to eradicate sectarianism. The battle against paganism took precedence, and the Church appeared more concerned with superficial adherence to the faith and recognition of clerical authority than with forcing all believers to accept a particular theology. In the eleventh century this situation changed, and already in 1022 some heretics led by Aréfast were executed at Orléans in the presence of King Robert the Pious of France. This had been the first execution for heresy in the West since the 383 execution of Priscillian. The Gregorian reform movement, which attempted to rid the church of many abuses, such as the buying and selling of clerical offices (known as simony), the marriage of the clergy (Nicolaitism), and investiture of the bishops by the laity, attempted to impose canonical uniformity of practice and belief after a long period of local autonomy.

This reform program led to the division of the church into three factions: the reformers, who accepted the papally-led reform program in its broadest lines; the reactionaries, who rejected the changes which had been suggested (the Greek Church, for example, balked at many of these changes as unscriptural, leading to the Great Schism of 1054); and the radicals, who sought to deepen the thrust of reform, often attempting a return to the principles of the apostolic church. During the eleventh and twelfth centuries this third group continued to grow, and we hear increasingly of small heretical groups, such as the Patarenes, Arnaldists, Petrobrusians, and others, advocating diverse and often contradictory points of view. Since much of our documentation concerning their doctrines and practices comes from Catholic sources, we cannot always be sure of its accuracy. Following an old polemical tradition, such heretics had been demonized and accused of sexual promiscuity and deviation, cannibalism, infanticide, alliance with the Devil or the Antichrist, Judaizing, witchcraft, and treason.

A variety of explanations have been sought for the sudden increase in heretical activity after the eleventh century. The rise of learning, centered first in the cathedral schools of northern France and later in the universities, created a cadre of students who had been introduced to ancient philosophy, classical literature, and Arabic science. Although such learning was intended to provide a rational basis to the received wisdom and revelation of the True Faith, such scholars as Peter Abelard increasingly cast doubt on some of the binding dogmas of the faith. The followers of Amaury of Bène (d. 1207), for example, a teacher at the nascent University of Paris, are regarded as the progenitors of the heretical (some would say anarchistic) Brethren of the Free Spirit (referred to in the report by Thomassa of Montefalco). The Paris-trained theologian Peter John Olivi was a leader of the apocalyptic beguin sect, while Gerard of Borgo San Donnino proclaimed the end of the visible church around 1260 and sought to replace the Gospel with a new dispensation based on the works of Joachim of Fiore (d. 1202). In addition to providing an intellectual foundation for many of the new sects, the universities also supplied the charismatic preachers who could spread the seeds of heresy.

The opening of Europe to the outside world as a result of the Crusades and the rise of commerce and trade led to greater contact with other faiths, including Islam, Judaism, and Greek Christianity. It has been cogently argued, for example, that Catharism was spread after about 1140 by Bogomil missionaries from Bulgaria, and shares much in common with other Byzantine sects, such as the Paulicians. Most of the new sects were centered in the urban regions of southern France, Italy, the Low Countries, and Rhine Valley, which were particularly open to outside influences. In order to achieve economic and political independence urban dwellers had organized communes in the eleventh century and had attempted to limit the traditional power exercised by the local bishop. The Patarenes of Milan, who opposed the selection of unworthy persons to clerical office, may have begun as a political movement which, as a result of conflict with the Church, was transformed into a heretical sect. The followers of Arnold of Brescia, who gained control of the city of Rome in 1147 and opposed papal influence in the city, may likewise be seen primarily as members of a political movement which sought to free Rome of its subservience to ecclesiastical authorities. This effort was defined as heretical by the Church. At the same time, urbanization also spawned new social problems such as a wider gap between rich and poor, the accumulation of ill-gotten wealth by merchants and bankers, and the creation of a population of unemployed or unemployable persons. City dwellers might easily be aroused by charismatic leaders such as Henry the Monk and Peter of Bruis (d. 1139/40), who had rejected the external forms of the faith and called for an end to clerical wealth. And, indeed, many of the heretical sects made use of Biblical imagery and precedent in their program of reform, preaching social, and even sexual equality. It would appear that women in particular were attracted to the new religious movements, which often rejected the special role of the male clergy, and like the Cathars, Waldensians, and Guglielmites (all of which are represented in this chapter) allowed women to preach and perform many of the "sacramental" roles usually reserved for men. The new orthodox emphasis on the celibacy of the clergy widened the gap between clergy and laity, which was particularly felt by female congregants.

The reaction of the church to the burgeoning phenomenon of heresy was slow. Local bishops were urged to identify the heretics and engage them in discussions aimed at restoring their faith. Theologians such as Peter the Venerable published polemical treatises against their errors; church councils issued condemnations of heterodox views and sought to mobilize the local clergy. In 1184 Pope Lucius III issued the bull *Ad abolendam* in order to encourage more active pursuit of heresy by the bishops and specifically condemning the Humiliati, Cathars, and Waldensians. By the late twelfth century, with the refinement of canon law, a more formal legal mechanism was put into place to bring heretics to trial. The Praemonstratensian and Cistercian orders had been particularly active in the battle against heresy. But the proliferation of Catharism in southern France led to the founding of the Dominican order in 1206, which regarded the battle against heresy through word and example as its central mission. As a result of the assassination of the papal legate Peter of Castelnau by Cathars in 1208, Pope Innocent III proclaimed the Albigensian Crusade, thereby mobilizing an army, made up largely of northern French nobility, against Count Raymond IV of Toulouse, the heretics, and their allies in southern France. The anti-heretical legislation enacted in 1229 (see below) following the restoration of peace to Languedoc, sought to provide detailed penalties for suspected heretics and those who assisted them. The murder of papal inquisitors, however, continued, with the deaths of Conrad of Marburg in 1233, Peter of Verona (known as Peter Martyr) in 1252 and some inquisitors at Avignonet in 1242.

The 1230s witnessed the establishment of the papal Inquisition, an independent investigatory body endowed with special powers to identify, try and imprison heretics and their abettors; the severest cases were transferred to the secular authorities for punishment. The registers of investigations undertaken by the Inquisition into heresy and the manuals written to guide its personnel concerning the views of the various sects and the means of pursuing them (such as Bernard Gui's *Practica inquisitionis*) represent perhaps our most important source for knowledge of these groups. The Church also undertook to mobilize the state in its war against the heterodox, with the result that secular law now imposed imprisonment, confiscation of goods, exile, and even execution of those found guilty of heresy. Not all secular rulers were equally cooperative; the Spanish kings and German emperors, for example, acted with reluctance; in England, heresy did not in any case become a problem until the late fourteenth century, with the appearance of the Lollards.

At the same time, all the ecumenical councils held during the central Middle Ages (1123, 1179, 1215, 1245, 1274, and 1312) specifically con-

demn one heresy or another and provide remedies for the ignorance of the
laity and the poor training of the clergy in the battle against heterodoxy,
such as the provision of yearly confession, the appointment of trained theologians in every diocese, and the enhancement of preaching. Confraternities
proliferated in which believers could meet, honor a local saint, receive the
sacraments and serve as local guardians of religious orthodoxy. Some of
these groups, like the Flagellants, may have themselves been infiltrated by
repentant heretics. The Fourth Lateran Council (1215) even recommended
the establishment of committees of local citizens who would identify sus-
pects and assist in their prosecution.

The testimony that was a result of inquisitorial hearings, besides detailing the beliefs and ceremonies of the heretics, provides a graphic view of
daily life among a population living in the shadow of a persecuting society,
forced to dissemble and even live on the geographical periphery in order to
survive. In some cases, such as those against the Dolcinists in 1304/5 and
against the Albigensians after 1208, a military crusade was undertaken to
wipe out the heretics. The agencies of persecution appear to have been
largely successful. The Guglielmites, Cathars, and most of the other sects
discussed in this volume disappeared by the mid-fourteenth century; only
the Waldensians, who have been regarded as progenitors of the Reformation, appear to have survived in remote regions of the French Alps.

The sources that follow represent only a small selection of documents
in which the heretics (or their opponents) speak for themselves. They
must, however, be read with caution. The testimonies of the Cathars Arnauda da Lamotha of Montauban and Beatrice of Planisolles, and the Guglielmite Flordebellina of Milan, were elicited by the Inquisition; after undergoing torture, even when applied with restraint, witnesses might be
willing to admit to any charge and incriminate others in order to be spared
the severest punishment. Nevertheless, these accounts are often supple-
mented by other sources that report the theological views and practices of
the heretics.

Peter Waldo, *Profession of Faith* (1181/82)

The following profession of faith was extracted from Peter Waldo by the
papal legate Henry of Clairvaux during a visit to Lyons, although by 1182
the Waldensians were excommunicated. Waldo himself had undergone
some kind of conversion experience in about 1173, having been inspired by

the example of St. Alexis, who abandoned his family in order to pursue the apostolic life. This document represents a summary of the principles of the Catholic faith, laying special stress on some of the false doctrines attributed to the Cathars and Waldensians. The final paragraph describes the way of life adopted by those Waldensians who have reconciled themselves to the Church. The text is based on the ancient *Statuta ecclesiae antiqua* (476/85), which was itself the product of early Christian attempts to counteract the doctrines of the heretical Arians, Nestorians, Sabellians, and others.

Source: Christine Thouzellier, *Catharisme et Valdéisme en Languedoc*, 2d rev. ed. (Paris: Presses Universitaires de France, 1969), 27–30.

Bibliography: Herbert Grundmann, *Religious Movements in the Middle Ages*, trans. Steven Rowan (Notre Dame, Ind.: Notre Dame University Press, 1995), 40–58.

* * *

In the name of the Father, the Son, and the Holy Spirit and the blessed and eternally Virgin Mary. Let it be known to all the faithful that I, Waldes, and all my brethren, placing the Holy Gospels before us, believe in our heart and understand by means of faith, confess with our mouths, and affirm in simple words: that the Father and the Son and the Holy Spirit are three persons. The one God and the whole Trinity of the Godhead co-essential and co-substantial, co-eternal and co-omnipotent, and each person being singly in the Trinity fully God and all three persons being one God, as is contained in the [prayers] "I believe in God," "I believe in one God," and "Whoever wants."[1] We believe in our heart and confess with our mouths that the Father, the Son, and the Holy Spirit are one God, about whom we speak, and is the Creator, maker, and governor and in a particular place and time, is the disposer of all things visible and invisible, celestial and in the air, in the sea, and on earth. We believe that the same and only God is the author of the New and Old Testaments, that is, the law of Moses, and of the prophets and the apostles, dwelling in the Trinity, as it is said, and created all things; that John the Baptist was sent by them as a saintly and just man to fill his mother's womb with the Holy Spirit. We believe in our hearts and confess with our mouths that the incarnation of the Godhead did not occur

---

1. These phrases are respectively the beginning words of the Apostles' Creed, the Nicene Creed, and the Athanasian Creed. A creed is a summary of religious belief or a test of orthodox faith. Various versions appeared in the early Church during the period of the persecutions and sectarian conflict.

in the Father or the Holy Spirit, but rather in the Son, so that He who was in the Godhead of God the Son of God is the true God from the Father, and is a true man from the mother; that He has true flesh from the loins of his mother and a rational human soul, while at the same time possessing both natures, both God and man, in one person. The one Son, one Christ, one God, with the Father and the Holy Spirit, is the ruler and author of all things, born of the Virgin Mary, in a true birth of the flesh. He ate, drank, slept, was tired, and rested from his journey. The true flesh suffered during the Passion; the true flesh arose at the Resurrection; and the true soul was reborn. In the flesh he afterward ate and drank, rose up into heaven, and sat at the right hand of God. We believe in our hearts and confess with our mouths that He will come to judge the living and the dead. We believe in one church, catholic, holy, apostolic, and immaculate, outside of which no one can be saved. Those sacraments that are celebrated in it, through the action of the inestimable and invisible Holy Spirit, may be administered by a sinful priest if the church receives him, whom we can in no way reject. Nor do we avoid the ecclesiastical offices and benedictions celebrated by him, but with a willing heart embrace them as from the most just of men. We therefore accept infant baptism, so that, should the children die after baptism but before having committed sins, we believe they can be saved. We believe that in baptism all sins, both the sin originally contracted and those committed voluntarily, are forgiven. We regard confirmation performed by the bishop through the imposition of hands to be acceptable as both holy and venerable. We firmly believe and simply affirm that the sacrifice, that is, the bread and wine, following the consecration is the body and blood of Jesus Christ, in the course of which nothing more can be done by a good priest, and nothing less by a bad one. We concede that those sinners who are penitent in their hearts and confess with their mouths and receive satisfaction for their deeds can receive pardon from God, and we willingly take communion with them. We venerate the [final] unction of the sick, consecrated with oil. We do not deny, according to the apostles, that carnal marriages may be contracted. We prohibit divorce from a formally contracted marriage, and do not even damn second marriages. We humbly praise and faithfully venerate ecclesiastical orders, that is, the episcopal and priestly, and others both lower and higher, and anything that is ordinarily read or sung in church. We believe that the Devil became evil not because of his nature, but out of his free choice. We do not in the least condemn the consumption of meat. We believe in our own hearts and confess with our mouths that this flesh which we bear and not any other, will be resurrected. We firmly believe and affirm that such persons will in the future be judged according to his own sins, which he has undertaken in his own body, receiving both rewards and punishments.

We do not doubt that the alms and the sacrifice and the other deeds of the faithful can be of benefit to the dead. Because according to the apostle James, faith "without deeds is death," we have renounced the world and have left it. As God has advised, we give charity to the poor and have ourselves become poor so that we do not care what the morrow brings, will take neither gold nor money from anyone, nor will we accept anything beyond our daily food and garments from anyone. We propose to serve the evangelical counsels as basic principles. We believe that those in the world but giving their possessions, alms, or other gifts out of their wealth, serving the principles of God, can be saved. We therefore ask that, at your discretion, if by chance it should happen that some come to you saying they are from us, if they don't follow this faith, you may know for certain that they are not from us.

Statutes Against Heresy (1229)

The following statutes were authorized by Count Raymond of Toulouse against the Cathars following the treaty of Paris, which ended the Albigensian Crusade. These statutes, which largely address confiscation and/or destruction of property belonging to heretics and those who aided or abetted them, indicate the severe economic and political liabilities under which the heretics lived, even in regions such as southern France, where they had received much sympathy.

Source: Jean Domenico Mansi, *Sacrorum Conciliorum nova et amplissima collectio*, 54 vols. (Graz: Akademische Druck- u. Verlagsanstalt, 1960–61), 23: cols. 265–67.

*   *   *

In the name of the holy and undivided Trinity. In order to exalt the Christian faith, extirpate the depravity of heresy, preserve the peace and the good condition of the entire country and make improvements for the better, we Raymond by the grace of God count of Toulouse, with the advice and consent of the bishops, all the prelates, counts, barons, knights, and other prudent men of our land, after considerable deliberation and following deep study of the matter, have decided to lay down these worthwhile regulations for the governance of our lands. As it is our firm intention to rid our land and our subjects of the depravity of heresy, we have decided to follow these regulations both carefully and faithfully.

We have decided that all of our barons, knights, bailiffs, and other persons should show great care and solicitude to pursue, investigate, capture, and punish the heretics, as we promised in the peace of Paris.

We have decided that without delay a legal investigation should be undertaken against those who have killed those persons who have pursued heretics or should do so in the future, and against all the villages and persons of our country who agree to their murder or should agree in the future. Justice should be done against such villages and such persons, and we want this matter to be pursued by us, our barons and our officials.

We have decided that in whatever land or district heretics may be found, in the cities, castles, villages, or even outside them, the men of said city, village, or castle, in whatever house they may be found, should pay one mark for every heretic found there.

We have decided that the aforesaid seneschals and bailiffs who do not act in faith will be removed without delay.

We have decided that all those houses, in which from the time of the peace of Paris a heretic has been found alive, or if this was known to the owner of the house (if he is an adult) or the heretics have preached in said dwelling, should be destroyed. All the property of the inhabitants should be confiscated, unless their lack of knowledge and ignorance of the matter can be clearly proven. Those persons captured in those buildings should be punished in accordance with the law and all those huts which are far removed from the common habitation of the castles, but which it is suspected have served as dwellings for such persons, should be destroyed; the caves should be blocked up; and the suspicious hiding places in those locations which have been so defamed should be utterly destroyed and burned down. In such places no one should dare to build any dwelling or to live in them. If anyone is found in such places after our edict, all his movable goods are to be confiscated and the lords of the castles in which such dwellings are found after the publication of our edict should be punished by having to pay a fine of twenty-five pounds of Toulouse.

We have decided that all the property of those who are heretics or will be in the future is to be confiscated and occupied. Their children and other intestate heirs, even if they are of the orthodox faith, may not inherit through the sale or gift of said goods or in any other way. If said property should be returned or in some other way held by them, it should be immediately taken away. The houses which the heretics have built since the time of said peace or which they may otherwise possess, and which they inhabit, should be destroyed without delay.

We have decided that the following persons should be punished by the confiscation of their goods by those who have the power to arrest: all those who keep inquisitors away from villages, houses, hiding places, or forests; protect heretics who have been found or help those who have found to escape; refuse to aid the inquisitors in capturing heretics when they have been requested by them to do so; or when called upon do not provide assistance, fail to protect those inquisitors who have arrived, or do not provide the assistance which has been demanded; or allow those who have been taken into custody to get away, especially if they are suspected of heresy. Such persons should also be subject to other legal penalties.

We have decided that if suspected heretics should be found, they should swear to be peaceable and accept the Catholic faith, abjuring all heresy. If they refuse to swear loyalty to the Catholic faith and to abjure heresy, they should be punished with the penalties laid down against heretics. If after having taken the oath, persons who have aided and abetted the heretics and have taken part in any way with them should be found, they should be punished in the same way.

We have decided that if anyone after death is found to have been a heretic, if this should be proven by law in the presence of the local bishop, all his property should be confiscated; and the houses which the heretics have built since the peace of Paris and may exist in the future, in which they have lived or will live, are to be destroyed.

We have decided that the lands which have been conferred upon the heretics should be immediately taken away from them unless they can prove that they have been reconciled by means of testimonial letters or it can be proven by other Catholic and upright persons, otherwise they should be confiscated. And even if reconciled, unless they undertake to wear crosses at the order of the bishop or by their own will undertake to wear them, since they ought to wear them prominently displayed on their outer garments on the upper part of their chest, but they are found to be hiding the crosses on their inner garments, they should undergo the same punishment, and whether they possess property or not, they should be forced to pay a similar debt.

We know that the followers of the heretics, when they have wanted to become "perfect ones"[1] in accordance with their hateful ritual, had in earlier times fraudulently sold their possessions and inheritance to the treasury, either giving it or having it pawned, or in other ways managed to get rid of it. We have therefore decided that, notwithstanding the contracts that were

---

1. The "perfect ones" were those persons who had undertaken to live according to the highest Cathar ideals of celibacy and asceticism illustrated in the text which follows, and who would no longer have to undergo earthly reincarnation.

undertaken, these goods should be confiscated. In light of the circumstances of such contracts and of those who undertook them, it appears to us
that those persons to whom these goods were transferred are to be regarded
as parties to fraud. We know that certain "believers" under the guise of
business or on the pretext of undertaking a pilgrimage have transferred
their wealth to heretics, so that because of their absence they manage to
avoid taxation and to remove their property from the treasury's jurisdiction.
If in the local bishop's presence their relatives or those who hold their
property in absentia should be asked or requested within a year to prove
that this action was illegal, in other words that there was no just and reasonable cause for those suspected heretics to be absent, action should be taken
against their relatives and the other persons holding their property, treating
them as if they are heretics, and their property is to be confiscated. If their
heirs or those who hold the property after it has been confiscated can prove
that there was a just and reasonable cause for their absence within the
aforementioned period of time, by law the property should be returned and
given back. . . .

Trial of Arnauda da Lamotha of Montauban (1244)

The most widespread heretical sect in medieval Europe were the Albigensians or Cathars, whose members were concentrated particularly in southern France and northern Italy. They had gained such wide public acceptance
in the late twelfth and early thirteenth centuries that they were able to hold
public councils of their bishops, establish convents, run several municipal
governments, and secure the protection of the nobility and episcopate. In
1208, taking advantage of the assassination of the papal legate Peter of
Castelnau, Pope Innocent III called a crusade against the heretics and their
protectors, enlisting the support of the northern French nobility. The recently established Dominican order had been created with the special aim
of rooting out heresy through word and example; and by about 1229 the
Inquisition had begun to undertake the systematic investigation, apprehension, and punishment of the heretics and their confederates. The following
testimony comes from one of the earliest surviving such trials of heretics,
held by the inquisitor Ferrarius in 1244, and describes the experiences of a
Cathar *perfecta*, who lived a life of stringent asceticism and spent some time
in a Cathar convent. Arnauda was also heard again in 1245/46 by the
Inquisitor Bernard de Caux; the trial protocol incorrectly labels Arnauda a

Waldensian. The most important of the Cathar rituals, the *consolamentum* and the *apparelliamentum*, are here described. As in many other heretical groups, women played a major role in the Cathar movement. Not all sites mentioned in the text can be clearly identified.

Source: Gottfried Koch, *Frauenfrage und Ketzertum* (Berlin: n.p, 1962), *Quellenhang*, 186–89, passim.

Bibliography: Malcolm Lambert, *Medieval Heresy: Popular Movements from the Gregorian Reform to the Reformation*, 2d ed. (Oxford: Oxford University Press, 1994), 105–46, esp. 135–38.

*   *   *

On July 30, 1244 Arnauda da Lamotha of Montauban, a *conversa* in the diocese of Cahors, was called to swear to the truth before all those living and dead, concerning the crime of heresy and Waldensianism. The witness testified that one day two heretical women, whose names she does not know, came to the home of her mother Austorga at Montauban and preached there. This witness, her sister Peirona, their mother Austorga, and Lombarda, the wife of the witness's uncle Isarne Daussac, were present. After the sermon, Austorga and Lombarda "worshiped" the two heretics by making three genuflections before them, and with each genuflection said to them, "Bless me," and they added, "Lord, pray to God for me, a sinner, that He may make me a good Christian and lead me to a good end."

And the heretics replied to each benediction, "May God bless you," and they added after the end of the benediction, "God grant that you become a good Christian and have a good end." When this was done, the heretical women left and went their way. . . . Not only the witness herself, but also her sister Peirona worshipped these heretics, more than thirty-five years ago.

One day, Raymund Aymeric, the heretical deacon of Villemur, and the heretic Bernard de Lamotha came to Montauban to the home of her mother, Austorga, and preached there. The witness, her sister Peirona, and their mother Austorga were present, and after the sermon, Austorga "worshiped" those heretics, as is said, and gave the witness and her sister to them. They took the witness and her sister from Montauban and brought them to Villemur to the home of the heretic Poncia and her heretical companions, who lived there openly. They remained with them for three years, eating at the same table from the bread blessed by the heretics and of whatever else was placed on the table. At any meal of whatever kind of food, at the first libation she said to each of them, "Bless me," and the heretical women replied to each benediction, "May God bless you." The witness and her sister Peirona frequently "worshiped" these heretics there, as is said.

They took the witness and Peirona to the house of Raymund Aymeric, the heretical deacon, who lived openly at Villemur. There the witness and her sister took part in the *consolamentum* in this way. First, the heretics asked the witness and her sister Peirona whether they wanted to devote themselves to God and the Gospel, to which they replied in the affirmative. Next, after being questioned by the heretics, the witness and her sister promised to abstain from eating meat, eggs, cheese, and anything oily, except olives and fish; that they would not swear or lie, give themselves to any passion throughout their lives, and never leave the heretical sect as a result of the fear of punishment by fire or water or any other kind of death. Afterward, the heretics placed their hands and a book over the head of the witness and her sister Peirona and read, making the witness recite a Paternoster in accordance with their ritual. These heretics made many genuflections in their presence and prayed and "gave them peace" with the book. Afterward, their shoulders turned sideways, they kissed them twice on the mouth in turns, and many heretics were present at this *consolamentum*. When this was done, the heretics, the aforementioned Poncia and her heretical companions, returned the witness and Peirona to their home. The witness and her sister remained in that house as members of the heretical sect for a year or more, eating, praying, fasting, blessing the bread at the table, taking part in the *apparelliamentum* ceremony,[1] worshiping those heretics, and doing everything else which male and female heretics are accustomed to do, more than thirty-five years ago. . . .

When she had been at Villemur for a year, crusaders came to that region, and out of fear Raymund Aymeric left Villemur with all the heretical men and women of the village. On the first day after leaving Villemur they came to Roquemaure to the home of the heretical women, whose names she does not know, stayed there, and then hid themselves early in a cave . . . whence they went to Lavaur . . . and stayed there for about a year. . . .

As a result of great fear of persecution, they returned to Montauban and abandoned the heretical sect, ate meat, and were reconciled by the bishop of Cahors more than thirty-two years ago [ca. 1212]. . . .

On a certain day the witness, her sister Peirona, and her mother, Austorga, who had fallen ill, gathered together with the heretical Bernard de

1. The Cathar confession ceremony, held monthly.

Lamotha and his heretical companion, left Montauban, and took the road to Linars, where heretical women lived in monastic garb. The women decided to receive the habit of the nuns and to visit the prioress of Linars and her heretical companion. They left Montauban with the aforementioned heretics and came to Linars and remained there. One day, Gerard Abit came along with his heretical companions, who performed the *apparelliamentum* for the heretical women, i.e., all those who lived in that house at Linars, as many as sixteen women . . . twenty years ago [1224].[2]

Beatrice of Planisolles (1320)

The trial of the accused Cathar Beatrice Clergue of Planisolles began on June 19, 1320. Her own testimony was elicited between July 23 and August 20, 1320 in the presence of Bishop Jacques Fournier of Pamiers and the Dominican friar Gaillard de Pomiès. The village of Montaillou, whose inhabitants were the chief objects of the trial, had passed into the hands of the counts of Foix in the thirteenth century and was clearly a hotbed of heresy. Beatrice herself was condemned to death on the walls of Carcasonne, but this sentence was commuted to wearing a double cross on her outer garments for the rest of her life as a sign of repentance and rejection of the Cathar heresy. Beatrice's case illustrates how persons living on the margins were often "guilty" of violating more than one taboo. Sexual nonconformity, egalitarian ideology, religious heresy, and the practice of witchcraft are all noted in her testimony. She was sentenced on March 8, 1321. After her testimony was read out to her, Beatrice in fact made corrections and changes, so that her account of Cathar belief is not wholly accurate; also, because the inquisitorial register does not survive in full, we cannot be entirely sure whether her remarks are complete.

Source: Jean Duvernoy, ed., *Le registre d'Inquisition de Jacques Fournier (1318–1325)*, 3 vols. (Paris: Édouard Privat, 1965–68), 1: 214–50 passim. For another translation see Patrick J. Geary, ed., *Readings in Medieval History*, 2d ed. (Peterborough, Ont.: Broadview Press, 1997), 500–519.

Bibliography: Emmanuel Le Roy Ladurie, *Montaillou: The Promised Land of Error*, trans. Barbara Bray (New York: Braziller, 1978).

*   *   *

2. Most of the testimony similarly describes the heretics' wanderings, their meeting places, and the network of believers who took part in the ceremonies and lived as *perfecti*.

Twenty-six years ago [1294] in August (she doesn't remember the day), when she was still married to the knight Berengar de Roquefort, the late chatelain of Montaillou, the late Raimond Roussel de Prades was the intendant and steward of his house, which was situated at the castle of Montaillou. Raimond Roussel often asked her to go with him to Lombardy to visit the good Christians [Cathars] who live there; telling her that God had said that one who abandoned father, mother, wife, husband, son, and daughter to follow Him will be given the kingdom of Heaven. When she asked him, "How can I leave my husband and children," he replied that God has ordered it; and that it is better for a woman to abandon a husband and children whose eyes are fouled than to abandon He who lives forever and grants the Kingdom of Heaven.

When the speaker asked him, "How can it be that God created men and women, since so many of them are not saved?" Raimond replied that only good Christians will be saved, and no one else; neither the religious [monks], priests, nor anyone except good Christians. For just as a camel cannot pass through the eye of a needle, so it is impossible for the rich to be saved. Therefore the kings and princes, the prelates and the religious, and all who possess wealth cannot be saved, only the good Christians. [He said that] they stayed in Lombardy because they do not dare live here, where the wolves and dogs persecute them, telling her that these wolves and dogs are the bishops and Dominican friars who persecute good Christians and drive them from this country.[1] He said that he had kept some of these good Christians. They were the kind of people who, once having heard them, one couldn't live without them; and if she were to hear them, she would belong to them forever.

She asked him how the two of them could flee and reach the good Christians, since if her husband found out, he would pursue and kill her. Raimond replied that, when her husband takes a long trip and is far away, they would be able to leave and visit the good Christians. Asked how they would live when they get there, he said that they would provide for them. When the speaker told him that she was pregnant and asked what she would do with the child she was carrying if she went away to visit the good Christians; Raimond replied that if she give birth among the good Christians the child would be an angel; with God's help he will be made a king and will be holy, for he will be born without sin, not having had contact

---

1. The Dominicans customarily referred to themselves as "dogs of God," derived from *Domini* ("of God" in Latin) and *cani* ("dogs" in Latin).

with persons of this world. They will teach him perfectly in their sect, because the child will not have learned from another sect.[2] She said that Raimond had told her that in the beginning all spirits were guilty of the sin of pride, believing they could know more and be higher than God. Such spirits later acquire bodies, and the world will not end until all of them have taken on the bodies of men and women. For that reason an infant's soul is as old as that of an old man.

He told her that the souls of men and women who have not been good Christians, having left their bodies, enter anew the bodies of other men and women nine times. If in one of these new bodies a good Christian is not to be found, the soul is damned. If it is the body of a good Christian, the soul will be saved.

When the speaker asked Raimond how the spirit of a dead man or woman can enter the mouth of an infant who is still in the womb, Raimond replied that the spirit can enter an infant still in its mother's womb through whatever part of the woman's body that it wants.

When she asked why children can't speak immediately when they are born, since they possess the old souls of other persons, Raimond replied that God doesn't want this. He said that God's spirits who have sinned live wherever they can. She said that Raimond encouraged her to leave with him and they went together to the good Christians, after he told her about several noblewomen who had also gone to them.

He said that Alesta and Serena, women of Chateauverdun, had put on makeup so they would not be recognized and had gone to Toulouse.[3] At a certain inn, the hostess had wanted to discover whether or not they were heretics. She gave them live chickens, telling them to prepare them since she had to go to town, and then she left the house. When she returned, found the chickens still alive, and asked why they hadn't been prepared, the women replied that if the hostess would kill the chickens they would prepare them, but they themselves wouldn't kill them. Hearing this, the hostess

2. A thirteenth-century heretical source, the *Anonymous of Passau*, argued that an infant among the Cathars could grow up to be a bishop if it were raised on almond milk and fish without eating meat.

3. This Alesta was Agnes de Durban, the sister of the count of Foix and wife of Pierre Arnaud of Chateauverdun. Serena was the wife of Athon Arnaud and sister of Pierre Roger of Mirepoix, the defender of the besieged fortress of Montségur. In the course of a war between Count Raymond VII of Toulouse and King Louis IX of France, a group of heretics from the fortress of Montségur, near Foix, killed several papal inquisitors at Avignonet. The royal seneschal besieged Montségur for nine months; over two hundred Cathars were captured, investigated, and burned. During this period, both Agnes and Serena were condemned to death as Cathars.

reported to the Inquisitors the presence of two heretics in her home. They were captured and burned; when they were about to be set ablaze, they asked for water to wash their faces, saying they didn't want to meet God with painted faces.

The speaker said to Raimond that it would have been better had those women rejected heresy rather than allow themselves to be burned. Raimond replied that good Christians don't feel the fire, since it can do them no harm. He said that one of those women, when she was about to leave the house at Chateauverdun, had a child in swaddling clothes whom she wanted to see before she left; she kissed him, and the child smiled. She began to leave, but returned, and the child laughed; this happened so often that she saw that she would be unable to leave the infant, and therefore instructed the maidservant to take him out of the house; when this was done, she left. He told her this in order to encourage the speaker to do the same thing.

Raimond told her that Stephania, wife of the late Guillaume Arnaud, a lady of Chateauverdun, had abandoned everything and had gone to the good Christians [ca. 1295] along with Prades Tavernier, who afterward, when he had become a heretic, was called André. He told the speaker all this in order to encourage her to leave. She replied that if two or three equal to her in social rank would join them, then she would have an excuse to leave with Raimond. Otherwise, she wouldn't be able to leave, since she was still young, and people would say that they'd left the country merely to satisfy their lust.

After having instructed her at various times and in different places concerning his heretical views, and after having induced her to leave with him, one night after they had eaten Raimond secretly entered the room where she slept and hid under the bed. After the affairs of the house had been dealt with, she went to bed; when she and everyone else were sleeping quietly, Raimond sneaked out from under the bed, and got under the covers with her, behaving as though he wanted to lie carnally with her. The speaker said, "What is this?"

Raimond told her to be quiet, to which she replied, "You bumpkin, why should I be quiet!" and began to shout and call her maidservants, who lay in the room beside her, telling them that there was a man in bed with her. When Raimond heard this he got out of the bed and room. The next day, he told the speaker that it was evil to run away with her. She replied, "I now see that you invited me to go to those good Christians only in order to have me and know me carnally. If I weren't afraid that my husband would

believe that something dishonest had occurred between us, I would immediately have you cast into a dungeon." . . .

She said that about twenty-one years ago [ca. 1299], about a year after
her husband's death, she went to the church of Montaillou during Lent to
confess her sins. When she was there, she went up to the rector, Pierre
Clergue, who was hearing confessions behind the altar of St. Mary. As she
bent down before him, he kissed her, saying that there was no woman in the
world he loved more than her. Much surprised, she left him without making confession. Later, during Easter, the rector often visited her and asked
to know her carnally. One day when he solicited her in her home, she said
that she'd rather know four men carnally than one priest, since she'd heard it
said that a woman who knows a priest carnally cannot see the face of God.
The rector responded that she was foolish and stupid, since a woman's sin is
the same whether she knows her husband or another man, the same for her
husband or a priest. The sin is even greater with one's own husband, since
the wife doesn't believe she is sinning with him, but is aware when she is
with another man. Therefore the sin is clearly greater in the first case.

She asked the rector how, as a priest, he could speak in this way, since
in church one is told that marriage was established by God, that it is the first
sacrament established between Adam and Eve, as a result of which there is
no sin when a man and wife know each other.

The rector replied, "If it is God who created marriage between Adam
and Eve, and he also created them, why didn't he protect them from sin?"
She remembered his saying that God had not created Adam and Eve and
established marriage between them. He added that the church often says
things which aren't true, and ecclesiastical persons say these things despite
the fact that they themselves don't believe or respect such things. For aside
from the Gospel and the Lord's Prayer, all the other texts of Scripture are
foolish [*affitilhas*], which is a word often used in the vernacular to refer to
something one simply believes oneself or has heard from others.

The speaker replied that in that case the ecclesiastics are misleading
the people.

On August 8 . . . continuing her confession, she said that with respect
to marriage Pierre said that many of the rules do not proceed from God's
will. God did not decide that a man ought not to take as a wife his biological
sister or another blood relative, because in the beginning of the world
brothers knew their own sisters. But when several brothers had one or two
beautiful sisters, each wanting to have one or both, many murders took

place between them. The church therefore decided that a brother should not know his own sister or any relative carnally. But in God's eyes it is as much of a sin to know another woman as to know own's own sister or another relative, since this sin is as great with one woman as with another, with the exception that it is not as great a sin between a man and his own wife . . . since married persons do not confess to having known each other and one does so without shame.

He said that marriage is perfect and complete when one pledges one's faith to another; what takes place in church between married persons — for example, the nuptial blessing — is mere worthless secular pomp, and was instituted by the church only for the sake of worldly pomp. The rector told the speaker that a man or woman may perform any sin while they live in the world and do as they please. It is enough for a man or woman to be accepted into the sect of the good Christians at the end of their lives for them to be saved and absolved of all sins they may have committed in their lives, because Christ told the apostles that he who abandons father, mother, wife, and children, and whatever they have to follow Him, will possess the kingdom of Heaven [Matthew 19.27, James 5]. Peter had replied to Christ, "If we abandon all and follow you, and thus have the Kingdom of Heaven, what will happen to those who are weak and cannot follow you?" The Lord replied to Peter that his friends would come to place their hands on the heads of the weak and they would be cured, and those who were cured would follow Him and thus possess the Kingdom of Heaven.

The rector said that these "friends of God" were the good Christians and those whom others call heretics; through the imposition of their hands, if men or women are near death, they are saved and absolved of whatever sins they may have committed. In order to prove that it might be better for the world if a brother were permitted to marry his sister, he said, "Look, we are four brothers, I am a priest and I don't want to marry. If my brothers Guillaume and Bernard had married our sisters Esclarmonde and Guille-mette, our lineage would not have been destroyed, because our sisters had to give a dowry. Otherwise, the house would have remained intact. With the assistance of the one woman whom our brother Raimond brought into the house, we would have had enough women, and the family would have been wealthier than it is. It would therefore be better for a brother to take his sister than a strange woman, or even that a sister should take her brother as a husband, since when she leaves her paternal home with a dowry to marry a stranger, the house may be ruined."

As a consequence of these and similar remarks, the speaker said that she consented to have relations with him one night in her home during the octave of saints Peter and Paul [July 6]; he knew her carnally for about a year and a half, and then two or three times a week at night she lay with him in her home near the chateau of Montaillou. She even came to the rector's house for two nights in order to have relations with him. One night during Christmas the priest knew her carnally and celebrated mass the next day, although no other priest was present.[4] When once this same Christmas night he wanted to have relations with her, she said to him, "How can you want to commit such a grave sin on such a holy night?" He replied that it is as grave a sin to have sex with a woman on Christmas night as it is on any other night. When on this occasion and on the other frequent occasions he celebrated mass the day after she had relations with him, he did not confess to any priest, because none were present. She often asked him how he dared to celebrate mass when he had committed such a grave sin the previous night without confessing to a priest; he replied that the only true confession is the one made to God, who knows about a sin before it has even been committed, and only he can absolve one of sin. The confession, on the other hand, made to a priest who only knows about this sin when it has been revealed to him and who cannot absolve one of sin, is not valid; it is only undertaken for show and pomp, since only God can absolve from sin and no man has such power.

The priest told the speaker that she should not confess to any priest about the sin she had committed with him because it is enough to confess to God, who knows all her sins and can absolve her, something no other man can do. In order to convince her to believe that no pope nor bishop nor priest under him has the power to absolve from sin, he argued that Saint Peter was not "apostolic" when he was alive, but only after he died and his bones were thrown into a well where they lay for many years. When his bones were found they were washed and were put in the throne on which the Roman pontiffs have their seat.[5] But since these bones of St. Peter do not have the power to absolve from sin, when they had been placed in the throne and "made apostolic," neither was Peter himself thereby made apostolic, nor did the Roman pontiffs who sit on the throne thereby receive the apostolic power to absolve from sin. Only the good Christians who are persecuted and suffer death like saints Lawrence, Stephen, and Bartholomew can absolve from sin. The bishops and priests subject to the Roman

---

4. This was presumably in order to impose absolution, as the priest was in a state of sin.
5. St. Peter's in Rome.

church, who are heretics and persecute good Christians, do not have the power to absolve from sin; for this power was taken from them by God and only given to the good Christians, who knew and predicted that they would undergo persecution.

She asked the priest, if it is true that since no confession made to a priest is of value, priests cannot absolve from sin, nor does the satisfaction meted out by them have any value, why does he hear confessions, absolve, and impose satisfaction? He replied that, although what he and other priests do is invalid, they do so because otherwise they will lose their incomes and nothing will be given to them unless they do what the church prescribes. Good Christians and others received by them after having adored[6] them can absolve others from sin. It is not necessary for those who have been absolved by them of their sins to confess their sins. They must rather give themselves to God and to the good Christians who will absolve them by placing their hands over their heads, and they will be absolved of all their sins. . . .

The priest then said that only God made the spirits and could not have made what is corrupted and destroyed, since the works of God are eternal, whereas the bodies we see and feel, the heavens and the earth and all that is in them, except for the spirits, were made by the Devil, the governor of the world. Because the Devil did this, everything will be corrupted, since he cannot do anything which is stable and permanent.

The priest told the speaker that when in the beginning God made a man who walked and spoke, after the Devil saw this, he made the body of another man who could neither walk nor talk. God then said to the Devil, "Why don't you make your man walk and talk?" The Devil replied that he couldn't, but asked God to make his man walk and talk. God replied that he would willingly do so provided whatever he placed in the Devil's man would belong to God. The Devil replied that whatever was placed by God in this man would indeed belong to Him. God then breathed into the mouth of the man made by the Devil, and the man began to walk and talk. As a result, man's soul belongs to God and his body to the Devil.

The priest told her that God had made all the spirits in heaven, which had then committed the sin of pride, wanting to be equal to God. Because of this sin, they fell from heaven into the air and the earth where they dwell, and enter into the bodies which they encounter indiscriminately whenever they can, so they enter equally into the bodies of brute beasts and human beings, with the exception that they can't speak when they inhabit the

6. This refers to the Cathar ceremony of *melioramentum*.

bodies of brute beasts. The spirits found in the bodies of brute beasts possess reason and knowledge, so that because of this it appears that they avoid what is injurious to them and desire and pursue what is useful. For this reason it is an equal sin to kill a brute beast as it is to kill a person, since both brute beasts and humans possess the spirit of reason and knowledge. All said spirits must enter some human body in which to do penance for the sin of pride; and this must happen before the world comes to an end. These spirits can do penance for this sin only while they dwell in human bodies, but not while in the bodies of brute beasts.

The priest said that those spirits that have sinned in this way are very happy if they are able to enter into the body of a good Christian. Immediately upon leaving their bodies they return to heaven, from whence they had fallen. But if they have not left the body of a good Christian, but rather that of another man or woman, when they exit that body they enter into the body of another man or woman if they can, and they enter nine bodies if they haven't succeeded again in entering the bodies of a good male or female Christian. Once entering such a body they immediately afterward exit and return to heaven from which they had fallen. But if after successively entering nine bodies such a spirit has not entered that of a good Christian man or woman, after leaving the ninth one such a spirit is lost forever and cannot be penitent afterward. This is generally the case, although those spirits which have consented to the betrayal of Christ, such as Judas and other Jews, after having exited their bodies, are immediately damned, unable to do penance afterward or to enter other bodies in order to do penance. But those spirits which were present at the betrayal of Christ and did not agree to that betrayal will in the end enter nine bodies, like the other spirits.

The priest told her that only those spirits which enter the bodies of good Christians will be saved, and no others, whether they be good Christians, Jews, or Saracens; and all good Christians and all who adore them, believe in them, and are accepted into their sect will be saved. Because of this his own mother Mengarde will be saved, for she did many good things for said good Christians. Na Roca and Raimond Roche his son, who were imprisoned for a while for the crime of heresy, received all their food from her house. Because these two persons were heretics and believers, his mother had been good to them.

The priest said that when such spirits were in heaven and sinned by rebelling against God, they were divided. Some of them had conspired to revolt against God and were the first to be expelled from heaven. Their sin was so serious that God had refused to receive their penance, and they would be destroyed in Hell. They are the demons. In contrast, the other spirits who did not plan to rebel against God nor openly showed contempt, but had rather wanted merely to follow those who had planned the rebellion, fell down to the earth and air, became incarnate in human and animal bodies, and may be saved or damned, as noted above.

The priest said that the good Christians do not believe that God makes the seeds which generate, flower, and grow those things which are born on earth. If this were the case, then God could equally make seeds grow on a naked stone, just as takes place in arable soil. Those seeds thrown on a stone could grow as well as those thrown on the ground. This rather takes place because of the enrichment of the soil, not because God has acted in some way.

The priest said that the good Christians do not believe that Christ was incarnate in the blessed Virgin or descended into her in order to take human flesh from her, since even before the blessed Mary was born, Christ existed from eternity.[7] He merely "adumbrated" himself in the blessed Mary, taking nothing from her. The word *adumbration* means that, if a man were inside a cask, he receives nothing inside the shadow of that cask from the cask itself, but is only contained therein. In the same way Christ dwelled within the Virgin Mary, receiving nothing from her, but was only in her as the contents is held within its container.

The priest said that when Christ ate with his disciples he never ate or drank, although he appeared to eat and drink.

Because Christ was crucified on the cross, no one should venerate or adore the cross, because so much vituperation was hurled at Christ when he was on it.

Swearing falsely on a book of the Gospels is not a lie, but only if one swears in God's name.

The Church of God exists only where there is a good Christian, because he is the Church of God, but otherwise there is no church of God, nor are other persons the Church of God.

When good Christians are burned because of their faith, they are martyrs of Christ.

When good Christians receive someone into their sect, they should afterward neither eat nor drink, except cold water. When they die weakly in this way because they don't want to eat, they become the saints of God.

7. See John 8.58: "Jesus said unto them, Verily verily, I say unto you, Before Abraham was, I am."

The fire in which the good Christians burn does not consume them, because God helps them not to be burned by that fire, and they do not suffer much.

She said that Raimond Rosselli told her that when a certain man was seriously ill, a priest came to him and asked if he wanted to see and receive the body of Christ. He said he wanted to do so more than anything else. The priest went to get the body of Christ and brought it to the sick man. After he took it out of its pix [a receptacle to hold the Eucharist] and held it in his hands, showing it to the sick man, and asked him about the articles of the faith, particularly if he believed this was the body of Christ, the sick man angrily said to the priest, "You stinking country bumpkin! If you are holding the body of Christ and it were as big as a large mountain, all you priests would have already eaten it." This sick man refused to accept the body of Christ.

The priest Pierre Clergue said that this visible world which the Devil made is totally corrupt, will become nothing, and will be destroyed. But before this happens, God will bring "his friends" [the Cathars] together and will gather them together to him, so that they won't witness a catastrophe as great as the end of the world and be destroyed. . . .

On August 12, 1320, she said that . . . while her husband was still alive, on a certain day, Raimond Clergue, alias Pathau, the natural son of Guillaume Clergue (who was himself the brother of Pons Clergue, who is the father of Pierre Clergue, the present priest of Montaillou), raped and carnally knew her in the castle of Montaillou. A year later, her husband, Berengar de Roquefort, died, and Raimond Clergue kept her publicly.

The rector, the brother of Raimond Clergue, knew perfectly well that Raimond had possessed her, but that didn't keep him from soliciting her to know him carnally. She asked how he could demand such a thing, since he know very well that his cousin Raimond had her, and she revealed everything.

The rector replied that it was neither by force nor very difficult, saying, "I know it's so and I can be of greater benefit to you and give you more than that faker." He told her that both he and said Raimond could both have her at the same time; to which she replied that she would in no way allow such a thing because of the dissension that would arise between them, and because one would treat her contemptuously because of the other. When the priest slept with her she didn't have relations with Raimond, although he occasionally made an effort.

She said that as a result there was a hidden hatred brewing between Raimond and the priest, which she was aware of.

She said that when she was at Dalou after having married her second husband, Othon de Laglieze, a marriage that took place on the Assumption of St. Mary, during the time of the fair, the priest came to Dalou, pretending he had come from Limoux. Coming to her home, he told her that her sister Gentille, who lives at Limoux, had sent her regards, and she let him in. They knew each other carnally in the basement while her maidservant Sibilla, former wife of Arnaud Teisseyre, stood guard at the cellar door. The night before she had given the speaker the veil of a blouse made in Barcelona, decorated with red and yellow silken lace, sent by Pierre, and she said he would come the next morning. . . . When the sin had been perpetrated, she led the priest out of her house. Near the outer gate she instructed him to give five sous to Bernard Belot . . . for the heretics. . . .

On August 22, 1320 . . . she said that . . . when she was living in Prades after her first husband's death, she dwelled in a small house situated between the home of Jean Clergue, rector of Prades, and the home of Pierre Guilhem. Since his house was adjacent to the priest's home, everything that happened could be heard in the neighboring dwelling. The priest Pierre Clergue of Montaillou, who had come to see her, said that on the next night he would send his student Jean (whose family name she didn't know) to look for her so that she could sleep with him, and she agreed. She waited for the student that night when the first hour sounded. He came and took her in the dead of night to the church of St. Peter of Prades, and they went in. There they found Pierre Clergue, who had prepared a bed in the church. She said to him, "How can we do something like this in the church of St. Peter?" To which the rector replied, "Damn St. Peter!"[8] They then went to bed and lay together in the church, having sexual relations. . . .

She said that when they began their relationship, she said to the priest, "What will I do if I become pregnant by you? I'll be dishonored and lost." The rector told her that he was in possession of an herb which, when it is taken by a man when he lies with a woman, acts so that the man cannot generate and the woman cannot conceive.

She replied, "What kind of herb is it? Is it what dairy farmers put over milk vats in which they have put rennet and which can retard coagulation while it is over the vat?" He replied that he didn't care what herb it was, but

8. This appears in the protocol in Provençal.

it had the aforementioned properties, and he possessed it. From that point onward whenever he wanted to know the speaker carnally he wore a certain object wrapped up and tied in a piece of linen cloth the size and length of an ounce, or of the first digit of the little finger of her hand, and which had a long string that he placed around his neck when he had sexual relations with her. This object, which was an herb, hung by a string between her breasts and rested on the opening of the speaker's stomach. Whenever he wanted to know her carnally he always wore this object and rested it on the speaker's neck. When he wanted to get up or she wanted to get up, he would take the object off her neck. Whenever he wanted to know her carnally twice in one night or more, before they had relations he would ask her where the herb was. She would take it by finding the string and place it in his hand, and he would place the herb in the opening of her stomach, placing the string between her breasts and in this way he had sexual relations with her in this way and in no other way.

The speaker said that when she asked the priest to give her the herb, he said that he wouldn't because she could then have sexual relations with another man and not get pregnant by him if she should wear that herb.[9] . . .

On August 25 . . . many suspicious objects for performing witchcraft were found among her possessions, which she knew to be hers and which she had, such as the umbilical cords of two children, which were found in her purse, some rags covered with blood, which appeared to be menstrual, which were found in a leather sack in which was also found colewort seeds; in addition there were, a certain amount of burned incense grains, a mirror and a small knife wrapped in linen cloth, the grain of a certain herb wrapped in muslin, a bit of dry bread known as "tinhol," and some writing on many pieces of linen. Because of this there was a strong presumption that Beatrice had used witchcraft and magic. She was questioned about these matters before the lord bishop.

She replied that the umbilical cords of children she had belonged to her daughters' sons, since a certain woman, formerly a Jewess but afterward baptized, had taught her that if she were to keep the umbilical cord of male children and kept them on her person, should she have a quarrel with anyone, she would not lose. For this reason she had these umbilical cords from her grandchildren with her and kept them. Within that period of time

---

9. After Beatrice's testimony was over, a summary was included, from which the final section is drawn.

she had had no quarrel with anyone, whereby she could prove the efficacy of the umbilical cord.

She said that the bits of cloth stained with blood was stained with the menstrual blood of her own daughter Philippa, because the baptized Jewess had said that if she had the blood which came out at her daughter's first menstruation, and gave it to her daughter's husband to drink, or to any other man, this man would afterward never care for another woman, except for the one whose first menstrual blood he drank.[10] Therefore, when her daughter Philippa had her first menstruation, knowing by looking at the girl what had happened, she asked her, and the girl replied that blood had come out of her body. She then remembered the words of the baptized Jewess, tearing off part of Philippa's blouse, which was covered with blood. Because it didn't seem as though there was enough on the rag, she gave Philippa another piece of soft cloth so that when the blood oozed out of her she would dip it into the blood and soak it completely. Philippa did so. She put aside those rags, intending that when Philippa got married she would give them to her husband to drink from the blood which had been soaked into those rags. In the course of the year that Philippa had gotten engaged to that man, she twice proposed to give Philippa's husband the blood to drink; but, as she said, she thought it would be better to do this when Philippa's husband had known her carnally, when Philippa would give it to him to drink. But because when the speaker was captured the marriage between Philippa and her husband had not yet been consummated, nor had the marriage itself been celebrated, she had therefore not yet given it to Philippa's husband to drink.

She said that the rags had not been placed in her bag with the grains of incense in order to perform some magic, but it just happened that way. She had it, she said, because her daughter Philippa had suffered an infirmity in her head that year, and the incense was mixed with other things in order to cure the infirmity. The grains of incense found in her bag had otherwise been left there, and she had no intention of doing anything else with them.

She did not have the mirror and small knife which had been wrapped up, or the bits of linen cloth, in order to carry out witchcraft or magic.

The grain which had been wrapped up and the grain which comes from an herb called *ive* in the vernacular had been given to her that year by a certain pilgrim. The pilgrim had said that the grain was powerful against

---

10. In his eleventh-century confessional code, Burchard of Worms imposed a penance of five years on women who placed their menstrual blood in their husbands' food in order to arouse their passions.

falling sickness. Since that year her grandson, the son of her daughter Condors, suffered from falling sickness, she wanted to make use of the grain, but
her daughter had said that she would take her son to the church of St. Paul,
where he would be cured of said disease. Condors did not want her to do
anything for her son for said illness; so that, as she said, she had not made
any use of said grain. . . .

Flordebellina of Milan and Others (1300), Disciples of Guglielma

According to her disciples, in about 1271, Guglielma, the alleged daughter
of the king of Bohemia, had appeared in Milan with a child in her arms. She
was surrounded by a corps of followers who wondered at her stigmata and
miracle-working powers. After her burial at the Cistercian monastery of
Chiaravalle in 1282, a cult under the patronage of the powerful Visconti
arose. In 1300, following the exhumation of Guglielma's bones, her disciples, including many noblewomen of Milan, were summoned before the
Inquisition. According to one of the sect's leaders, the Archangel Raphael
had announced the incarnation of Guglielma to Queen Constance of Bohemia. The head of her church was one Manfreda, a cousin of the Visconti;
while the cardinals of the sect were female devotees, who would succeed the
Roman hierarchy after the Second Coming. As the incarnation of the Holy
Ghost, Guglielma had supposedly infused her disciples with the divine
spirit. Politically, these Guglielmites were avid opponents of Pope Boniface
VIII and supporters of the Visconti faction, themselves accused of black
magic and other evil deeds. Many were also apparently members of the
order of the Humiliati, a primarily lay organization of urban religious devoted to handicrafts and the simple spiritual life. The following selection,
drawn from the protocol of the trial held between April 19, 1300 and
February 12, 1302, illustrates the appeal of heresy to women. In this sect,
the deity and the priesthood are female.

Source: Felice Tocco, ed., "Il processo dei Guglielmiti," in *Rendiconti della Reale
Accademia dei Lincei*, Memorie della classe di scienze morali, storiche et filologiche
Ser. V, vol. 8 (Rome, 1899), 309–42, 351–84, 407–32, 437–69.

Bibliography: Steven Wessley, "The Thirteenth-Century Guglielmites: Salvation
Through Women," in *Medieval Women*, ed. Derek Baker, Studies in Church History,
Subsidia 1 (Oxford: Blackwell, 1978), 289–303.

*   *   *

Sister Flordebellina . . . was asked if she ever believed or was taught that Guglielma, who is buried at Chiaravalle, was a saint, that she might be the Holy Spirit and the third person of the Trinity. She answered that she had heard this, but no longer. Asked if her father Andrew Saramita believed these things, she said that even Andrew believed this in Manfreda's day, which was a long time ago, but not now. Asked if Manfreda herself had preached about the Gospels and the Epistles, she said that she sometimes spoke good words concerning the Gospel, St. Catherine, and St. Margaret. Asked how many were present at the sermon, she said that about ten or twelve women were present. Asked if she knew any women who had led others to the cult of St. Guglielma, she said no. Asked if she partook of the host that was brought from Chiaravalle and was placed above the tomb of Guglielma, she said, "Franceschino Malcozati frequently brought the host, gave it to his mother, and even to me, Flordebellina, and I ate three times out of devotion to St. Guglielma." Asked how many times they held festivities devoted to St. Guglielma, she said twice: once on the feast of St. Bartholomew, and at another time on the day of the translation of St. Bartholomew in October. Asked if she believed or was taught that St. Guglielma would return before the general resurrection and ascend into heaven, she said that she did not believe this and had never heard it said. Asked who was responsible for the garments, preparations, and all else necessary for the cult of St. Guglielma, she said that her father Andrew Saramita had these things made and procured them. Asked if she knew any other person who had procured these things or made payments for this purpose, she replied that she did not know anyone else besides Andrew. Asked if she saw any of the water in which St. Guglielma was washed at death, she said that she had, in the house of Blasso, of the order of the Humiliati.[1] . . .

Asked if she ever heard or was taught or believed that this Guglielma would ascend into heaven just as Christ ascended, she said that she had heard this frequently, and was taught and believed and heard this from her father and from sister Manfreda. Asked if she had ever heard it said or was taught that sister Manfreda would be pope on earth as vicar of St. Guglielma, just at St. Peter was the vicar of Christ on earth, she replied that she heard this frequently, and believed and was taught and heard this from her father and from sister Manfreda. Asked if she heard and was taught

1. A religious order of lay and clergy founded in the late twelfth century centered in northern Italy. It was condemned at first as heretical, but a recognized order was established under Innocent III, although some of its members continued to reject ecclesiastical control.

and believed that the aforesaid St. Guglielma would redeem and save the Jews, Saracens, and false Christians, she answered that she had heard this frequently. . . .

Mistress Petrea de Alzate and Mistress Katella de Gioziis . . . said and confessed that they heard . . . that St. Guglielma, who is buried at Chiaravalle, was the Holy Spirit, and that in her resides the substance of the holy and divine spirit. . . . This Guglielma is supposed to appear again bodily and visibly and in the presence of many people will ascend into heaven. They said that the Jews and Saracens would be saved by her, just as Christians were saved by Christ. They said that Andrew especially taught that . . . Manfreda . . . should have the power of loosing, just as St. Peter did, because the Holy Spirit had come in the form of a woman in this Guglielma; so that sister Manfreda ought to be the vicar of the same Guglielma in the form of a woman. They said that sister Manfreda gave them the host, which she blessed, and even gave it to two other women, and it was brought from the tomb of St. Guglielma, and the witnesses ate and gave some to their sons to eat. . . .

Mistress Petra . . . answered that Manfreda sometimes said to them and to others, "If you are cited by the inquisitors, you should not enter their presence before you have spoken to me, nor should you speak the truth except as I direct you." . . .

They said that when they went to Manfreda's house, they and other women kissed first her foot and then her hand. They said that Manfreda told them that just as Christ had sent the Holy Spirit to the apostles, so all of the devotees of St. Guglielma would receive the Holy Spirit. They said that Manfreda had said that all of the devotees of St. Guglielma ought to perform baptism and ought to be the apostles of Christ. . . .

Thomassa (1318), Disciple of Clare of Montefalco

The following comes from the testimony of Sister Thomassa at the canonization hearing devoted to Clare of Montefalco (1268/75–1308), also known as Clare of the Cross. Despite her many reported physical infirmities, Clare had battled heretics in her native Umbria. Her verbal battles with the Fraticelli, a radical apocalyptic and anti-papal offshoot of the Franciscan order and with the Brethren of the Free Spirit are here described. The Free Spirit allegedly advocated free love and held the view that one could live without sin. The penitential Flagellants, still regarded as orthodox and

also alluded to here, had begun roaming about central Italy in 1260, flagellating themselves in anticipation of the Second Coming in order to punish
their souls for sin and purge their bodies of desire. Clare is here depicted
using her power to assist the Inquisition in the persecution of such heterodox groups.

Source: Livario Oliger, ed., *De secta spiritus libertatis in Umbria saec. xiv. Disquisitio et
documenta* (Rome: Edizioni di "Storia e letteratura," 1943), 103–19 passim.

Bibliography: Robert Lerner, *The Heresy of the Free Spirit in the Later Middle Ages*
(Berkeley: University of California Press, 1972).

*　　*　　*

Sister Thomassa, daughter of the deceased Master Angelo de Montefalco,
said that she had heard from St. Clare herself that, in a certain place and at a
certain time, she had seen in the valley of Spoleto naked men flagellating
themselves, going through the cities, villages, and countryside in disorderly
groups saying that they were doing this as penance and because of their
reverence for God. St. Clare had a revelation in which she saw a great house
in which was standing a crucified demon. Many people stood around this
crucifixion in reverence. This crucifixion emitted a heat that seemed to
excite those who stood about to indulge in vices and carnal pleasures. St.
Clare reported this vision to this witness and to some other sisters, and
spoke to them, especially to this witness, saying, "You will see that from this
congregation of Flagellants much evil will arise." After that time, from a
number of these Flagellants there came and developed the followers and
teachers of the error of the Free Spirit. She said that Clare predicted many
things concerning these Flagellants through divine revelation, concerning
which it is not reported.

The witness reported that she had heard from St. Clare that she had
refuted a certain Franciscan brother named Joannuctio de Mevania of the
Friars Minor, concerning the devilish temptation or illusion of the Devil
which he had experienced. The sisters of the monastery did not know that,
as a result, he came to the monastery more frequently in order to celebrate
mass more often than had been his custom.

Quite often she had heard Clare preaching about persons who would
come to the monastery in order to spread poison under the guise of sanctity
but with a false heart. People of this ilk afterward did come to the monastery. Before they came, she warned the women to beware and not to speak

to them unless she were present, fearing for them as for her flock. Clare told the sisters that those brethren and false religious would at first speak with subtlety about the spirit, so that they might afterward more easily achieve their false purpose. Asked if she recalled the appearance of some of those who came, she said that she did not remember individuals, but recalled well that Clare warned them to beware of some Fraticelli and Franciscans who roam about and adhere to the heresy of the Free Spirit. . . . This warning occurred at the time when many flagellated themselves.

Asked how she knew, the witness said that she had seen and been present when Clare spoke at length with brother Bentivenga;[1] and among the many things which brother Bentivenga had said at the beginning concerning God and spiritual matters, and which she heard afterward, Clare reported that he had mixed in much that sounded like and contained the error of the Free Spirit. Having heard these things, Clare had answered this brother with great fervor, reprimanding him about his error and refuting much. . . . Brother Bentivenga said to Clare, among other things, "Don't you believe that it is possible for a man to be with a woman a whole night and know her, and still celebrate mass with his hand?" Clare replied that she didn't believe it was possible. They exchanged many words and much disagreement over this matter.

Asked if the friar then posed any other question, she replied and said that he had, as follows, "Which do you believe is more pleasing to God, the sin of Magdalene or the virginity of Agnes?" Clare replied, "The virginity of Agnes is more pleasing to God because sin never pleases God. But I cannot tell whether the repentance of Magdalene pleases God more than the virginity of Agnes." The witness said that she had then seen Clare crying a great deal, feeling pity for the misery and deception of this friar Bentivenga, and ordered the sisters to pray for him so that he might extricate himself from that error; because should he remain long in error, he might subvert many people as a result of his beautiful and subtle rhetoric and spiritual appearance.

The witness said that she had heard from Clare that brother Joannuctio of Mevania, called Pulcino, had spoken to her. She had words with him because he had said that the soul may possess such complete peace in itself that it is disturbed by nothing. Clare said to him, "If this soul appears to offend God, is it never troubled?" The friar replied that it is not. . . . Clare

---

1. Bentivenga of Gubbio was a radical Franciscan who had been associated with a number of heretical sects, including the flagellating Disciplinati, the Apostolic Brethren, and the Brethren of the Free Spirit.

asked the sisters to ask God to save him from this error and told them not to have any contact with him. . . .

Clare had spoken to the inquisitor friar Andrew of Perugia with great fervor and excitement, saying to him, "Since you are an inquisitor, why don't you punish the heretics and Patarenes among you, and particularly brother Bentivenga?" Friar Andrew said, "How can I? I cannot catch him in sermons since he is so full of raillery and I don't have a witness against him."

Clare spoke to Bernard of Pesauro with many tears, saying to him, "What can you do with Cardinal Master Napoleone Orsini[2] in order to capture and punish friar Bentivenga, so that the heresy he follows can be destroyed? For this friar can cause many evil things unless some man opposes him, since this heresy is so evil, and he is so subtle. Unless there is one heart which possesses the spirit of God, no man can guard himself from his deception."

2. Cardinal Orsini (d. 1342) was a leading opponent of Pope Boniface VIII and patron of many of the more marginal apocalyptic religious groups, such as the Spiritual Franciscans.

VI

Insiders and Outsiders:
Liminality and Integration

In addition to the formalized marginality inflicted on Jews, lepers, sexual outlaws, heretics, and the mentally unstable, exclusion from the body politic may be observed during those temporary periods of separation from the faithful that occur in the course of the transitions in the life cycle, from infancy through to childhood, adolescence, adulthood, old age, and death. At each stage, the believer becomes detached from his or her age or social group, often by means of ritual ceremonies, including confirmation, marriage, initiation into the priesthood or religious orders, and last rites. Such observers as the anthropologist Arnold van Gennep have described the cycles of separation, transition, and reintegration that characterize such "rites of passage."[1] The phases are bridged by an ambiguous phase of liminality, during which the participants find themselves outside normative family and social structures, acquiring the skills and abilities needed to redefine their position. In the course of the trauma that may accompany the liminal condition, such persons may be endowed with special religious authority or sacred power and make decisions which will determine the future direction of their lives.

Many of the persons whose accounts are included in this chapter found themselves facing such a critical phase in their lives and temporarily found themselves at the edges of the traditional family and social structure. In these personal accounts, they describe the experience of the passage from one stage of their lives into another. Such processes often endow the participants with feelings of empowerment and sanctification, and those who undertake such a journey of self-realization have been described as liminal personalities. They have abandoned their homeland, family, property, priv-

1. Arnold van Gennep, *Les rites de passage: Étude systématique des rites*, rev ed. (Paris: Éditions A. and J. Picard, 1981).

ileges, and social status, rejecting the values and mores that have governed the environment in which they were reared. They often find themselves involved in the early stages of a new religious movement or cult, which generated and liberated enormous creative energy. A catalog of some of the characteristic features of liminality would include egalitarianism, a quest for anonymity, the absence of property, sexual continence and a minimization of sex distinctions, humility, the absence of rank or status, unselfishness, suspension of kinship ties, mysticism, and the possession of sacred knowledge. Many of these features find expression in the following texts.

Each of these characteristics is likewise paralleled by the opposite elements of the normative society from which such liminal persons have excluded themselves, including respect for structure and status, pride, wealth, defined sex roles, family ties and obligations, learning, and secularity. The liminal personality flies in the face of accepted norms, placing him- or herself outside of civil society, much as the Christian hermit or monk had done at the inception of monasticism in the third century. By the central Middle Ages, however, monasticism had become well integrated into the social structure; many of the monasteries possessed vast wealth, thus were populated by members of the propertied classes, and their members reached high positions in the ecclesiastical hierarchy. The new religious orders such as the Franciscans, on the other hand, sought to break down the sharp distinction between lay and clergy, to strip the model monastic community of its dependence on feudal landholding.

Clare of Assisi and Salimbene, for example, whose odysseys are described in this chapter, took Francis of Assisi as their role model. They pursued an egalitarian, apocalyptic vision and undertook a violent break with their families by placing themselves in the liminal stage between the upper bourgeois life of the Italian commune and the new family of mendicant religious who identified with the poor. Clare of Assisi had been born into a prominent family, which would expect their daughter to undertake the responsibilities of marriage and childbearing. In her youth, following the example of Francis, she fled her home to seek a life of chastity and poverty in accordance with the ideal of mendicancy. She cut off her hair, dressed in modest garb against the wishes of her parents, and repeatedly expressed the desire to undertake the same burdens of wandering, preaching, individual and collective poverty, and ministry to the poor and the dispossessed which characterized the male order of poor friars. Not only did she reject the highborn class identity, she also voiced a more textured gender identity, undertaking the tasks normally assigned to men. In the end, after a period of marginalization, her order, the Poor Clares, was reintegrated into the church and their way of life was given recognition by the papacy.

Salimbene likewise turned his back on family responsibility, fleeing his home to join the Franciscan order. Although his father belonged to the Parman aristocracy and was a partisan of the Holy Roman Emperor Frederick II, who at that time was engaged in a bitter struggle with Pope Gregory IX for influence in central Italy, Salimbene allied himself with the church, and by entering the Franciscan order he denied his father the heir he so desired. His father prevailed on the emperor and the Franciscan minister-general Elias to have his son returned to him; but Salimbene made use of the arguments of Scripture and succeeded in remaining within the order. Family continuity was at the very foundation of the social order in the Italian city, and Salimbene's act of defiance at first placed him outside the consensus. Nevertheless, in the end his conversion to the Franciscan movement served as an example to other members of the family, who followed his lead into the order.

The selections from the testimony of Joan, daughter of the sheriff Adam of Marden and his wife Caecilia, and Berardo Appillaterre, a notary of Tolentino, both taken from canonization trials, provide direct first-hand evidence of the pattern of separation, transition, and reintegration that disease or danger can initiate. The events surrounding Joan's drowning in a village pond and alleged resuscitation were recorded in September 1307 at Hereford by the notaries investigating the miracles of Bishop Thomas of Hereford. The witnesses who appeared about eighteen years after the accident (which took place in 1289 or 1292, depending on the witness) included Joan, her parents, her godmother and spouse (who were the parents of John, the little boy who had accidently pushed Joan into the pond), the owner of the beer tavern where the event occurred, and other bystanders. When the girl's body was found, it was suggested that the corpse be illegally moved and thrown into a local brook in order to avoid the unpleasantness of a royal inquiry into a possible homicide. Joan was eventually revived by prayers to Thomas. But as a result she devoted her life to the saint, refused to marry and was labeled by the community as "St. Thomas's virgin."

Berardo, who appeared at the canonization trial of the Augustinian friar Nicholas of Tolentino in 1325, was a frequent witness to the distress suffered by former prisoners, the possessed, and the physically disabled and diseased who flocked to the saint's tomb from near and far. He himself, despite the high status accorded a notary in imperial service, who acted much as do modern solicitors, was equally the victim of the vicissitudes of medieval life. Many of his children did not survive childbirth, while those who did had various diseases which demanded frequent visits from friar Nicholas while he was still alive, and afterward to his shrine. His late wife saved the water from Nicholas's bath as a balm against disease, and the horse belonging to his son-in-law (a merchant and notary, no doubt much in need of a horse) was likewise saved by the saint. Berardo's eyewitness testimony thus reveals the creation of a small cultic community of believers, consisting of the speaker's family and others of Tolentino, whose lives had been transformed by contact with the saint.

While focusing on persons who found themselves facing personal trag-edy, near death, or temporarily excluded from the community, at the same time these documents provide us with a valuable glimpse into the norma-tive community of the faithful, which is the foundation of the Christian polity. The sense of cohesion and shared values that bound together various "members of the body of Christ" in a shared religious experience often focused on a series of rites, such as baptism and communion, a common burial ground, festive occasions, and religious feasts. The testimonies of the notary Berardo Appillaterre and of Joan of Marden illustrate the shared community interest in the welfare of the young. A high rate of infant mor-tality, coupled with the need to produce offspring in order to till the fields, help with household duties, and provide security in old age, prompted great concern for their survival. The desire to baptize children as soon as possible also indicates concern to ensure their eternal salvation (and per-haps to relieve the fear that eternal consignment to Limbo would be on the parents' conscience), while at the same time serving as an antidote to devil-ish mischief. The largest number of miracles deal with the vagaries of in-fancy and childhood and testify to faith in the supernatural as the ultimate means of protecting the young against accidents, disease, and death. The aftermath of Joan's accidental drowning illustrates how an entire commu-nity was mobilized to pray for her resuscitation.

In order to identify those to be labeled with the badge of infamy and worthy of exclusion from the community of believers, and at the same time to assist in the reintegration of those deserving inclusion, perhaps the most effective tool of social control exercised by the church was the sacrament of confession and penance. This ensured a clerical monopoly over the forgive-ness of sin and the admission of believers into Heaven (although the hereti-cal sects rejected the Church's authority to act as a surrogate for God). Confession allowed the Church to cement its contact with the believers and to identify sinners and heretics more readily. Although in the primitive church public confession seems to have been the rule, in the early Middle Ages private confession was introduced and a detailed catalog of sins and their suitable "cures" was developed. The Fourth Lateran Council (1215) required every believer to confess at least once a year to his or her local priest; while the scholastic theologians, often working at the University of Paris, undertook to provide reliable, standardized manuals of penance for use by the clergy, like the manual for confessors attributed to Robert of Flamborough that appears in Chapter 3. Such works contain a systematic breakdown of the genres of sin, their punishments, and the citation of the canonical authorities on which they rest. The forms of penance included prayer, charity, pilgrimage, fasting, and vigils, and their fulfillment became the foundation for many of the religious institutions that flourished in the central and later Middle Ages, such as hospitals, orphanages, and pilgrimage churches. The penitential orders (some of whose regulations are given below) which thrived in the later Middle Ages, became an important agency for focusing and mobilizing the spiritual energy of the faithful through the meetings, festivals, charitable enterprises, church building, and artistic patronage they organized. They also provided an avenue for the readmission of heretics, political enemies, and the infamous to the community of the faithful.

Those who diverged from the prevailing Christian consensus by expressing reservations about the faith, or by going so far as to perform acts of sacrilege, were made to suffer as God's means of demonstrating his power to the faithful. Although in a moment of anger the believer might be led to utter blasphemous remarks against God or the saints, divine retribution could mark him among those cast out from the body of the faithful. Along with paganism, heresy, Judaism, and apostasy, Thomas Aquinas classified blasphemy among the forms of disbelief; while in the Christianized Roman law code of Justinian blasphemy was regarded as the kind of sin which, like the various sins against nature, could lead to pestilence, famine, earthquake, and death. The blasphemer's doubt and disbelief might be expressed through thoughts, words, publications, or acts. Ezekiel 30, referring to those who deny the laws of God, contained a frightening prophecy of the fate of such blasphemers: the fathers would consume their children, some would die of pestilence, perish by famine, or die by the sword; those who were left would be scattered to the four corners of the earth. Although the blasphemer might suffer capital punishment in secular law, more often he was subjected to flogging, immersion in water, imprisonment, or mutilation.

In hagiographical sources, one often encounters reports of the punishment for such deeds as the failure to honor a feast day, scorn toward a saint or his relics, sacrilegious theft from a church, and desecration of a holy place; the greatest blasphemers included those who murdered a potential saint such as Thomas à Becket. This chapter contains such an example of a believer whose faith had grown cold, who uttered blasphemous remarks, was punished, was restored to the community after becoming penitent, and became a supporter of the saint's cult he had formerly mocked. Thomas de Mathia was a canon of Salerno who visited the relics of Thomas Aquinas, which had been deposited at San Severino, but doubted their value. After being duly punished and expressing remorse, he supported the cult, and continued to carry with him a scent he believed to be that of sanctity, which adhered to his cloak after it had brushed against the dead saint's hand. The tale is here presented in several eyewitness versions, taken from Thomas Aquinas's canonization hearing. While the commissioners' aim was to demonstrate the effectiveness of Thomas's relics and his ability to perform post mortem miracles, at the same time this report illustrates the kind of liminal situation in which a believer whose faith had been tested might find himself: Thomas de Mathia passed through the three phases of exclusion, separation, and re-integration that were also experienced by Clare, Salimbene, and the others heard in this chapter.

The Orders of Penance at Bologna (1244) and Bergamo (1265)

Source: *Statuti dei penitenti (Bologna, 12 June 1244)*, in G.-G. Meersseman, "Études sur les anciennes confréries dominicaines," *Archivum Fratrum Praedicatorum* 20 (1950): 65–66.

Bibliography: Hans-Georg Beck et al., *From the High Middle Ages to the Eve of the Reformation*, ed. Hubert Jedin and John Dolan, trans. Anselm Biggs, Handbook of Church History 4 (Boston: Crossroad, 1980), 172–84.

Statutes of the Congregation of St. Dominic at Bologna (June 12, 1244)

To all the faithful in Christ, members of the society of the brotherhood of St. Dominic of Bologna, brother John, by the grace of God bishop and master of the Order of Preachers [the Dominicans], may they proceed worthily, through deeds of beneficial grace, in the presence of God and man.

May the grace of divine refuge enlighten your hearts, having been provoked by the examples of the blessed Dominic, whose patronage you have relied on for assistance, gathered together in one congregation, with the aim of performing pious deeds, through which the suffering of the needy will be relieved, and the health-giving indulgence of souls is procured. Whose devotion and fervor of spiritual thoughts are devoted to God, while in his saints we note a wondrous God, who through the example of one person, like a small seed buried in the earth, makes a crop of faithful to flourish, let us judge your life and ordination, which is contained in the following chapters, to be holy, fruitful, and useful, and may it be pleasing and acceptable to God, a life whose tenor is as follows:

This is the fraternity or congregation of the confessor St. Dominic, which has been established for his reverence, and for the salvation of souls.

1. Whoever wants to join this fraternity, may be received, unless he is infamous or suspected of an error of the faith and then he may not be admitted until his reputation for good behavior has been restored.

2. On the last Sunday of each month all the members are to gather together (if this is possible) to hear a mass at the church of St. Dominic in his honor, and to hear the word of God, if it is preached to them, and there each member of the congregation should give one *denarius* to the alms collectors of the fraternity, and if they cannot come they should do so through someone else sent.

3. There are to be four alms collectors of the fraternity, if possible, one for each quarter, whose job will be to do the following. They are to settle discords peacefully. They are to visit wards, widows, orphans, the sick, the imprisoned, the poor, and other oppressed persons, with the aid and assistance of brotherly charity. They are to spend the monies from these oblations for the aid of such persons, and so that this can be accomplished more easily, on that Sunday after nine o'clock the alms collectors should gather in the church of St. Dominic in order to handle these affairs and similar matters, so that Jesus will want to inspire them.

4. Every year on the solemn day of the feast of the blessed Dominic all members of the fraternity are to gather together with reverence and the devotion of their souls in the church of St. Dominic in order to hear masses; and each person is to give a candle, in accordance with his position, and everyone is to honor and praise Our Lord Jesus Christ and the blessed Dominic. We have said these things, unless by just necessity they are hindered from doing so.

5. Every member of the fraternity should repeat the Lord's Prayer seven times for the remission of his sins.

6. Every member of the fraternity should say the Lord's Prayer seven

times for the sake of one dead member of the congregation. They should also do this for the sake of one dead friar preacher by going to the church of the blessed Dominic of Bologna.

7. When called upon to do so, if this is convenient, they should attend the funeral of the dead brothers and sisters; if this is inconvenient, they should provide the expenses for the prayers.

8. A light should always be burning before the altar of the blessed Dominic.

9. They should provide two large candles, placed in the sacristy of the blessed Dominic, to be carried at the funerals of dead members of the fraternity. . . .

Statutes of the Congregation of Mercy of Bergamo (1265)

Source: Lester K. Little, *Liberty, Charity, Fraternity: Lay Religious Confraternities at Bergamo in the Age of the Commune*, Smith College Studies in History 51 (North-ampton, Mass.: Smith College, 1988), 112–13. Text edited by Sandro Buzzetti.

1. Who ought to be received into the congregation

First we ordain that members of the congregation should be persons of honest, legal status, neither gamblers, nor drunkards, nor impostors, nor infamous persons, but rather suitable persons who behave in a good and honest way. No brawler, infamous person, one noted for the foulest vice, or heretic or believer in heretics should be accepted into this congregation unless he wants to return to the faith of the holy church. No infamous person publicly guilty of usury who wants to do so should be received because of his position or profession. The same applies to women, adding that an infamous public prostitute [should not be admitted]. Any man or woman who wants to perform true penance will be received when the conclusive signs appear in them. A man who wants to join this congrega-tion should not be immediately recorded in the book, but should be re-corded in a line above, and the day and time when he was first written down on the list should be recorded. Such persons should remain there for a year, so the brethren can see and learn about their suitability, and whether they are capable of undertaking the burden of this holy congregation. At the beginning of the year the minister of the congregation should gather to-gether the councilors and four alms collectors, but if all of them are not interested in this, the minister can then, with the advice and agreement of those present, support [the candidacy of] those who appear suitable to them. If he whose name appears will be suitable and is pleasing to them, he will be received and inscribed in the book. If he will however not be suitable, he will leave. Women should not be recorded in the same book as the men, but in another book, so that the minister and the councilors will be able to find out what can be known about such women, and sometimes ask them to give charity. Whoever is supposed to make a testament should do so when he is supposed to, and should summon three brethren, or at least two of the congregation, and make the testament with their advice, ordering it according to the grace given to him by God. If a man or woman who is not a member of the congregation wants to come to the preaching of the fraternity and to offer charity, they may participate alongside members of the congregation so that God may illuminate their hearts in penance. . . .

Filippa di Leonardo di Gislerio (1254), Disciple of Clare of Assisi

Clare (1193/4–1253), foundress of the Order of Poor Clares, was born to Ortolana and Favarone di Offreduccio, members of the local aristocracy of Assisi. The night following Palm Sunday in 1211 or 1212, saying a definitive farewell to her paternal home, she left secretly for Portiuncula, on the plains of Assisi, together with her confidante Bona di Guelfuccio. She was greeted by Francis and his companions, among them her own relatives Rufino and Silvestro. After that, dressed in a coarse gray outfit, she went to San Bastia, to the Benedictine monastery of San Paolo; she later moved to the Benedictine house at Sant'Angelo in Pansa, joined by her sister Agnes. Made an abbess in 1215, she maintained a lifelong devotion to the Franciscan ideal of absolute poverty, both individual and collective. Clare obtained the "privilege of poverty" from Pope Gregory IX, which allowed the sisters to accept no property, not even in common. This privilege was again ratified three days before her death by Pope Innocent IV. Clare was canonized in 1255 by Pope Alexander IV. Although some of Clare's letters have survived, the best testimony of her life was given by her followers at the canonization trial held in 1254, which also became the basis of later biographies, particularly the life by Thomas of Celano. The testimony of Sister Filippa, the fullest direct report of Clare's life, is characteristic of the remarks made by others involved in the great flowering of female piety during this period.

Source: "Il processo di canonizzazione di S. Chiara d'Assisi," ed. Zefferino Lazzeri, *Archivum Franciscanum Historicum* 13 (1923): 452–59 (Witness no. 3).

Bibliography: Caroline Walker Bynum, *Holy Feast and Holy Fast: The Religious Significance of Food to Medieval Women* (Berkeley: University of California Press, 1987), 13–30.

*   *   *

Sister Filippa, daughter of Messer Leonardo di Gislerio, and nun at the monastery of San Damiano, said that when Clare had already been in religion for four years, as a result of the preaching of St. Francis, she herself also assumed the habit in 1215. The saint had pointed out to her how Our Lord Jesus Christ had suffered the passion and had died on the Cross for the sake of humanity; she therefore agreed to undergo penitence with Clare, and remained with Clare from that time until her death, that is, thirty years.

She further testified that the saint's holiness of life and honesty of behavior were inexplicable to everyone. Already as a child, she had decided to become a bride of Christ. Before entering religion, she was considered saintly by all who knew her, as a result of her honest life, great virtue, and the grace with which God had endowed her.

Before entering religion, God increased Clare's virtue and grace; she was always very humble, devout, kind, and a lover of poverty, having compassion for the afflicted. She was assiduous in prayer; her conversation and speech always seemed to concern godly matters, to such an extent that neither her tongue nor her eyes took heed of worldly things.

She chastised her body with harsh garments; on several occasions she had clothes of horsehair and horsetails made for her, and had a tunic and cloak of harsh wool. Her bed was made of vine-twigs, and she was content with this at all times.

She chastised her body three times a week, on Mondays, Wednesdays, and Saturdays, and on other days, lunched on only bread and water.

She was no less cheerful before God; untroubled and angelic, she received so much grace from God that, many times when the sisters were ill, she made the sign of the cross with her hand and cured them.

She especially possessed the grace of many tears, having great compassion for her sisters and the afflicted, and cried when she received the body of Christ.

When asked how she knew all the aforesaid, Filippa replied that she was Clare's third sister, had known her since childhood, had always been with her since then, and saw all these things.

Such was the humility of this beloved mother that she deprecated herself before everyone, and put herself behind the other sisters, making herself inferior to everyone, serving them, giving them water for their hands, washing the chairs of the infirm sisters with her hands, and even washing the feet of the servants. Once, when she was washing the feet of one of the servants, she wanted to kiss the servant's feet, but the maid withdrew; nevertheless, in the course of her withdrawal, she grazed the holy mother on the mouth. Her humility was such that, not content with this, Clare kissed the maidservant's sole. Asked how she knew these things, Filippa replied that she saw them, for she had been present.

When asked which sisters Clare had cured with the sign of the cross, she replied that among them was sister Benvenuta da Madonna Diambra, who had a deep sore on her arm for twelve years, that is, a fistula, which disappeared after the sign of the cross accompanied by an invocation to Our Lord, the Lord's Prayer.

Another was sister Amata, a nun of the same house, who was gravely ill with dropsy and fever, and had an enlarged stomach. The holy mother made the sign of the cross and touched her with her hands; the following morning she was cured, so that her body returned to its former small size, like a healthy person. Filippa said that she had seen the holy mother make the sign of the cross and touch her; she saw that Amata had been ill for a long time, and she saw that she had been cured.

She corroborated the testimony of sister Benvenuta concerning the freeing of brother Stephen.[1]

She also said that Clare was such a lover of poverty that when the alms-collectors of the monastery brought whole bread as charity, reproving them, she sought them out and said, "Who brought you this whole bread?" She said that this was because she preferred to receive crumbs rather than whole loaves as alms.

Nor could she be induced, neither by the pope nor by the bishop of Ostia, to receive any possessions. She held the privilege of poverty which had been granted to her in great reverence, guarding it well and diligently, fearing its loss.

The infant son of Messer Giovanni de Maestro Giovanni, the sisters' procurator, had a grave fever and was taken to the holy mother Clare. After receiving the sign of the cross from her, he was cured. Asked how she knew this, Filippa replied that she had been present when the child came and

---

1. This refers to the cure of a brother suffering mental illness, sent to Clare by Francis of Assisi.

when the blessed mother touched him and made the sign of the cross, and it appeared as though he had been cured thereafter. . . .

She reported that when sister Andrea de Ferrara was suffering from scrofula of the throat, Clare knew mystically that she would be tempted with the desire to cure her. Therefore, one night when sister Andrea was below the dormitory and was strenuously squeezing her throat with her own hands so that she lost the power of speech, the holy mother knew this mystically. Distraught, she summoned the witness, who was asleep nearby, and said to her, "Go down quickly beneath the dormitory where sister Andrea is gravely ill; warm her an egg and give her a drink; and after she has recovered her speech, bring her to me." This was done. When Clare asked Andrea what was wrong and what she had done, Andrea did not want to say; at which point, this memorable madonna told her everything in the order in which it had occurred, and this was divulged among the sisters.

This witness also said that mother Clare freed a sister named Christina from long-standing deafness in one ear.

She also said that at the time of the war in Assisi, when the sisters feared the coming of the Tartars and Saracens and other enemies of God and the Holy Church, the blessed mother began to comfort them, saying, "My sisters and brothers, do not be afraid, for if God is with us, these enemies cannot hurt us. Commit yourself to Our Lord Jesus Christ, for he will free us. I want to be your guardian, so that we will suffer no evil. If they should show themselves, place them before me." Whence, one day when the enemy appeared in order to destroy the city of Assisi, some Saracens scaled the wall of the monastery and fell into the cloister, where the sisters stood in fear. The most holy mother comforted and strengthened them all, saying, "Do not be afraid, for we cannot be harmed." Having said this, she returned to the small oratory chapel for the customary prayer. The power of this prayer was so great that the Saracen foes, without making an attack, left as though they had been chased, and they did not touch any part of the house. When asked how she knew these things, Filippa replied that she had been present. When asked the month and day, she said she couldn't remember.[2]

She also said that when Vitalis of Aversa, at the order of the emperor [Frederick II], had come to attack the city of Assisi with a great army [1243], there had been much fear. The matter was reported to the madonna Clare, that the city was under siege and endangered, for Vitalis had said that

2. This episode refers to the use of mercenaries by Emperor Frederick II in the course of his wars against papal supporters in Umbria. The siege occurred on a Friday in September 1240. Although not confirmed in the sources, artists usually depict Clare driving away the Saracens by holding up a monstrance.

he would not leave until he had captured the city. When the madonna understand the state of affairs, confiding in the power of God, she called together all the sisters, had ashes brought, and covered her shaven head with them. She then put the ashes on the heads of all the sisters, and ordered them to beseech the Lord to free the city. It happened in this way: the following day, Vitalis left by night with his entire army.

This witness also said that when the madonna and holy mother was approaching death, one Friday night, she began to speak, saying thus, "Go in peace, for you will have good fortune; since He who created you first sanctified you; and then, when He created you, placed you in the Holy Spirit, and has always cared for you as a mother for her little sons whom she loves." And she added, "You, O Lord, be blessed, you who have created me." She said many things concerning the Trinity, so subtly, that the sisters could not easily understand her.

This witness said to one of the sisters who was present, "You have a good memory; keep in mind what the madonna is saying." The madonna heard these words, and said to those sisters who were present, "You are going to remember only as much as he who is putting these words in my mouth permits you to remember."

A sister named Anastasia asked the madonna with whom or to whom she was speaking these words. She replied, "I speak to my own soul."

The witness added that, on the night before she died, she admonished the sisters to pray for her. In the end, she made such a beautiful and good confession, unlike any this witness has ever heard. Clare confessed that she had no doubt that she had in some way offended the faith promised in baptism.

When Pope Innocent [IV] came to visit her, although gravely ill, she said to the sisters, "My daughters, praise God, since neither heaven nor earth could equal this gift which I have received from God. Today not only have I received Him in his sacrament, but have also seen his vicar." Asked how she knew these things, Filippa replied that she saw them and was present. Asked how long before Clare's death this had happened, she said that it was a few days.

This witness also said that Clare was so devoted to contemplation that on Good Friday, deep in thought over the passion of the Lord, she stood as if insensible for the whole day and the greater part of the following night.

Concerning the vase of oil, she said the same things under oath as the other witnesses had reported.

Asked about the other sisters who had been cured, she replied that the others who were cured were no longer alive, but had died.

This witness also said that Clare had told the sisters that when her mother was pregnant with her, she had gone to church. While standing before the cross, carefully praying and beseeching God to aid and assist her during the pangs of birth, she heard a voice saying, "You will give birth to a moon which will illuminate the world."

Clare also reported that, once, in a vision, she saw herself bringing St. Francis a bowl of hot water and a beaker with which to rinse his hands. She ascended a steep staircase, but proceeded as lightly as though she were walking on level ground. When she reached Francis, the saint proffered her one of his breasts, and said, "Come, receive and suck." After being suckled by him, the saint bid her to suck again; she did so, and what she received from him was so sweet and tasty, that she could in no way describe its power. After the opening of the breast had fully bestowed its nourishment, the milk still remained between her lips; seizing with her hands whatever had remained in her mouth, it seemed as clear and lucid as gold, as if in a mirror.

Clare also told how on the night of the Nativity, which had just passed [December 25, 1252], when she was unable to raise herself out of bed in order to attend chapel because of a grave illness, the sisters all went to matins in the usual way, leaving her alone. With a sigh, Clare said, "Oh Lord, I have been left alone with you in this place." She then suddenly began to hear the musical accompaniment [*organa*] and responses and the entire office sung by the brothers in the church of St. Francis of Assisi, as if she were present.

This witness reported these miracles and others known to her and through hearsay, concerning Clare. Clare was the first mother and abbess of the monastery of San Damiano, and she was the first member of this order, of noble background and parentage, rich in the things of the world. She loved poverty so much that she sold all her inheritance and gave it to the poor. She loved this order so much that she did not want to relax even the slightest aspect of the observance, even when she was ill.

At the end of her life, Clare called all her sisters together and reminded them of the privilege of poverty. She very much desired to maintain the *Regula bullata*[3] of the order, to such an extent that one day she would be able to place the bull in her mouth and then die the next day. Just as she wanted, it happened in this way. She asked a friar to come with the *Regula*

---

3. The papal bull issued by Pope Innocent IV prior to her death granting the privilege of poverty to the Poor Clares, a subject of dispute. This kissing of the bull occurred on August 10, 1253.

bullata, which she reverently took, although approaching death. She then placed the bull in her mouth in order to kiss it. The following day Clare passed to God, truly pure, without any stain, without the aura of sin, to the clearness of eternal light. This witness, the other sisters, and all others who knew her sanctity corroborated these things without doubt.

Salimbene de Adam (d. ca. 1287), *Cronica*

Salimbene was a member of a non-noble bourgeois family, related by marriage to the local nobility of Parma and associated with the Ghibelline or pro-imperial party. His own bias is indicated by the statement that "the world is destroyed by the people and saved by noblemen and soldiers." In addition to effectively ending the male line in his family, his decision to join the Franciscan order in 1237 identified him with the Guelf or pro-papal opposition party. The conflict between Salimbene and his family details a critical turning point in the passage from the secular to the mendicant (and primarily clerical) world of the friars. Salimbene's *Cronica* represents a major source for our knowledge of Italy in the thirteenth century and reflects the moderate, apocalyptic Joachitic view common in Franciscan circles, as opposed to the more radical, heretical Apostolic Brethren. The historian Placid Hermann described him as "an incorrigible busybody and, besides, being rather vainglorious, he delights in giving us a multitude of details about himself and his kindred." The following personal testimony is especially illustrative of the tendency to prove the value of Scripture as a guide to everyday life.

Source: Salimbene de Adam, *Cronica*, ed. Oswald Holder-Egger, *Monumenta germaniae historica: Scriptores* 32 (Hannover: Hahn, 1913), 34–40, 54–55. Another recent translation is in *The Chronicle of Salimbene de Adam*, trans. Joseph Baird et al., Medieval and Renaissance Texts and Studies 40 (Binghamton, N.Y.: Medieval and Renaissance Texts and Studies, 1986).

Bibliography: Robert Brentano, *Two Churches: England and Italy in the Thirteenth Century* (Princeton, N.J: Princeton University Press, 1968), 326–46; Placid Hermann, *XIIIth Century Chronicles* (Chicago: University of Chicago Press, 1961), 195.

*   *   *

In the year 1221 the blessed Dominic died on the eighth day before the Ides of August [August 6]. I, brother Salimbene de Adam of the city of Parma, was born during the same year in the month of October, on the seventh day before the Ides of October [October 9], on the feast of Sts. Dyonisius and Doninus. Lord Balian of Sidon, a great baron of France who had come from across the sea to the army of Emperor Frederick II, raised me from the holy font at the baptistery of Parma, situated near my home, so they tell me. Friar Andrew, a Franciscan, who came from across the sea at Acre, who was with said lord, was a member of his retinue and had been his companion on the journey, saw and reported these matters, and he told me.

My mother [Imelda de Cassio] told me that at the time of the great earthquake [1222] I had been alone in my cradle. She took my two infant sisters under her arms, leaving me in my cradle, rushing to the home of her father [Gerard de Cassio], mother [Maria], and kinfolk. She claimed to have been fearful lest the baptistery fall on her, because it was near my home. Since that time, I haven't much cared for her as I did before, since she should have been more concerned about me, as a boy, than about her daughters. But she said they were easier to carry because they were bigger.

My father, Guido de Adam, was a handsome and valiant man, who had crossed the sea in aid of the Holy Land at the time of Count Baldwin of Flanders, whose journey I have described above. I had not yet been born. I have heard from my father that when the Lombards[1] asked soothsayers overseas about the condition of their homes, my father didn't want to inquire about that subject. When he returned, he found all peaceful and comforting in his home, while the others found sadness, as they had heard from the soothsayers. I have also heard from him about the beauty and goodness of his steed, which he took to the Holy Land and which was superior to all others of his company. And I have heard from my father that when the baptistery of Parma was built [1196], he had laid the foundation stone as a sign and memorial. [He reported] that the baptistery had been built on the site of the homes of relatives who had gone to Bologna after the destruction of their homes, became citizens there, and are called the Cocca family. My family's name had been Grenone, and I have found in old documents that they were afterward called de Adam. There are other persons named Grelone in the city of Parma, whose name is spelled with the letter "L," who live at the foot of the bridge on the street which leads to Borgo san Donnino. They owned a well-known elm tree, named after Giovanni Grelone, situated in front of their house. It is said that Oliverio de Grenone created the society of Santa Maria of Parma. He was the same

1. Italians, largely from northern Italy.

Oliverio de Adam who was the father of the aforementioned judge Bernardo Oliverio de Adam. Bernardo Oliverio had two sons, one of whom is called Oliverio de Adam, and the other, Giovanni de Adam. Oliverio de Adam had two sons, the aforementioned Oliverio and Rolando Oliverio. Bernardo Oliverio had Leonardo, Emblavato, Bonifacio, and Oliverio, and four daughters: mistress Aica, a nun at St. Paul's, mistress Ricca, mistress Romagna, a Poor Clare in Bologna, and Mabilia, who died a virgin. Rolando Oliverio had six sons, Bartholomeo, Francesco, Oliverio, Guido, Pino, and Rolandino. He had two daughters, Mabilia and Alberta. Giovanni de Adam had two sons: Adamino, a strong, courtly and benevolent man, who died without sons, and Guido de Adam, who had four sons, the first of whom was friar Guido de Adam, who remained in the Franciscan order until the end of his life. He had a noble wife named mistress Adelasia, the daughter of lord Gerardo de Baratti, by whom he had a daughter named Agnes. Both mother and sister were to end their lives in a praiseworthy way in the Poor Clare convent of Parma. Friar Guido had been married in the secular world and had been a father and a judge. In the Franciscan order he became a priest and preacher. The Baratti clan prides itself on being related to Countess Matilda of Tuscany. They do service to the commune of Parma with forty knights (*milites*) of their house. The second son of Guido de Adam the elder, called Niccolo, died in childhood, as it says, "While I was still growing, he cut me off" [Isaiah 38.12].

I, Salimbene de Adam, am the third son. When I began to study the Pythagorean method, that is, when the three lustral[2] periods were over, which three periods make up the cycle of the indiction I entered, I entered the order of the Friars Minor,[3] in which I have served as a priest and preacher for many years, have seen many things, dwelled in many provinces, and have taught much. In the secular world, some call me Balian de Sagitta (meaning "of Sidon") because of the aforementioned lord, who raised me from the sacred font.[4] My friends and family call me Ognibene.[5] I spent a year's probation in the order [February 4, 1238–February 1239]. When I left the March of Ancona in order to live in Tuscany [April 1239], I passed through Città di Castello and found in the hermitage a certain aged and long-lived friar [cf. Genesis 25.8] who had four sons who were knights

2. A lustral period is five years; therefore, three such periods is fifteen years. The indiction is the method of calculating the year according to the date of Easter. Salimbene's calculations are incorrect.

3. Salimbene entered the Franciscan order on February 4, 1238.

4. Served as Salimbene's godfather in 1221.

5. *Omne-bonum* in Latin means "Good in all things."

(*milites*) in the secular world. He was the last friar whom the blessed Francis had inducted and received into the order, as he told me. Hearing that I am called Ognibene, he was surprised, saying to me, "Son, 'no one is all good except God alone' [Luke 18.19]. Otherwise, your name should be Salimbene, since you have taken the right step by entering a good religious order."6 I happily knew that he made good sense, and that the name had been given to me by a holy man. The name that I did in fact like the most I did not possess. I wanted to be called Dyonisius, not only out of reverence for the distinguished doctor, who had been a disciple of Paul the Apostle, but also because I was born on his feast day. And thus I saw the last friar whom the blessed Francis had received into the order; after him he neither received nor inducted anyone. I also saw the first one, friar Bernard of Quintavalle, with whom I spent the winter at the friary in Siena [ca. 1241]. He was a close friend of mine, and told both me and all the young folks many wondrous things about the blessed Francis; and I have heard and learned many good things about him.

All my life my father was much grieved by my entrance into the Franciscan order, and couldn't be consoled by not having a son who would succeed in his inheritance. He complained to the emperor, who had come to Parma [November 1238] that the Friars Minor had taken his son from him. The emperor then wrote to the Franciscan minister-general Elias, requesting him to kindly obey him and return me to my father. Brother Elias received me when he joined the emperor at Cremona, having been sent by Pope Gregory IX in 1238 [February 4]. My father then visited brother Elias at Assisi, placing the imperial letters in the general's hands. This is the introductory line of those letters: "In order to fulfill the desires of our faithful Guido de Adam, etc." Brother Illuminato [d. 1281], who was Elias's secretary and scribe at the time, who had gathered together in a notebook all the beautiful letters which the princes of the world had sent to the minister-general, showed me the letter at the time when I lived with him at the Sienese friary [1241–43]. Brother Illuminato afterwards served as a minister in the province of St. Francis [Umbria], was later made a bishop [July 23, 1274] and spent his last days at Assisi. Having read the imperial letters, brother Elias immediately wrote to the brethren at Fano where I had been living [February 1238–February 1239] that, should I be willing to return to my father's authority, they should let me do so without delay. Otherwise, if I was unwilling to join my father, I should be protected

---

6. This is a play on words, since *Bene salisti* in Latin means "you have taken the right step."

"as a pupil in the eye" [Psalms 16.8]. Many soldiers showed up at the friary of Fano in order to put an end to the affair. I was made a "spectacle" for them [1 Corinthians 4.9], and they were "a source of eternal salvation" to me [Hebrews 5.9]. The brethren therefore gathered together in chapter with the seculars and exchanged many words. My father brought many of the minister-general's letters and showed them to the brethren. When these had been read, the guardian friar Jeremias said to my father in their presence, "Lord Guido, we appreciate your grief and are ready to obey our father's letters. He is your son. 'He is of age; let him speak for himself' [John 9. 21]. You may ask him. If he wants to go with you, let him go in God's name, if we haven't strengthened him enough to go with us."

My father therefore asked if I wanted to go with him or not. I replied, "No, because the Lord says in Luke 9.62, 'No one who sets his hand to the plough and keeps looking back is fit for the kingdom of God.'"

My father answered me, "You don't care for your father or mother, who suffered much for you."

I replied, "I don't care, since as the Lord says in Matthew 10.37, 'No man is worthy of me who cares more for his father or mother.' About you He even said [Matthew 10.37], 'No man is worthy of me who cares for son and daughter above me.' Father, you should therefore beware of the One who hung on the cross for our sakes, so that He might grant us eternal life. For it is He who said in Matthew 10.35–36, 'I have come to set a man against his father, a daughter against her mother, a son's wife against her mother-in-law; and a man will find enemies under his own roof. Whoever then will acknowledge me before men, I will acknowledge him before my Father in heaven; and whoever disowns me before men, I will disown him before my Father in heaven'" [cf. also Matthew 10.32–33]. And the brethren were amazed and cried out in praise that I should say such things to my father.

Then my father said to the friars, "You have bewitched and deceived my son so that he won't agree with me. I will go back to the emperor and minister-general about you. Permit me to speak to my son without your presence, and you'll see that he'll come without delay." The brethren allowed me to speak with my father without them, since from previous remarks about myself they somewhat trusted me. They "kissed me before the wall," as we say. They trembled like rushes in the water, lest my father tempt my soul with his blandishments. Not only did they fear for the safety of my soul, but even feared lest my departure serve as an excuse for others not to join the order.

My father therefore said to me, "Beloved son, don't believe these 'pissin-tunics' who have deceived you; but come with me, and I will give you everything."[7]

I replied and said to my father, "Go away, go away, father! The wise man of Proverbs 3.27 says, 'Refuse no man any favor that you owe him when it lies in your power to pay it.'"

My father replied tearfully, saying to me, "What shall I tell your mother, my son, who continually suffers because of you?"

I said to him, "Tell my mother the following: Your son says, '*My father and mother have deserted me, but the Lord takes me in*' [Psalms 26.10]. Jeremiah 3.19 says, 'You shall call me father and never cease to follow me.' For, 'It is good too for a man to carry the yoke in his youth'" [Lamentations 3.27]. Hearing all this, my father despaired of my ever leaving the order and prostrated himself before the friars and laymen who had come with him and said, "May you swallow a thousand demons, cursed son, both you and your brother Guido who is with you, who has deceived you. My eternal curse be with you, commending you both to the spirits of Hell."

He departed very much disturbed. We remained, consoled, giving thanks to God, saying to Him, "'Let them be cursed, and you be blessed' [Psalms 108.28]. For [Isaiah 65.16] 'he who invokes a blessing on himself in the land, may he be blessed by God. Amen.'" The laymen also left, very much edified by my constancy. But the brethren rejoiced, for the Lord had manfully nourished his little boy through me, and they knew that the words of God are true which appear in Luke 21.14–15, "So make up your minds not to prepare your defense beforehand, because I myself will give you the power of utterance and a wisdom which no opponent will be able to resist or refute."

The following night the Blessed Virgin repaid me as I lay prostrate in prayer before the altar, as the brethren are accustomed to do when they wake up for matins. I heard the voice of the Blessed Virgin calling me. My face uplifted, I saw the Blessed Virgin seated above the altar in the place where the host and the chalice are placed, and she held her little child on her knees, offering him to me, saying, "Come without fear and kiss my son, you who gave witness yesterday before men."

While fearful, I saw that the little boy opened up his arms to receive me. Sure of the speed and innocence of the boy, and of the benevolence of his mother, who had been so great as to come to me, I embraced and kissed him. And the kindly mother, after some delay, left him to me. Since I was

---

7. See the words of the Devil to Jesus in Matthew 4.9.

not satisfied by this, the Blessed Virgin blessed me and said, "Go away, beloved son, and take a rest, lest the friars, who are getting up for matins, should find you with us." I acquiesced, and the vision disappeared. But in my heart, such a sweetness remained, that I could not put it into words. In fact, I have never experienced such sweetness in this world. I now knew the truth of what is written in Scripture, that for one who has tasted the spirit, all flesh lacks flavor.

At the same time, when I was still in the city of Fano, I dreamed that the son of lord Tommaso de Armari of the city of Parma had killed a monk, and I reported the dream to my brother. Several days later, on his way to Apulia, Amico de Amicis passed through Fano in order to collect some money. Since he was an acquaintance, a friend and a neighbor, he came to the friary to see us. After discussing some other matters, inquiring how things were going with such-and-such (he was called Gerardo Sencani), he told us, "Things are going badly for him, since the other day he killed a monk." We thus know that dreams are sometimes true.

At that time, when my father passed through Fano on the way to Assisi, the friar used to hide my brother and me in the home of Martin of Fano, who was a master of laws.

My paternal grandmother was called mistress Ermengard, and she lived to be a hundred. I lived in my father's house with her for fifteen years. She taught me to avoid evil company and to associate with good persons in order to become wise, good, and well-behaved. She did this very often. She was buried in the aforementioned tomb which belongs to us and to members of our clan. My father, however, had his own new monument built, since the old one was totally full. No one had yet been buried in it, and it is situated in Vetere square, at the gate to the baptistery.

My father's fourth son, born of his concubine Rechelda, is named Giovanni. He was a handsome man and a great warrior. He freely left Parma [1247] and joined the imperial party. But he made a pilgrimage as a penitent to St. James of Compostella. When he returned he remained freely at Toulouse. There he became a citizen and married a woman who bore him both sons and daughters. After this, "he took to his bed" [1 Maccabees 6.8] and died after confessing to the Franciscan friars; he was buried at the Franciscan church of Toulouse.

My mother, Imelda, was a humble woman, devoted to God, who fasted frequently and often gave alms freely to the poor. She was never angry, nor did she ever strike any member of her family. During the winter she would always take in a poor mountain girl whom she gave food and clothing, even though she already had enough female servants to do the housework. Pope Innocent IV gave me a letter for her at Lyons [1249] so she could join the order of St. Clare. On another occasion he gave me a letter for my brother friar Guido when he was sent by the Parmans to the pope. She was buried at the Clarissian convent. May her soul rest in peace for the mercy of God!

I, brother Salimbene, and brother Guido, destroyed our house, with its male and female lines, by entering religion. May we raise it up again in heaven!

Joan of Marden (1307), Follower of Bishop Thomas of Hereford

The following miracle is one of hundreds of miracles attributed to the post-humous intervention of Bishop Thomas of Hereford (d. 1282), largely among the village folk of the region. After a large number of witnesses testified to its authenticity, and the commissions weighed the evidence, questioning the signs of death and of revival, this case was included among the miracles cited in Thomas's bull of canonization as follows: "A five-year-old girl remained drowned and dead in a deep pond for a long time and was taken out completely cold and stiff; showing no sign of life; after a vow was made to the saint in order to resuscitate her, she was restored to life as before." The fish pond in which Joan was drowned, sometime between 1289 and 1292 (depending on the witness), was probably situated in the small hamlet of Wisteston. She had accompanied her parents on Sunday afternoon to the local beer tavern, where a large number of people were engaged in drinking and dancing. The children had wandered off to play beside the pond situated behind the tavern, when Joan was accidently pushed into the water by John, who was nine months her junior. When her body was eventually discovered submerged in the pool, some of the bystanders suggested throwing the corpse into a nearby brook, so that there would be no suspicion of homicide, which would entail a royal inquiry. Still unidentified, the body was at first believed to be that of the daughter of a poor beggar-woman, who had been thrown into the pool by her mother because of anger and distress over their impoverished condition. But when Joan's identity was clear, her godmother immediately disrobed and jumped into the pool to rescue her. Assumed dead, her body was taken to a nearby hearth to be warmed. After all joined in prayer, the child came back to life and the parishioners bore the child to the church at Hereford. Joan's case was corroborated by a large number of witnesses including her parents, and provides a graphic description of village life at the end of the thirteenth century.

Source: *Processus de probatione miraculorum*, in *Vatican Lat. Ms.* 4015, fol. 123ʳ–123ᵛ. Another recent translation appears in Ronald C. Finucane, *The Rescue of the Innocents: Endangered Children in Medieval Miracles* (New York: St. Martin's Press, 1997), 172–74.

Bibliography: Barbara Hanawalt, *The Ties That Bound: Peasant Families in Medieval England* (Oxford: Oxford University Press, 1986), 171–87.

* * *

Joan le Schirreve,[1] daughter of Adam le Schirreve, was brought by the procurator of the cathedral chapter of Hereford, took an oath and was asked if she was a member of lord Thomas of Hereford's family.[2] She replied that she was not. Asked how old she was, she replied that she was about twenty years old. She was asked to report what she knew about the miracle that had taken place in her person. She said that when she was about five years old she had been playing with John, who is now dead, the son of Thomas Schonk of the parish of Marden. Both of them were on the bank of a pond situated on the land or property of Walter de la Wyle of the same parish.[3] In the course of a game, the child John playfully pushed her into the pond, whose bank was about four feet above the water, and which was so deep that she fell into the water. Her hands reached for the brittle branches along the bank as she cried out. But because there was no one present who could hear her, except the little boy, as she grasped the branches she fell into the water and died, as she was to hear from her parents. They said that she lay drowned in the water from right after nones [about 3 p.m.] until sunset. After she had been discovered and taken out of the water, her parents made a vow and measured her for St. Thomas.[4] They promised to bring her to Thomas's tomb with a waxen image, if he would remember her. She said that she had heard from them that she was revived and, following said

---

1. Her father was presumably the local sheriff. His testimony indicates knowledge of local law, according to which those finding a dead body are to wait for the arrival of the coroner and attend the royal court for a preliminary hearing.

2. The term *familia* suggests membership in the episcopal household, as an official or in some other capacity.

3. The fish pond was in fact situated behind a beer tavern to which Joan's parents had gone on Sunday afternoon to dance and drink. The children had tagged along.

4. This is a peculiarly English custom. The victim's body is measured with a wick, which is then inserted into the candle to be brought as a votive offering to the saint's shrine.

revival, her parents took her with the image to the church at Hereford, and
made that miracle public during the year following her revival on a Sunday
around the feast of St. George [April 23]. All the girl's neighbors came
barefoot in procession to the church of Hereford with offerings because of
the miracle, and the bells in the church and city of Hereford were rung.
Concerning the year, month, and day because of which she came to the
church of Hereford with a waxen image, she testified that she did not
remember.

Asked if she remembered seeing, hearing, or feeling anything while she
lay drowned in the water, and how long she remained submerged, she said
she didn't recall.

Asked if following said revival she experienced any vision or revelation
of the lord Thomas, she replied that she often saw herself in a dream near
the tomb of lord Thomas, and that she prayed or undertook a pilgrimage
to him, or otherwise showed devotion to him. Nevertheless, neither lord
Thomas nor an angel nor a saint appeared to her in her sleep or otherwise as
far as she knew or understood.

Asked about the life led by her mother and father, the witness said that
they led good and honest lives by means of their lands and animals. They
gave charity within their means, frequently attended church to hear divine
service, and had five sons and three daughters.

Asked if as a result of the miracle she had become more religious and if
her parents and their neighbors praised and glorified Thomas as a result, she
answered in the affirmative. She said that she and her father and mother
went barefoot twice a year as pilgrims to Thomas's tomb, and intended
doing so as long as they lived. Because of this devotion, up to the present
time [1307] she had refused to marry, although urged by her parents and
others to marry a man suitable to her.

Asked if in her parish the neighbors and others publicly say that the
witness had been miraculously revived due to the merits of lord Thomas,
she replied in the affirmative, and that she is generally called in public "St.
Thomas's virgin."

Asked if she was acquainted with all the other witnesses who had
sworn and come to testify together with her, she replied that she was, and
that they were from the same parish from which she came, that they were
free persons and were considered of good faith, and did not come from the
temporal estates of the bishop or cathedral chapter of Hereford, but rather
from the estates of the baron Roger Mortimer. She did not know that he
was a member of the family of said lord Thomas.

She was finally asked whether she had testified out of fear, hate, or love, had been bribed or promised a bribe, whether she had been taught or instructed what to say, or whether she had conferred with the other witnesses in order to testify in this way. She replied in the negative. Let it be known that she testified in English.

Recorded in said chapel of St. Catherine in our presence, the notaries of this trial.

Thomas de Mathia, canon of Salerno (1319), Disciple of Thomas Aquinas

The following miracle, which appears in the 1319 canonization acts of Thomas Aquinas (canonized in 1323), was reported by several witnesses and appears in several versions. These selections include the testimony of both the recipient of the miracle himself, Thomas de Mathia (also spelled Marchia), and other witnesses, along with the version that appears in the contemporary biography of Aquinas by William of Tocco. It illustrates how direct personal experience could become the basis of legend, since this miracle appears among the papally "approved" miracles cited in Thomas's bull of canonization, and was employed by many later preachers as an illustration of the saint's power, thus becoming known to a wide circle of believers. At the same time, Thomas de Mathia's punishment for failing to recognize Aquinas's sainthood and the efficacy of his relics indicates how the wrath of God could injure and mark those who strayed from the divinely-ordained ideological consensus. Thomas de Mathia was a canon, a cleric living a disciplined semi-monastic life.

Sources: Antonio Ferrua, ed., *Thomas Aquinatis vitae fontes praecipuae* (Alba: Edizione Dominicane, 1968), 265–67, 301–2, and William of Tocco, *Vita S. Thomae Aquinatis*, in *Acta Sanctorum*, ed. Socii Bollandiani, 69 vols. (Paris: V. Palme, 1863–1940), 11 February I, 6.

Bibliography: Leonard W. Levy, "Blasphemy," in *The Encyclopedia of Religion*, ed. Mircea Eliade, 16 vols. (New York: Macmillian, 1987), 2: 238–42.

* * *

On that same day [July 31, 1319], Abbot Thomas de Mathia, a canon of Salerno, was called as a witness and swore to tell the truth regarding said inquiry in accordance with the form noted above. First asked about the life and behavior (*conversatio*) of friar Thomas, he said that he had heard it reported publicly that brother Thomas was a man of good life and upright behavior, and that he did not know any more.

Asked about the miracles of friar Thomas, he said that once, in order to praise God and the Holy Cross, he began to build a chapel at the site of the cross [*in loco Crucis*], and with great care sought relics of the saints in order to collect them for the chapel. He came to the chapel of San Severino in the diocese of Salerno, and there he found Lord Matthew de Adiutorio, the chaplain of the chapel. He asked Matthew to show him whatever relics of the saints he might have; and the chaplain showed him many relics, which he looked at with reverence. The chaplain said afterward that he had in his possession even more precious relics. Asked which ones, he replied that he had the hand of friar Thomas Aquinas of the Order of Preachers. The witness reacted with derision and jokingly said that friar Thomas is not a saint, but had been a preacher. He refused to look at it; and he immediately began to shake, and it seemed to him that his head had swollen up in size like a very large and heavily ulcerated sore.

Regretting what he had said and his expression of disbelief, he began to cry out and asked the priest of the chapel for leave, and repenting his contemptuous words about friar Thomas, asked the priest to provide him with help. After this, he went devotedly to pray and to kiss the hand; in the course of kissing and venerating it, the witness was suddenly freed of the shaking and the swelling of his head and became healthy and experienced a great fragrance emanating from the hand. Because the hood he wore over his shoulders touched the hand, he and his hood continued to emit an aroma so that for a long time afterward it seemed to others with whom he spoke that he was carrying honey with him. From then on he was in the habit of reporting all that had happened and the miracle.

He said that he then experienced such a feeling of consolation and was so tearful that ever since he has had a great faith in friar Thomas. As a result, whenever he has been tempted by carnal desire and after much thought has considered sinning carnally, the thoughts disappear after he has commended himself to friar Thomas. Whenever he suffers temptation, whatever it may be, he invokes the name of friar Thomas and receives aid, and whatever desires may have welled up in him disappear.

Asked about the time, month, and day of said miracle and his liberation, he said that it was in the seventh year of the indiction [1316], in a month and day which he did not remember. Asked who was present with him in the course of the miracle, he said the aforementioned chaplain, who is dead, Maffeo Acconzaioco de Revello, and Maffeo's servant, whose name he didn't know. Asked about the place, he said the *castro*[1] of San Severino in the church of the castro. Asked what words he had used in his prayer to friar Thomas, he said the following: "O blessed Thomas, I consider you a saint, and I repent of the things I said about you, and I lied. I commend myself to you. Help me."

After the prayer had been uttered, he was immediately freed and made healthy. Asked how long he had experienced shaking and heaviness in his head; he said for as long as he was confessing and returned to the altar and made his prayer. Asked for how long afterward he had remained well, he replied that he has been well ever since. Asked how friar Thomas's hand had reached the church of San Severino, he said that the chaplain had told the witness that the countess, the wife of Lord Roger, count of San Severino, and friar Thomas's sister, out of the devotion and love which she had for friar Thomas, had the hand given to her by the abbot and convent of Fossanova. He said that afterward the countess placed the hand in the church. Asked if it was whole, he replied that he saw it complete with skin, flesh, bones, tendons, and sinews, only missing a thumb. Asked if said miracles were publicly known, he replied that because he had reported the above events afterward, they were known in the castro.

On the same day [August 4, 1319] Aconzaioco de Barello[2] was called as a witness and swore in the form prescribed concerning the inquiry, to tell the truth and was first asked about the life and behavior of friar Thomas. He said that he himself knew nothing about those things for certain, but had heard from many elderly clergy and laity that friar Thomas was a man of holy life and behavior, and that God had performed and performs many miracles due to the merits of this friar Thomas.

Asked if he knew about any of Thomas's miracles, he said that he had himself gone with Abbot Thomas de Marchia [Mathia], a canon of Salerno, to the castro of San Severino, to the church of San Severino which is situated in the castro, he would sometimes go to see certain relics of saints, which are in that church, among them the hand of friar Thomas. In the presence of Abbot Thomas he had venerated the relics, along with the hand of friar Thomas, because he was and is very much devoted to friar Thomas

1. A walled-in town or castle, usually including both a residential and commercial quarter and castle.
2. Variant spelling for Acconzaioco de Revello.

as a saint. The abbot made fun of him for venerating Thomas's hand. After
this derision, Abbot Thomas suddenly began to shake all over and said, "I
can't see."

He immediately called for the priest, to whom he confessed with great
contrition and tears. After he had confessed and received absolution, he
venerated the hand, his shaking stopped immediately, and he recovered his
sight, as this same abbot said publicly.

Asked how he knew all this, he said that he had witnessed Abbot
Thomas trembling all over after his derision; and after his confession, absolution, and veneration, in the presence of the witness, he saw Abbot Thomas
freed from his shaking. The witness said that he didn't know about the
absence and recovery of his sight, except by means of Abbot Thomas's confession, who reported this to him and the church's chaplain. Asked who was
present, he said that no one was there with Abbot Thomas except for the
witness and the church's chaplain, who is now dead. Asked to what priest
said Abbot Thomas had made confession, he replied to that chaplain. Asked
about the time, month, and year, he said that he didn't remember. Asked if
he had been healthy ever since that infirmity, he replied in the affirmative.

When the aforesaid hand of the doctor had been preserved with reverence in the chapel of the castle of San Severino, which belonged to said
mistress,[3] a canon of Salerno, very devoted to God, who was made procurator of the rector of the chapel at a certain point, came out of devotion to
view the relics which had been preserved there with reverence. After venerating them with reverence, the doctor's right hand was presented to him by
the chaplain so that he might venerate it; he laughed, refused to venerate
and look at it, and was suddenly gripped by a great shaking. As he turned
around, because of the contempt he had shown in refusing to venerate the
saint's hand, he suddenly shook so that there was a great change in his body.
He looked down at the priest's feet in penance, humbly and contritely
asking to be absolved of the contemptuous words he had uttered against the
saint. He was absolved by him, and after having received penance, while the
punishment of his shaking continued, he asked to be shown the said hand
of the saint, so that as a penitent he might return the debt he owed the saint
by having refused to look at it. Genuflecting, he tearfully venerated it,
asking to be absolved by God of his criminal lapse, because of the saint's
merits, and to be freed of the punishment of shaking with which he had

3. The sister of Thomas Aquinas.

been inflicted. Approaching with reverence, urged by God and the saint, he kissed the hand, which gave out a fragrance which he recalled never having experienced before. The shaking of his body ceased immediately, a marvelous [*mirabilia*] divine change came over him, so that he was more devoted in his heart. As a result of the touch as he kissed the holy hand, he felt that the odor adhered to the hood on his shoulder as it touched the pouch in which the sacred hand was kept. When he donned that hood, he often recalled that miracle because of the odor and was often asked by those he met, "What is that fragrance which accosts anyone who approaches?" As a result, in the course of the day he often had to tell about his liberation and the miracle of the fragrance so that his guilt for the contempt he had shown for the saint was turned to the glory of the saint. That miracle occurred in the forty-second year [1316] from the doctor's death, so that during the long period since then the arm had remained intact and the divine virtue was miraculously preserved and appeared in it by means of the strong odor. The cleric reported that he was aided by the odor against the dangers of temptation, and whenever he felt himself in combat with the Enemy, even if he had already decided in his mind to give in, after invoking God's help he felt that by means of the continuing merit of the saint he was freed from every danger and kept secure, having appeased God.

Berardo Appillaterre, notary of Tolentino (1325)

The following testimony provides graphic evidence of the continuing patron-client relationship that bound members of the Appillaterre family to the Augustinian hermit Nicholas of Tolentino, who could be called upon for assistance in time of stress. The testimony begins with a long report concerning the saint's penitential life and reputation among local residents. The speaker was presumably involved in the establishment of the saint's cult and may have been a member of one of the many confraternities found throughout Europe, which bound together persons of the same professional, familial, and geographical origin under the saint's patronage. Although this narrative is spoken by a leading notary, it nevertheless voices the extreme insecurity which was the common lot of many. Nicholas's canonization trial called 217 witnesses between July 23 and August 9 and on September 9 and 10, 1325.

Source: N. Occhioni, ed., *Il processo per la canonizzazione di S. Nicola da Tolentino* (Rome: École Française de Rome, 1984), 123–30.

Bibliography: André Vauchez, "Patronage of Saints and Civic Religion in the Italy of the Communes," in *The Laity in the Middle Ages. Religious Beliefs and Devotional Practices*, ed. Daniel Bornstein, trans. Margery J. Schneider (Notre Dame, Ind.: University of Notre Dame Press, 1993), 153–68.

*   *   *

Master Berardo Appillaterre, notary of Tolentino in the diocese of Camerino, aged fifty or more . . . [served] in the province of Romagna; for six months as an official in the cities of Rimini and Forlì; in the cities of Cesena, Forlimpopoli, and Faenza, and in other places, villages [*castri*], and cities of that province. He was an official in the province of Tuscany, in the cities of Siena and Florence; in the province of the duchy of Spoleto, including Foligno, Bevagna, Montefalco, and Spello, where he was an official; and in many other cities and villages of those provinces. In the kingdom of Sicily, especially in Manfredonia, Baroli, Trani, Naples, Blandutia, Bari, and many other places in that country, he served as an official to King Robert [of Anjou] for eighteen months. In the province of the March of Ancona he served in the cities of Ancona, Iesi, Fano, Pesaro, Ascoli Piceno, and Macerata. . . .

The witness said that [on several occasions] . . . when he suffered from a continuing fever friar Nicholas would visit him and place his hand on the witness's head and recite the Evangel of St. John, "In the beginning was the Word" [John 1.1]. Sometimes when he was suffering severely from this fever, Nicholas placed his hand on his head and he seemed to be cured. Once, when the witness had fever after he had been ill, Nicholas came to visit him at vespers [6 p.m.] and placed his hand on his head, his fever seemed to disappear, and at that moment the bell rang for vespers. When the friar removed his hand from his head it felt as though the fever had returned. He said, "For God's sake, friar Nicholas, put your hand on my head again, since it soothes me." He then replied to him, "I have to go to vespers. I can't remain with you all the time. Console yourself and ask God to help you." After Nicholas had left, the fever left him immediately and never returned. Asked when this had happened, he said that it was before friar Nicholas's burial [September 9, 1305]. But this happened so long ago that he couldn't remember the month and day.

He said that when he was more than twelve years old, having come to the church of Sant'Agostino [at Tolentino] where friar Nicholas is buried, a noblewoman of Fermo[1] came with a large number of knights and a little girl about twelve years old, whom the woman claimed had died and had been

---

1. Situated about twenty miles from Tolentino.

revived due to the prayers and merits of the blessed Nicholas. She had made a vow to bring her daughter or have her brought to the tomb of the blessed Nicholas, and to offer him all the clothes her daughter wore and the locks of her hair. She swore on the Holy Gospel of God by touching the book in front of all who were present that this was the truth. The witness, who was present at the time, saw and heard it. The girl's mother offered the girl's clothes, a pair of multi-colored garments, and cut her daughter's hair in front of everyone. . . . Many were present. . . .

He said that during Nicholas's obsequies, at different times and for many years, he was present, day after day, from time to time when persons from different countries, provinces, and places would come to the territory of Tolentino and to the convent of Sant'Agostino where the blessed Nicholas is buried and to his tomb. They would publicly declare, some that they could no longer see, others that they couldn't walk; some said that they had been invaded or attacked by demons; while others were captives or prisoners; and others said that they were deaf or mute, and there were those who said they had suffered all kinds of maladies and had been cured due to the prayers and merits of the blessed Nicholas. They confirmed under oath that it was the truth and they had made an offering which was noted in their vow.

He reported that when he had been an official at Florence in the month of May during the present year [1325] . . . a Florentine hunchback, [partly] paralyzed, who had been ill for ten years according to his own testimony, vowed to the blessed Nicholas that evening and remained in the church of the Holy Spirit of Florence where the friars of the order of the Augustinian hermits dwelled.[2] He was cured by morning and everyone saw that he was cured, and the witness himself saw that he was cured. He saw the paralyzed man swear and affirm on the Holy Gospels of God that all of this was true. Asked how he knew, he replied that he was the very same official [before whom he swore]. He was present along with the other officials belonging to Ponzio of Florence when the bell had rung announcing the miracle, and he went with the other officials to the convent. Asked if he had seen this paralyzed man before the miracle, he said he had not, but he had heard it said by the man and by many other residents of Florence that they had seen him both ill and paralyzed. But a notary belonging to said Signor Ponzio of Florence was asked along with other Florentines to record the declaration made by the paralyzed man in the presence of a large crowd of men and women.

He said that his wife, mistress Margarita, now deceased, had given

2. This church was situated in the Oltrarno quarter of Florence. The hermitage was established in 1250/51 and placed near this church, which was destroyed by fire, but reconstructed at the end of the fifteenth century.

birth to many children, some dead, some who barely survived. Margarita, who was very much devoted to friar Nicholas, said, "Friar Nicholas, beseech God for me that those children who will be born by me will not lose their souls, and they will be born alive, and that I will not suffer great grief." He then replied, "Calm down, and don't be in doubt. You are going to give birth to a girl who will live a long time, and as long as I live she will bring me food from you." After that a daughter named Berardesca was born. . . . He knew this from his wife. . . .

One of his sons, named Nicolucio — this name was given to him out of the love of the blessed Nicholas — suffered a hernia for six months. The witness's wife, Margarita, beseeched the blessed Nicholas to cure him for the sake of the services she had performed for him and for the love which she had for him. She asked that he not be cut with a hot iron because she couldn't see him suffer. She brought her son to Nicholas's tomb, saying she would make an image of wax if he should cure her son. She then brought him home, and Nicolucio began to walk better; he was completely cured within eight days. Asked how he knew this, he said he was present when his wife made her vow. But he was not present nor did he accompany her when she brought the boy to the church. Asked when this had happened, he said after the burial of friar Nicholas, although he didn't remember the year or month. Asked who was present when the vow was uttered, he said that along with him there was mistress Bellaflora, mistress Gualterucia of Tolentino, and many others whose names he did not remember. Asked where the vow was made, he said in his own home, located in the San Catervo quarter, and he was present.[3] After his wife had made her vow, it was made a second time at the church of Sant'Agostino beside the tomb of St. Nicholas. Asked about the invocation which led to this miracle, he said, as above, at his wife's invocation. Asked about the words, he said as above. . . .

One of his daughters, named Ceccha, had a severe throat ailment, and her throat was so inflamed and swollen that it was as large as her head. The doctors wanted to cut her throat with an iron, and his wife, Ceccha's mother, was much distressed and cried that her daughter should not be cut in the throat. While she was crying, friar Nicholas, who was himself ill, felt the woman's grief, before she had even told him anything about it. He called for two friars who were with him, saying, "Brethren, go and visit mistress Margarita, who has served me so much, and continues to serve me

3. The town of Tolentino was divided into four quarters, S. Catervo, S. Maria, S. Martino, and S. Nicolò.

and who is so grieved due to her daughter's illness, and comfort her in my name." The brethren visited the woman and comforted her in his name, saying, "Why are you sad and crying so much?" She replied, "Because the doctors want to cut my daughter in the throat, she will be so injured by the wound that she will be cursed." The brethren left and returned to friar Nicholas. After listening, he said, "Go back and tell her from me that if I could I would willingly visit her, but she knows I can't walk because I'm ill; she should visit me and bring her daughter Ceccha, and not let her be touched by any iron." The woman took her sick daughter and gave her to a servant named Specia, and the witness' wife and her daughter Berardesca came to friar Nicholas. Friar Nicholas then said to the woman, "Don't be sad, mistress Margarita. Confide in God and the blessed Biagio [St. Blasius], since your daughter Ceccha will be cured without the iron and the advice of physicians. Go with her to the church of San Biagio in the parish of Tolentino and bring three offerings: since the blessed Biagio is a better doctor than all of them." The witness's wife did as friar Nicholas had said, taking her daughter to the church of San Biagio in the parish of Tolentino where the feast of San Biagio is celebrated. She devotedly begged for her daughter to be cured, she offered a candle, an egg, and a silver *denarius*, and they returned to friar Nicholas. Friar Nicholas touched Ceccha's throat and blessed her, saying, "Go with God to your home, and have no doubt that with the help of God and San Biagio, the girl will be cured." This happened one day at vespers; and the next morning his daughter, when she got up, was totally cured. . . .

The witness had a son named Tucio who suffered from epilepsy and he consulted many doctors in order to free his son, but nothing helped. His wife, Margarita, said, "I want to have recourse to the blessed Nicholas, who loved me so much while he was alive. Just as he aided me concerning our other son Nicolucio." . . . He was freed.[4] . . .

He said that he heard from his son-in-law Antonio Thomasii[5] that last year on the first day of the month of November his horse had died as a result of some illness, and lay dead from the evening to the next morning and was completely swollen. When Antonio saw the horse lying in this way, he vowed him to the blessed Nicholas, saying, "O blessed Nicholas, who assisted in so many dangers, help me not to lose this horse. I promise when I get up in the morning to immediately buy a pound of wax and bring it to

4. Nicholas also aided another infant born to Mistress Margarita, who appeared to be dead at birth.
5. A merchant and notary of Tolentino.

your tomb." When the vow had been uttered, the horse immediately gave one neigh, got up, began to eat, and was freed. . . .

When friar Nicholas died, Berardo's wife, mistress Margarita, went to see friar Nicholas, washed his hands and feet, and saved the water used to wash his hands and feet in a vial. She kept this water, and it always remained clear as though it had just come from a fresh, clear fountain. This water was displayed before the venerable lords bishop.[6] . . . His wife preserved this water as though it were a relic . . . and whenever some member of the household, or someone else, or when his wife had eye or stomach problems or difficulties with any part of her body, she had the water brought with great devotion by one of the young children and applied it to the suffering member; and the person was often cured. Asked who was cured thanks to this water, he said mistress Flordalisia, wife of Francesco of Sant'Angelo in Pontano, a resident of Tolentino, who had stomach problems and was cured of incontinence when the water was placed on her stomach. When his wife had a pain on her right side, as though she had a growth inside, she called on her daughter Berardesca to bring the water and placed it on the suffering spot. When this was done the pain disappeared. . . . This happened eight years ago [1317] after the octave of St. Martin. . . .

6. Frederick Sanguini, bishop of Senigallia, and Thomas, bishop of Cesena.

Selected Bibliography

The following list includes works not previously cited.

Allard, Guy-H. et al. *Aspects de la marginalité au moyen âge*. Montréal: L'Aurore, 1975.

Casagrande, Carla and Silvana Vecchio. "Clercs et jongleurs dans la société médiévale (XIIe et XIIIe siècle)." *Annales: Économies, Civilisations, Sociétés* 45 (1990), 913–28.

Davis, Natalie Zemon. *Fiction in the Archives: Pardon Tales and Their Tellers in Sixteenth-Century France*. Stanford, Calif.: Stanford University Press, 1987.

Douglas, Mary. "Witchcraft and Leprosy: Two Strategies of Exclusion." *Man* n.s. 26 (1991), 723–36.

Edwards, John, ed. and trans. *The Jews in Medieval Europe, 1400–1600*. Manchester: Manchester University Press, 1994.

Geremek, Bronisław. *The Margins of Society in Late Medieval Paris*. Trans. Jean Birrell. Cambridge: Cambridge University Press, 1987.

Germani, Gino. *Marginality*. New Brunswick, N.J.: Rutgers University Press, 1980.

Ginzburg, Carlo. *Ecstasies: Deciphering the Witches' Sabbath*. Trans. Raymond Rosenthal, ed. Gregory Elliott. New York: Pantheon, 1990.

Hamerton-Kelly, Robert G., ed. *Violent Origins: Ritual Killing and Cultural Formation*. Stanford, Calif.: Stanford University Press, 1987.

Horrox, Rosemary, ed. and trans. *The Black Death*. Manchester: Manchester University Press, 1994.

Jacquart, Danielle and Claude Thomasset. *Sexuality and Medicine in the Middle Ages*. Trans. Matthew Adamson. Princeton, N.J.: Princeton University Press, 1988.

Leclercq, Jean. "Modern Psychology and the Interpretation of Medieval Texts." *Speculum* 48 (1973): 476–90.

Moore, Robert I. *The Formation of a Persecuting Society*. Oxford: Oxford University Press, 1987.

——. *The Origins of European Dissent*. Toronto: University of Toronto Press, 1994.

Muir, Edward and Guido Ruggiero, eds. *Microhistory and the Lost Peoples of History*. Baltimore: Johns Hopkins University Press, 1991.

Nirenberg, David. *Communities of Violence: Persecution of Minorities in the Middle Ages*. Princeton, N.J.: Princeton University Press, 1996.

Richards, Jeffrey. *Sex, Dissidence, and Damnation: Minority Groups in the Middle Ages*. London: Routledge, 1991.

Robert, Ulysse. *Les signes d'infamie au moyen âge*. Paris: H. Champion, 1891.

Schmitt, Jean-Claude. "L'histoire des marginaux." In *La nouvelle histoire*, ed. Jacques Le Goff et al. Paris: CEPL, 1978. 344–69.

Turner, Victor. *The Ritual Process: Structure and Anti-Structure*. 1969. Reprint New York: Aldine, 1995.

Vauchez, André. *Sainthood in the Later Middle Ages*. Trans. Jean Birrell. Cambridge: Cambridge University Press, 1997.

Vodola, Elisabeth. *Excommunication in the Middle Ages*. Berkeley: University of California Press, 1986.

Waddell, Helen. *The Wandering Scholars*. 1927. Reprint Garden City, N.Y.: Doubleday, 1955.

Waugh, Scott and Peter Diehl, eds. *Christendom and Its Discontents: Exclusion, Persecution, and Rebellion, 1000–1500*. Cambridge: Cambridge University Press, 1996.

Weintraub, Karl Joachim. *The Value of the Individual: Self and Circumstance in Autobiography*. Chicago: University of Chicago Press, 1978.

Index